# FACTS AGAINST FICTIONS OF EXECUTIVE BEHAVIOR

# FACTS AGAINST FICTIONS OF EXECUTIVE BEHAVIOR

## A Critical Analysis of What Managers Do

*Joe Kelly*

**QUORUM BOOKS**
Westport, Connecticut • London

**Library of Congress Cataloging-in-Publication Data**

Kelly, Joe.
    Facts against fictions of executive behavior : a critical analysis
of what managers do / Joe Kelly.
      p. cm.
    Includes bibliographical references and index.
    ISBN 0-89930-737-X (alk. paper)
    1. Chief executive officers—United States—Case studies.
2. Executives—United States—Case studies. 3. Executive ability—
Case studies.    I. Title.
    HD38.25.U6K45   1993
    658.4'09—dc20      92–41607

British Library Cataloguing in Publication Data is available.

Library of Congress Catalog Card Number: 92-41607
ISBN: 0-89930-737-X

First published in 1993

Quorum Books, 88 Post Road West, Westport, CT 06881
An imprint of Greenwood Publishing Group, Inc.

Printed in the United States of America

∞™

The paper used in this book complies with the
Permanent Paper Standard issued by the National
Information Standards Organization (Z39.48–1984).

10  9  8  7  6  5  4  3  2  1

# Contents

# Tables and Figures

## TABLES

## FIGURES

# Preface

This book has two audiences in mind: executives who wonder what is going on around them and business professors and personnel professionals who are puzzled by the problems of reconciling what they read in management texts and business magazines with what executives actually do. The aim is to reconcile scientific "facts" with the "fictions" of actual executive life, as revealed by experience, such as those revealed in Lee Iacocca's autobiography. To get these facts and fictions of executive life together in a meaningful and understandable way, this books develops a new view of executive behavior that focuses on the classical and existential models of the manager.

An earlier and extremely successful book, written in 1973, was *The Nature of Managerial Work* by Henry Mintzberg. Since then, research by John Kotter (*General Manager* 1982) and practice as exemplified by Lee Iacocca, Jack Welch, Steven Jobs, John Sculley, and others have developed considerably, sometimes in divergent ways. A new approach is now available that allows us to form a critical view of executive life, its facts, fictions, and paradigms, that will allow the executive to make things happen efficaciously. "Efficacious" in this context implies not only "good things happening in an executive sense" but also "things happening in a way meaningful to researchers."

To get detailed answers to these issues, it is necessary to find answers to specific questions: What does the manager do? How does he or she allocate time? How much time is spent in planning or in meetings? How much time do managers spend with superiors, peers, and subordinates? What about alone time? What are preferred communication methods? We know many of the answers, but how can we reconcile them with the facts of executive life as revealed by the careers of Iacocca, Welch, and Jobs?

We know from observation of executives that managers have a preference for immediate, concrete, and specific problems, which they immediately simplify through some model. The scheduled meeting is the mainstay of their days. Two fundamental types of managers are considered, the classical and the existential. In the classical view, the manager organizes, coordinates, plans, and controls. We know from observational studies of existential executive behavior, however, that managers are not in fact reflective, regulated workers who are kept informed by sophisticated systems. They prefer soft information often collected through the grapevine of gossip.

To manage is a verb, a doing word. But what do managers do? They talk. We know that they spend long hours working, mostly interacting. These interactions involve fleeting, superficial, often distracting contacts with their bosses, sending "OK—carry on" signals. The classical theory views executives as players in the great game of realpolitik.

Chapter 1 introduces the basic concept of executive behavior, namely the notion that behavior can be observed, measured, analyzed, and categorized. It sounds scientific, and it is. But so much of what managers actually do can only be described as behaving in nonmanagerial ways, such as vice presidents who nod in agreement when the boss spells out the reasons for firing them. Of course, CEOs are quite expert in winning consent. To do this, CEOs focus on people's behavior on the task to be achieved, structuring their space, processing their behavior, and forming their values.

To get to the meaning behind such happenings, it is necessary to compare and contrast classical and existential executive styles of management. The old classical style with its emphasis on organization charts, role descriptions, corporate planning, management by objectives (MBO), organization development (OD), and all the acronyms of the 1960s is still there but fading. This now passé style, as exemplified by ITT and its then chief executive Harold Geneen, is being replaced by an existential style where the emphasis is on creative decision making, risk taking, and participation. Management has become a much more exciting experience, through which great things can be done. The new-style managers include Jack Welch of General Electric, John Sculley of Apple, Steven Jobs of Next, and Bill Gates of Microsoft.

Part I deals with the behavior of executives and covers four levels of managers: chief executives, general managers, middle managers, and supervisors. Starting at the top with the imperial chief executive, this is a review of the scientific evidence of chief executive behavior. This intense, demanding life of ad hoc, brief, fragmented encounters is compared with the facts and fictions of top management life as revealed in autobiographies and interviews. The question is why the CEO is perceived as the main problem in American business today. The crisis in management is right at the top of the organizational pyramid.

At the next level, of general manager, research in the 1980s has provided a more positive and encouraging portrait of success by diligence, not by going by the book but by agenda setting and networking. The portrait is essentially existential. General managers who are hard workers use an informal network, establish good relations, and do favors to get the job done. The main finding is that mangers are successful not because they have MBAs but because they have detailed knowledge of the industry and its technology, and also enormously important, they have a large informal network.

Looking at middle managers, a different message comes through. Successful middle managers are experts in politics and communications; effective middle managers focus on their job but are more likely to be passed over. Middle managers in many companies are the fall guys of the system. Making up less than 10 percent of the organization, they make up almost 20 percent of firings. Supervisory activity, which gets the actual work done, is redolent with ambiguity and confusion; again, their activities are rarely managerial because they spend so much time trouble-shooting and doing the jobs of their subordinates. Computers, automation, and participation of shop floor people are eliminating the need for supervisors. Quality of Work Life Programs require supervisors to operate as coaches, mentors, developers, and trainers.

Part II deals with executive selection, leadership, communication, and pay. The aim is to review how managers are chosen: at the top of the tree they are chosen through rotating these high flyers through the roles of COO, president, vice chairman, CEO, and chairman; at a lower level, the interest is in assessment centers and interviewing.

Executive leadership deals with a quantum theory of influence, showing how style changes as a manager ascends the hierarchy. Junior managers have a human relations approach that gives way to human resources management for middle managers. Top managers use a transformational style. Communication styles of executives are discovered in the videos of actual meetings, described and transcribed in part herein, revealing existential dramas and traumas. This study of executive meetings reveals the paradigm of corporate drama that integrates the structure of roles (the actors), the process of events (clarification, evaluation, decision), and values (democratic and task). Pay and performance are reviewed in the light of the evidence of the nineties, providing a more complex answer, where perception is more important than reality. The question is not whether CEOs are paid too much, but how pay and performance can be linked in a meaningful way.

Part III draws together the facts and concepts deployed and developed earlier in the book and begins with a fuller explanation of the new executive style. The final chapter takes the form of a critique of executive behavior that spells out the methods, models, and limitations of this approach.

The overall objective of the book is to present an updated picture of what managers at different levels do, of how they are selected, how they lead, and how they are rewarded. But the picture is changing. My hope is that the readers—professional managers and students—will see the executive world with fresh eyes and recognize that the classical and existential are the obverse faces of the same coin whose reconciliation will enable managers to make a new beginning.

# 1

---

# Executive Behavior: Classical and Existential

Executive behavior is simply what managers do. Managers do two things: They get things done, and sometimes they even get great things done; the better managers do these things with such style and elegance that others get a kick out of working with them. The best managers not only manage efficiently (''doing things right'') and effectively (''doing the right thing''), but they also achieve a vision for their organization, which can transform society and nearly always transforms the visionaries. Like Lee Iacocca or Jack Welch, they communicate their vision by their actions and their behavior. Thus, executives never simply behave.

Other business executives (standing next to Iacocca or Welch) wonder what is going on around them and are puzzled by what is happening ''up front.'' Talking more generally, an easy way of confounding adherents of traditional management is to ask them to define management. The answers tend to be somewhat clichéd: ''Management is getting results through people''; ''Management is the coordination of such functions as planning and organizing to reach a measured objective''; ''Management is . . . '' What is managing? Two answers are discussed here: the classical and the existential.

## WHAT IS MANAGING?

### The Classical Answer

For the traditional classical manager, ''Managing is the art of delegation'' and ''Managing gets results through people.'' For the classical manager, "Managing is the formulation of and executing of policy through the functional activities of *planning, organization, leading, and evaluating,*" or POLE. All this POLEing leads to "managing as teamwork where people really matter." At the shop-floor level, following F. W. Taylor, "Managing is discovering how tasks should be performed and seeing that they are performed in that way."

## The Classical Manager as the Organization Man

This view sees the manager as the person who sets objectives; plans the work; organizes the people into tasks according to their ages, aptitudes, and abilities; leads them in a way that turns work into fun; and evaluates performance in a way that ensures correspondence between plan and action. That is, the manager does things through people: he or she plans, organizes, leads and evaluates the efforts of other people.

We know from scientific studies of executive behavior that they spend tremendously long hours working (twelve to fourteen hours a day plus "homework"), and most of this is what psychologists call "interacting time." The time spent with others is made up of myriad fleeting, superficial, often distracting contacts. A lot of these contacts are in meetings, but most are swift base-touching signals that terminate with the manager's "OK—carry on" signal.

This managerial lifestyle can be disturbing to outsiders. They are likely to view managers as having sold their services to the highest bidder (usually the image of a bloated capitalist smoking a cigar is invoked) or as a kind of powerbroker who gets people together to do what the manager wants.

One such outsider was W. H. Whyte, Jr., an editor of *Fortune* magazine, who, in 1956, wrote a brilliant and widely read book called *The Organization Man*. Managers like to think of themselves as tough guys who go in and do it their way, win the order, get a coronary, are fired—then make it all the way back to become chairman of the board. Whyte painted another picture, however: a guy with a crewcut, in a buttoned-down collar, gray flannel suit, and polished leather shoes, who drives a Buick or an Oldsmobile (a Cadillac would be conspicuous consumption), tutors his wife on how to toady up to the boss, and is an all-around conformist.

## A Behavioral Portrait

One of the first studies of American chief executives was made in fact by Whyte, who reported a study of fifty-two company presidents, twenty-three vice presidents, and fifty-three middle managers identified as "comers." Whyte found that they worked excessive hours, included evenings in their work time, and spent most of their time interacting with or influencing people. The question was not how much executives work, but how they find time to work.

The findings of a later study, reported in 1960 by Dale and Urwick, largely confirmed Whyte's data. Dale and Urwick studied ten executives and analyzed in detail the working week of a bank president. More than half of his time was taken up with outside contacts, and a lot of time was spent on public relations.

The whole idea of making executive behavior studies by observation was invented by Sune Carlson (1951), a professor of business studies in Sweden. Carlson was preoccupied with the idea that management studies were largely theological, sterile, and based to a large extent on anecdotes. Carlson was fighting the idea, then and still widely held, that what a manager did could be summed up in the acronym POLE. Carlson asked, "How do you recognize a manager when he is POLEing? What are his behavioral characteristics? Does he have an identifiable profile?" When nobody could answer him, he set out to find out for himself. Carlson collected his data under five headings: place, person, technique of communication, question handled, and action taken.

What Carlson found confirmed the cliché. He discovered that top executives worked long hours, rarely visited their factories, spent long hours traveling, were slaves to their diaries, and had little time for leisure and contemplation.

Henry Mintzberg, a professor of management at McGill University, set out in 1968 to study the work of the chief executives of five large US corporations. Using a technique called structured observation, he observed each CEO for a period of one week. Mintzberg showed that the American chief executive was on the surface a very superficial person who worked long hours, largely because he was a node in a complex information system. Virtually everything in the business, usually in digested form, had to cross his desk.

What Mintzberg is telling us is that grand theories of management are irrelevant: Managers don't act; they react. Managerial life seems to be made up of "brief encounters" and "brief activities" (49 percent of executives' activities in Mintzberg's study lasted less than nine minutes). To get their business done, managers concentrate on issues that are current, well-defined, and nonroutine; they work mainly through the spoken word, with few letters, apparently.

### Behavior

Behavioral studies of executives indicate beyond all reasonable doubt that managers feel compelled to work excessive hours at an unrelenting pace, with few opportunities for breaks or recreation. This critical executive fetish becomes more pronounced at higher levels in the hierarchy and must be regarded as a function of the kicks, rewards, and challenges that senior executives get out of their jobs. The manager's life is suffused with brief contacts and fleeting interactions; it is highly fragmented, with a fair level of noise. Managers appear to operate at several levels simultaneously, or at least in rapid succession.

Managers apparently spend most of their time communicating, mostly by the spoken word and mostly at meetings. For most, writing letters is not a major activity. Managers have a preference for the immediate, concrete, and specific problems they immediately simplify through some model. The scheduled meeting is the mainstay of their days.

### The Manager's Job: Fact and Fiction

In the classical view, the manager organizes, coordinates, plans, and controls. We know from observational studies of executive behavior, however, that managers are not in fact reflective, regulated workers who are kept informed by sophisticated systems.

### "The Game Is the Thing"

The classical imperialist drama theory of the organization views executives and their hangers-on as players in the great game of realpolitik. The great thing about the metaphor of game playing is that by reducing personal responsibility, it frees individuals to make decisions.

These Top Dog executives, whether in business, government, education, or the church, have power, understand the drama of power, and use it. These Top Dogs maneuver and manipulate in order to get the job done and, in many cases, to strengthen and enhance their own position. They revel in being seen as "fascists," but only in a humorous sort of way— "He is somewhat to the right of Attila the Hun." Success is dependent on the manipulation of the vast intricacy of human relationships that make up the political universe of these Top Dog executives. They know how to play the game.

In terms of leadership style, the essentially male classical mode of command, coordination and control is being supplemented by a more feminine human relation mode of pragmatic, less confrontational style of management. Managers in executive development courses are being guided towards a more androgynous form of influence which combines the best features of the male and female modes. But not all female managers follow this non-confrontational model.

Carol Bartz, CEO of Autodesk, which is the sixth-largest personal computer software company, has shifted her organization from an exclusive reliance on consensus decision-making to a more top-down management. Autodesk, which was known in the computer industry as a gaggle of hackers, has profited from the establishment of a proper hierarchy.

## ORGANIZATIONAL PRINCIPLES

"The organization as a whole" has a logic that is peculiarly its own and that, when it is working effectively, is a sight to be seen. Sustained by ideological fictions ("this place is more than brick and mortar, it has a heart"), serving both unique ("makes a big buck") and accessory ("keeps you out of the cold") functions, held together by powerful coalitions ("the inner circle") whom none will challenge, organizations can only be understood in their own terms. "*You* don't believe, but believe that everybody else believes" is what everyone believes. With this kind of pluralistic ignorance, organizations are not only hard to buck, but on occasion are capable of mobilizing and directing resources in such a way that dramatic achievements become the order of the day, leaving both participants and spectators gasping in awe. And further, to add horrors to horrors, organizations can get people to overcome their anxieties and learn to love them. Why? Mainly because the organization has principles!

1. Organizations exist: They are bigger than people; they may be immortal. Organizations can be managed through human resource management.
2. Organizations have "structure, process, and values." Organizations affect perception, emotions, and behavior of individuals and groups. Organizations develop a culture.
3. Organizations can be designed and managed.

## MOVING BEYOND THE CLASSICAL CEO

### The Classical Chief Executive Officer

Classical CEOs make extensive use of organizational charts, role descriptions, and rule books; and they make certain assumptions about organization. Basically, what is assumed is that an organization is like an orchestra, with the chief executive as the conductor who runs the whole show because only he or she knows the whole score. The classical type of CEO is still the most widely employed.

For example, until very recently the North American auto companies organized along classical lines with maximal task break-down and with individual effort tied to the speed of the assembly line. On the other hand, Volvo in Sweden has come up with an existential auto assembly line where people work in teams that allow job enrichment and job exchange.

The first step in the classical model is to define the job in terms of duties, physical and mental requirements, and tools; this means job analysis. The next step is to organize the jobs into groups according to some principle. For example, the jobs can be organized according to function or geographical area. The old type of organization is called bureaucracy; a new type of organization is called adhocracy.

## The Existential Chief Executive

Realizing the limitations of the classical approach, chief executives, not behavioral scientists, switched their efforts to redefining the CEO's style.

The superior advantage of the existential approach is that it does not reject the organization model built on the accounting and industrial engineering analogy but goes beyond it to give pride of place to the transformational style.

## The Executive Personality

Why don't CEOs concentrate their efforts on production? When we ask such questions regarding executive behavior, we are trying to explore questions of motivation. Motivation is concerned with the study of the direction and persistence of action. Executive personality is the organizing center around which both people's motives form a unified and integrated system and the strategy of the firm becomes manifest.

The aim here is to present an organized review of some of the outstanding contemporary chief executives that may be of interest to the executive, indicating their relevance for the study of executive behavior and personality.

Gordon W. Allport, in *Personality: A Psychological Interpretation* (1937), examines a mass of different definitions and gives the neatest, most penetrating, and most frequently cited definition: "Personality is the dynamic organization within an individual of those psychophysical systems that determine his unique adjustments to his environment."

For Allport, personality is dynamic and describes something that is always in the process of becoming. Executive personality is seen as an expanding system seeking new and better levels of order and transaction. Thus his definition emphasizes the ideal of organization, of how people perceive themselves and the world.

Executive personality of the chief executive is a crystallizing focus around which the other managers' behavior, attitudes, and motivations form a unified and integrated system. For a firm to function properly, the subordinate managers must have some insight into how the CEO's personality works, especially if they wish to mobilize their energies and resources to focus them in a productive way.

## The Existential Answer

For the modern entrepreneur, the time has come to talk of many things, of how the new entrepreneurial society has revealed entrepreneurship and existentialism to a new executive (a young upwardly mobile manager, or Yummy), and of why he or she often feels that the organizational sea is boiling hot with opportunity.

The ancients compared the plot of a drama to the tying and untying of a knot. Corporate life has become a knot, and existentialism offers a way of untying that knot.

The Pepsi Generation of executives are young in years, seasoned in experience, and knowing about conflict.

## Managers Are Ballet-Dancing Samurai

New types of managers, who have a different optic and a distinct perspective, have joined the team (see Table 1.1). Existentialism, as an executive style and a manner of thinking, is of great interest to these entrepreneurial managers because so much of contemporary consumer choice is mandated by the new existential ways that "creative people" have consciously and unconsciously built into ads, both electronic and print.

The Yummies' cognitive style places its emphasis on lateral thinking and the search for an alternative. Existentialists want to stand out, to "*exister*," to move beyond self-actualization. All this means a new value system and new attitudes. Yummies do not fear Freud (castration complex, for example); they fear moving down market.

The new managers have a different attitude to authority, computers, women, minorities. They do not function in a crisply defined black-and-white geometrically defined environment. In the world of "organizational Alice," they use intuition and in particular the right hemisphere of the brain. Because organizations and markets behave in counter-intuitive ways, it is useful to cast a glance at the executive as ballet-dancing samurai, where existentialism, entrepreneurship, intuition, and disciplined analysis are all necessary. A good example of a ballet-dancing samurai is John Sculley. Sculley is excellent in the Art of Corporate Self-actualization. To achieve this corporate self-actualization John Sculley had to reinvent Apple. Three years after Sculley arrived at Apple, he was in a quandary. Just as Moses went to the mountain and came back with the Ten Commandments, Steven Jobs went to the mountain and came back with the Macintosh. "But," as John Markoff points out in "John Sculley's Biggest Test" (*New York Times*, Sunday, February 6, 1989), "Can John Sculley go to the mountain and come back with something unique?" In January 1986, after its most disastrous year, Sculley had to reinvent the

**Table 1.1**
**Characteristics of Classical versus Existential Executives**

| CLASSICAL EXECUTIVE | EXISTENTIAL EXECUTIVE |
|---|---|
| **Structure** | |
| Hierarchical, pyramidal, multi-level -limited access | Controlled anarchy and adhocracy - almost unlimited access |
| **Style** | |
| Three piece suit | Shirt sleeves |
| **Process** | |
| POLES (plans, organizes, leads, evaluates) | Agenda setting networking |
| Reflective, systematic planning | Brief encounters, full of wit, gossip, soft info. all at high speed. Brevity, variety, discontinuity |
| **Information** | |
| MIS complex print outs, sales reports, etc. | Highly verbal as well as non verbal, electronic mail, faxes |
| Long monthly, quarterly meetings | Extremely short one-on-ones and brief meetings |
| **Values** | |
| "No-nonsense, let's get on with this job." "We are one big happy family." Denial of political dimension | "Work smarter not harder." Exploit visibility like Iacocca to sell cars |
| **Incidentals** | |
| No computer hands-on skills, apprehensive about women and minorities | Computer skills, gets along with minorities, high tech ambiance, modern attitudes toward marriage. |
| Cars: Caddies and Lincolns Sports: golf | Cars: German Driving Machines Sports: tennis and skiing |

**BOTH**

High pay, rich in stock and acquisitions; age indeterminant; social and geographical origins anywhere; both can co-exist and indeed do.

| **Patron Saints** | |
|---|---|
| Harold Geneen Reginald Jones | Jack Welch Lee Iacocca Steven Jobs |

Apple vision while giving a decent burial to the messy departure of Steven Jobs. As Frank Rose points out in *West of Eden* (1989), Sculley, the ultimate package goods guy and the marketing guy behind the "Pepsi Generation," had some hot ideas about communicating intangibles. A leap of faith was necessary to go from intangible benefit to intangible product—this was what the Apple Vision was all about.

### Yummies Are from the Pepsi Generation

John Sculley's background at Pepsi-Cola prepared him for Apple. A good example of consumer psychology in action emerges from a swift comparison of how Coca-Cola and Pepsi-Cola have been marketed. Coca-Cola's slogans, such as "It's the real thing; Coke" emphasize the product. Pepsi-Cola's statements, like "Come alive, you're the Pepsi generation" emphasize the consumers, especially young people. At the beginning, Pepsi used to compete with Coke by offering twice as much. An unsubtle class difference developed between Coke and Pepsi drinkers, as "The Pepsis" was used to describe the ethnic class that was at a social and economic disadvantage. But in the 1970s, Pepsi began to emphasize its slogan "Think Young." Cokes' riposte was to emphasize the tradition of Coke. Pepsi-Cola in the late 1970s began to emphasize the idea of the Pepsi Generation. Nature became the key thing; the new campaign was based on self-actualization, and existential life styles took the consumer beyond Watergate and the Vietnam War. A new generation of Pepsi-like managers and organizations was emerging. These Pepsi-managers or yummies want to change the world.

Sculley, the perfect Pepsi-manager, found it difficult to invigorate practical business methods at Apple, since most people at Apple had never worked in business. So Sculley, a master of marketing and management who had worked in business, set out to show that Apple could be trusted by businesspeople. He set out to transform Apple from a small technology company to a blue-chip giant without losing the creative and existential passion of its "wild ducks." To get Apple's "wild ducks" to spread their wings, and yet fly in formation, Sculley set out to make Apple the most exciting corporation in the world. As Frank Rose quotes Sculley in *West of Eden*: "It requires a genuine passion to want to change the world." John Sculley sees himself as the apostle of the information age who will lead Apple beyond the PC to the promised land of commercial electronics. And in the process, by 1993, Sculley has made Apple with $7 billion in revenue as large as Pepsico, which he left a decade ago.

Another extremely successful Pepsi Generation chief executive is Anita Roddick who is the managing director of The Body Shop International, a successful cosmetics manufacturer and retailer with no marketing department and no advertising. The Body Shop, which has a very serious commitment to its mission of environmental responsibility, is seen as a model for organizations of the future, because of its financial success and its capacity to retain the loyalty of its customers. The company mission which is available in all its shops, states, "We will be the most honest cosmetics company around." Many CEOs are trying to follow in the footsteps of The Body Shop's success by getting their companies to become environmentally friendly and socially conscious.

### The New Manager's Patron Saint: Jack Welch

A new change in management style is sweeping American business. A good example of this new-style manager is John S. ("Jack") Welch, Jr., Chairman of General Electric Company, who is in the process of dismantling the organizational structures built by his predecessor, Reginald Jones. Jones had built up General Electric in the 1960s and 1970s through the use of classical organizational structure and formal strategic planning. For example, he made a major effort to reduce the number of levels in the organization so that the number of layers going from the lowest rung to the president would be only six or seven. Jones also introduced the idea of strategic business units (SBUs), which were developed solely for the purpose of strategic planning. Each of these SBUs had to have a unique business mission with a clearly identified set of competitors and the ability to accomplish strategic planning and implementation relatively independent of the other SBUs. The strategic manager in charge of a particular SBU must be able to make crucial decisions to ensure the success of the SBU. This strategic planning in General Electric represented a formalized process for establishing the corporate goals and turned out to be extremely successful. It is widely accepted that Jones's formal, almost bureaucratic strategy in his approach to the organization was appropriate for the 1960s and 1970s.

Now, in the 1990s, Jack Welch, in a series of dramatic moves, is making a major effort to modernize the company by shutting down the unproductive plants, which he describes as marginal. Welch's approach is that a plant must either be "fixed" or "sold" if it is marginal, and the financial evidence shows quite clearly that General Electric is moving quite briskly.

This new entrepreneurial and dramatic style of Jack Welch is in strong contra-distinction to the bureaucratic style of Reginald Jones. General Electric had an outstanding reputation for using modern management techniques including value analysis, strategic planning, and new decentralized organizational structures. Welch is now redesigning the company using a personal drama style that is much more informal but rigorous and more appropriate to the highly competitive environment of the 1990s. What Welch is trying to do is to turn General Electric into a high-flying entrepreneurial organization, which he feels must grow to succeed. Welch's tough, hard-nosed style has earned him the reputation of being one of the hardest-charging managers in the United States. Welch's predecessor, Jones, was perceived as a polished, disciplined, and rather formal man who rose through General Electric from its accounting and finance departments. Welch, on the other hand, is a much more ''shirt-sleeves''-type manager. According to Thomas J. Lueck, Welch exudes confidence that the company will reign supreme in foreign markets. ''We have the smarts and the money,'' he said. ''We ought to be able to win.''

### Translating Top Management Policy into Shop-Floor Practice

At the same time, however, Welch is trying to run his company like a small business. Welch's view is ''you've got to take out the boss element.'' In his mind, managers will have to set aside their own powers of POLEing and take on the responsibility as coaches and team leaders. As Welch points out, ''we're going to win on our ideas not by whips and chains.'' For Welch it is a question of ''speed, simplicity, and self-confidence.''

As Thomas A. Stewart points out in ''GE Keeps Those Ideas Coming'' (1991), Welch has no intention of sacrificing profit for new management ideas. Welch believes that a hard-nosed reputation for superior performance can go along with soft concepts like employee involvement. The idea is that power in the executive system has to be dismantled and allocated to ''process-mapping'' people who could be in any level in the organization but who are the people responsible for getting the stuff out the gate. General Electric uses three techniques: work-out, best-practices, and process-mapping. Work-Out is meant to get employees more involved in the decision-making process; Best-Practices is meant to get General Electric looking elsewhere for good ideas; and Process-Mapping is a technique for specifying the actual procedures used to produce or manufacture a particular product. This latter technique is used to identify where the actual holdups are.

### General Electric Changes Culture

What Welch is trying to do is to challenge his employees to develop new ideas by taking the boss element out of management. Yet Welch, himself, is quintessentially a boss. He is often described as *capo di tutti capi*. Welch believes the future in management lies in the ability to mobilize employees' good ideas. The organization focus is on these ideas to get things done.

This represents a radical departure for General Electric, which introduced such concepts as strategic planning, decentralization, and market research. In many respects GE was the corporate lab for a whole spectrum of management techniques. When Welch took over in 1981 the company operated 350 different product lines; Welch has squeezed them into thirteen big businesses. So effective was he in reorganizing General Electric that he received the title "Neutron Jack" after the neutron bomb, which will kill people but leave buildings intact. But Welch wasn't only removing 100,000 jobs, he was designing a new style organization too.

What Welch is trying to do is to change GE's culture. The objective is to get GE's hierarchy to wither away and replace it with a horizontal structure, but with accountability built in. In this system, as Welch points out, a manager's functions "are comfortable facilitating, greasing, finding ways to make it all seamless, not controllers and directors. Work-Out is fundamental underpinning of the training of the next generation managers."

## THE NEW MANAGERIAL STYLE

The turmoil in the offices of CEOs is forcing senior executives to undertake a radical reassessment of their understanding of management concepts. The complexity of events and the complicity of players have made change and crisis the two constants in corporate life. CEOs are marching to a new drum beat of rapid technological change and global competition. Three things matter to the CEO: market leadership, high profits, and a stand-out stock price. Loyalty is one characteristic that has changed (or even evolved) with the new CEO. *Business Week* (1989) asks and answers the question, "What influence will their past have on their executive style?"

Some argue that these business leaders will be less loyal to companies and more appreciative of leisure and family. Their views on environmental issues will differ from those of earlier generations. And others note that this group of executives will be the first to feel comfortable dealing with computers and the other trappings of the Information Age.

These CEOs are learning to deal with uncertainty and paradox. To cope with these difficulties, CEOs are focusing on the nitty-gritty details of business with short time horizons; they are acting differently and refusing the straitjacket of corporate hierarchy. A new interpersonal climate is emerging where the emphasis in on *we* rather than *I*. But something else is happening.

It is becoming increasingly obvious to Top Management that a new style of management is required if business is to succeed in the 1990s. Companies are beginning to realize that when something is in fact accomplished, it is, as Peter F. Drucker puts it, "by a mono-maniac with a mission." Contrary to conventional wisdom, business decision making is not entirely rational; rather, a great deal depends on intuition, hunch, and experience. If chief executive officers are to be successful, they must become mono-maniacs with vision who can in fact drive their companies forward. The essence of the matter is really that the CEO is able to infuse the system with his or her values. To ensure these values are absorbed by the organization, the CEO has to develop a new management style.

*The Marks of the New Management Style*
1. Uses a transformational style of leadership
2. Cuts an existential figure
3. Is a charismatic visionary
4. Can handle conflict
5. Has a different value system

# Part I

---

# The Behavior of Executives

# 2

---

# The Chief Executive

## THE IMPERIAL CHIEF EXECUTIVE

It is amazing to many outsiders that the chief executives of many companies behave in a very imperial way. Many of them continue to hold on to power, even when the company is floundering and the stock price is plummeting.

As Steven Prokesch points out, there is a widespread movement in the United States arguing that chief executives ought to be held accountable for financial and comparative performance and for the general behavior of their companies (Prokesch, 1986). But most boards are made up of executives from their own companies and outsiders selected by the CEO. These very executives who sit as the directors are very reluctant to be aggressive and challenging to the chief executive officer. American chief executives are rarely held fully accountable for the performance of the company, primarily because few executives believe that the chief executive is in complete control of the corporation. Matters are somewhat different in Europe, for corporate ownership is in far fewer hands and the chief executive has to account for much more. In Japan, chief executives are also held accountable. For example, the president of Japan Air Lines (JAL) apologized to the victims' families and resigned after a JAL jumbo jet crashed in 1986.

The same cannot be said for the chairman of Morton Thiokol. The chief executive did not even think of resigning after the space shuttle *Challenger* exploded. In Japan, chief executives are expected to accept moral responsibility for the performance of their companies, but in the United States chief executives are not, as it is widely believed that no single executive can control the operations of a very large organization.

Lack of managerial accountability, in this country, is explained by how boards operate: The chief executive and the members of the board often come from the same background, went to the same schools and universities, are members of the same country club, and are often close personal friends—indeed, intense mutual admirers. Thus, members of the board are extremely reluctant to call into question the performance of the chief executive, perhaps one of their colleagues. In addition, directors are very reluctant to oust the chief executive even when there has been a dramatic failure in performance, and many chief executives in fact receive pay without performance.

Even the threat of litigation and liability provide little inducement for members of boards to take action to oust incompetent chief executives. Directors of companies are liable, especially when they fail to exercise good judgment in regard to decision making. The argument seems to be that CEOs are not likely to admit responsibility for mistakes. Their view is that they would be fools to apologize or to admit guilt for an accident or for a product failure. The chief executive officer of Morton Thiokol, when asked if he should resign, snapped back: "You explain to me why I should." The ultimate explanation for this lack of corporate accountability lies in the American culture. Americans do not expect the CEO to accept responsibility for his corporate misdeeds or his mistakes. A widely held view, in the United States, is that the chief executive often does not know enough about what's going on to be held accountable.

### John Akers and IBM

In 1992, IBM was in a disaster mode. Its stock was falling and its profits were falling. At one time IBM stock was the bellwether for the Dow Jones industrial average. Now IBM is performing well below expectations. In the fourth quarter of 1992, IBM reported a loss of $5.5 billion, its first quarterly operating loss.

John Akers' answer to the charge that IBM is in crisis is simply that IBM is caught up in an industry that is moving so fast that it is difficult to adjust quickly enough. The problem is that IBM is fighting for its life and the company has failed both in product development and marketing.

Akers is going to be remembered as the man who let IBM falter. Akers has had a career of accomplishments, first as a navy flier, then as an outstanding IBM salesman and junior executive; he was picked out as a star. The trouble was twofold: When Akers took over IBM from his immediate predecessors, Frank T. Cary and John R. Opel, he took over a company that was fat and overconfident, and IBM has 50,000 competitors, most of whom are niche players. IBM is often described as asset-heavy, people-laden, and bureaucracy-ridden. For many years IBM has been operating like a huge citadel surrounded by a moat; now that moat is drying up, and IBM has to face harsh criticism from its many competitors. No longer can it depend on its history.

The computer that has been giving IBM the most problems is the personal computer (PC) that sells in a soybean-sowbelly price driven market, just like any other useful commodity. Teaming up with Apple in an attempt to overcome some of the technical difficulties that IBM PCs face in the marketplace because they are not seen as user friendly. All this interest in PCs has come at a time when IBM has still focused its major effort on mainframes.

How Akers manages information flow for the company is of considerable interest. On about the fifteenth working day of each month, IBM's management information people deliver to Armonk, New York, headquarters a quarterly forecast based on orders received. For example, in 1991 business in January and February was poor but the February forecast showed that IBM could still have had a reasonable quarter bolstered by sales in March. But nothing is certain in the world of computers. When it got to "white knuckle time," a term IBM people use to describe the waiting days of a quarter, the business wasn't there.

The essence of the matter is that for IBM, marketing has always been more important than technology. For example, Thomas J. Watson, Jr., the son of the founder of IBM, spells out how technology has always been less important than sales and distribution methods. Young Tom relates how his father, Thomas J. Watson ensured, starting with the competition from Univac (which had a better computer than IBM), that IBM was able to out-perform Univac simply because in fact he had marketed IBM's service skills. What the elder Watson's salespeople had was the ability to install the machine properly and to hang on to customers once they had them with expert service. Unfortunately, Akers cannot manage to mobilize IBM's marketing resources effectively to get the kind of performance needed to stop IBM's stock market price from plummeting. In an interview reported in *Fortune* magazine in July 1991, Akers said that the company is facing reality at last. The article, "Can John Akers Save IBM?" by Carol J. Loomis, highlights IBM's enormous staff and the major problem of how to reduce it. Having always pursued a policy of job security for its employees, IBM now has invented a whole bureaucratic language to explain how it overcomes problems of assured job security while still having the right to fire people. This IBMspeak includes such terms as MIS, or management initiated separation. This term is used to describe a reduction in the work force not caused by voluntary resignation or retirement. Translation: "You're fired." Another example cited by Loomis is the verb "non-concur," meaning to withhold for approval as in "I non-concur with this proposal." Another term used in IBMspeak is "tree-hugger," which refers to an employee who resists a move or any other change. Technically IBM's well-established principle is full employment, that is, "no lay-off system in place." Nevertheless, in the era of Akers, the company has been forced into the use of MIS.

Akers has been compared unfavorably with Jack Welch of General Electric, who really is running a revolution in his company. Akers answers that this is simplistic, "You can't compare IBM and GE." But Akers does admit that IBM was slow in getting into personal computers, that he missed the boat in mid-range systems, and that they were late in work stations. To counter all these criticisms Akers is cutting IBM's expenses to the bone and is striving for growth in software services to what is called OEM—original equipment manufacturing—meaning production by IBM of its hardware for resale under another company's name. Akers has also declared war on IBM's competition. "We're going to ship one spiffy product, and we're going to price it to maintain or gain market share" (Loomis, *Fortune* 1991). But in 1993 Akers is being blamed for taking IBM from being one of the world's most profitable companies to one of the biggest loss-makers in corporate history.

### Iacocca and His General Managers at Chrysler

The image presented to us of Lee Iacocca on television—eyes glinting behind aviator frames, chin jutting forward, and finger poking the air excitedly—is an image that has alerted America to the idea that Chrysler cars are made in America and worth considering. Now in the early 1990s Chrysler is facing a real crisis again.

The trouble for Chrysler has come because Iacocca failed to follow his own maxims. As he pointed out in his autobiography (1984), "In the end, all business operations can be reduced to three words: people, product and profits. People come first. Unless you've got a good team, you can't do much with the other two." At Chrysler Lee Iacocca had a good team, which included Harold Sperlich, who helped design the Mustang. Sperlich has always been an outspoken maverick as well as a very creative executive who would have been weeded out in a more conformist-oriented corporation. Iacocca, himself, is a very demanding boss. He is willing to fire people who don't measure up to his standards, but he was able to manage this unique group of people he had brought together. Indeed the recovery of Chrysler was spearheaded by Sperlich who designed the K-car, which provided the platform from which all other early 1980 products came, including the minivan.

Because of the K-car, the narrow, fuel-efficient, front-wheel drive vehicle that Sperlich had started designing when he came to Chrysler from Ford, Chrysler's share of the North American market went from 7.8 percent in 1980 to 10.8 percent in 1985. The enormous success that Chrysler enjoyed turned Iacocca into a celebrity and a glamorous party-goer. Indeed his autobiography, projected to sell a few hundred copies, sold nearly six million and stayed on the best seller list for a year.

Unfortunately Iacocca did not stick to his knitting but decided to engage in a series of acquisitions. For example, Chrysler owned 24 percent of Mitsubishi Motors, but Iacocca's appetite for expansion was merely whetted. In 1984 he decided to buy a 3.5 percent share in Mazarati to begin a joint development of a luxury sports car, the TC. In 1986 he upped Chrysler's stake in Mazarati to 15.2 percent. Also in 1986 he bought Gulf Stream Aerospace for $637 million. In 1987 he bought an Italian sports car manufacturer, Lamborghini. Again in 1987 he bought American Motors for $757 million.

While Iacocca was making all these acquisitions, Sperlich argued strongly for the building of a new car "platform." Such a platform, like the K-car, can provide the basis for a whole series and models. Unfortunately, Iacocca wasn't willing to get involved in developing a new platform at that time. When Iacocca first set out to rebuild Chrysler, he brought in strong-willed, dynamic executives particularly from the Ford Motor Company to help him form a strong team, with Sperlich and Gerald Greenwald as the two most important members of this team. To keep these general managers happy, Iacocca created a new set of prestigious titles. Now Iacocca was just the man to manage a creative team such as Sperlich and Greenwald: he was able to command their loyalty yet spend sufficient time to smooth their egos and reconcile competing visions.

In "The Guru Who Forgot What He Said" (1990), John B. Judis points out that once he became a celebrity, Iacocca spent less and less time in Detroit because he was busy raising funds for the Statue of Liberty and spending a lot of time with other celebrities. Iacocca also began a whirlwind courtship with former flight attendant Peggy Johnson. They were married in April 1986 and divorced a year later. It seemed as if Iacocca was in fact in need of distraction.

In the middle of all Iacocca's comings and goings, the product-minded Sperlich and the bean counter and accounting genius Greenwald entered a real conflict. Sperlich was fighting for a new platform in 1985–1986, but he was opposed by Greenwald. Unfortunately, Iacocca wasn't around to resolve this conflict to refocus their attention on the survival of Chrysler. In the middle of the fight, Sperlich opposed the 1987 purchase of AMC mainly because he believed the money was needed to build a new platform if Chrysler was in fact going to succeed. Iacocca asked Sperlich to step aside, so that "a new team could be formed." By this move Chrysler lost a brilliant product man who had a genius for marketing and who had been behind many of Iacocca's successes: the Mustang, and, via the K-car, the minivan.

Iacocca lost not only Sperlich but also Greenwald, who left Chrysler in 1990 to join United Airlines. Of the original trio who rebuilt Chrysler—

Iacocca, Sperlich, and Greenwald—only Iacocca was left. Faced with these problems Iacocca was forced to sell off many acquisitions and indeed to make a major investment in building a new platform. In 1992 Iacocca was eased out of office because of Chrysler's failures.

These development problems at Chrysler and the personal difficulties that faced Iacocca made it seem as if history would repeat itself. When Iacocca was president of Ford, under Henry Ford II, a major personal conflict broke out between Ford and Iacocca. When they were quarrelling, Ford completed the argument simply by suggesting to Iacocca that he take a trip outside the building and look to see whose name is actually out there on the wall, and then come back in and give his opinion again. It is widely believed that Ford was jealous of Iacocca's accomplishments. Cooler minds in the 1990s can believe that Iacocca's self promotion became a threat to the company. Much the same thing has happened at Chrysler. Now Iacocca is gone. Iacocca had been unable to handle his general managers, and he had been unable to fuse together a product genius and an accounting genius into a successful team that could continue to function over a long period of time. Instead he became caught up in the celebrity business and got away from the day-to-day attention to "people, product, and profits." For a company to be successful, executives have to stick to the knitting and keep working at what, in fact, they do best. In Iacocca's case this was the designing, manufacturing, and marketing of cars. When he allowed himself to be sidelined into restoring the Statue of Liberty and following celebrity tracks, he lost sight of what he should have been doing.

### William H. Gates and Microsoft

In his mid-thirties, William H. Gates is chief executive of Microsoft, one of the fifty most valuable companies in the United States according to *Business Week* magazine. Microsoft was the major provider of key software for IBM and provided MS-DOS operating systems for IBM personal computers. Microsoft corporation is now the world's largest software company, with revenues in 1990 of $1.3 billion. But Microsoft's relationship with IBM is in a shambles after a falling out over the joint development of the successor to MS-DOS. Each company is now trashing the other's product in public. As Andrew Pollack points out in "One Day, Junior Got Too Big for His Boots," Gates has worked at a relentless pace since he dropped out of Harvard at the age of eighteen in 1975 to start Microsoft. Now Gates is sending out more than one hundred electronic mail messages each day. Many of his colleagues receive mail at two in the morning. Some of his thirtysomething executives have now started to marry and have families, and they find it difficult to cope with this onslaught of electronic mail. Gates, by all descriptions, is a very demanding boss and will blast any employees who come to him unprepared; they may well leave with their heads in their hands. "At least three times in a meeting, he said 'that's the stupidest thing I ever heard,'" said Paul Maritz, vice president for advanced operating systems. According to Gates, new organizations in the 1990s will have to utilize new technology (NT), which runs on powerful personal computers using a new version of Windows, which was clearly inspired by Apple's work with the MacIntosh line of computers. Microsoft is the largest supplier of personal computer applications software such as wordprocessing programs and spreadsheets, and it continues to expand into new categories such as software for the home and small business.

## THE EXECUTIVE: HIS OR HER BEHAVIOR, BEHAVIORALLY VIEWED

If you wanted to study executives, you could do three basic things: Ask them what they do (interview); look at work records (examine documents); or study them in action (observe).

What do we already know about the behavior of American chief executives? We know a great deal about such giants as John Akers, Lee Iacocca, and Jack Welch from newspaper gossip columns. But what do we know about the American chief executive through observational studies?

### A Behavioral Portrait of Top Management

One of the first studies was made by William H. Whyte, Jr., of *Organization Man* fame (1956), who, while studying company presidents, found out that they worked long hours, often into the evenings, mostly interacting—doing a "Dale Carnegie" and influencing people. The question puzzling social scientists was how top management found time to work. What about their families, their personal lives? But the key question is "What is the underlying paradigm?"

Thirty years ago, Whyte described his paradigm, the corporate conformist who worked for the organization. These organization men were dominated not by the work ethic of getting to the top but by the social ethic. The basic propositions of the social ethic are three: a belief in the group as a source of creativity, a belief in "belongingness" as the ultimate characteristic of the individual, and a belief in the application of science as a method *par excellence* of solving society's problems.

The whole idea of making executive behavior studies by observation was invented by Sune Carlson, a professor of business studies at Uppsala University in Sweden.

## Carlson's Managers and the Arapesh

The most famous executive behavior research is the study by Carlson of nine Swedish managing directors and one French managing director reported in *Executive Behaviour* (1951). In the preface, Carlson makes a revealing reference to the Arapesh in Margaret Mead's *Sex and Temperament in Three Primitive Societies*. A mountain people, the Arapesh are characterized by friendliness and a readiness to help each other. What struck Carlson as interesting is that they apparently have great difficulty in finding people to act as leaders. In their view, "big men" have to plan, have to be willing to start things up, "have to strut about and swagger and speak in loud voices," and in general act in a boastful manner like modern day managers. Carlson's conclusion is that the chief executives he observed have something in common with the "big men" among the Arapesh.

Carlson was preoccupied with the idea of getting management studies beyond the pre-Galileo stage. He felt the field of management was too theoretical, academic, and sterile, based to a large extent on anecdotes—and, worse still, anecdotes with a sample size of N = 1. In an attempt to get away from these "ought-axioms" and to get to some "is hypothesis," Carlson tried to get "the facts." What he was against was the idea that management can be summed up in acronyms such as POLE, MBWA (management by walking about), OD (organization development), SWOT (strengths, weaknesses, opportunities, threats), and so on. Carlson set out to find out for himself what managers do by actually observing managers.

The chief executives he observed worked all hours, rarely inspected factories (although not doing so made them feel guilty), and had no "alone time." The lack of this "alone time" for thinking things out worried Carlson. This is a constant finding of social scientists looking at executives. Professors need a lot of "alone time" ("are they in a state of withdrawal in the asylum of the university?"), whereas executives like a lot of "interaction time." Perhaps one person's behavioral cocktail is another person's poison. Carlson was also worried about their lack of opportunity to go to the theater or to read books. Carlson ended up by noting that this study only confirmed the cliché about executives. But what *was* Carlson's cliché in paradigm?

## Carlson's Cliché

While admitting that the managing directors may have *desired* to change their behavior, Carlson felt that the choice was not theirs. On the score of choice, Carlson concluded:

In several respects we could check the data collected for the observation period against similar data covering a full year, and also against the evidence obtained from the interviews with subordinates. Indeed, even had the executives wanted to change their behavior, they did not have much chance to do so. The content of their working day is determined only to a small extent by themselves, and it is difficult to change it without making considerable alterations in the organizational structure of which they are part. Before we made the study, I always thought of a chief executive as the conductor of an orchestra, standing aloof on his platform. Now I am in some respects inclined to see him as the puppet in a puppet-show with hundreds of people pulling the strings and forcing him to act in one way or another.

### The Strategic Fit Model

A different approach suggests that executive behavior is misleading. Ibrahim (1986, 1989) proposed a paradigm shift that focuses on the fit between executive behavior and personality on one hand and the corporate strategic direction on the other hand. The author identifies two distinct executive behaviors: the visionary and the missionary (see Table 2.1) that match different strategic directions. Ibrahim's study clearly indicates that our corporate prima donnas are not ''in'' for a lifetime but rather have to fit the firm's strategic directions.

### Corporate Mythology and the Chief Executive

Unfortunately, many CEOs are blinded by their own grandiose self-images and are unable to make rational choices in regard to the economic realities facing their companies. Abraham Zaleznik, a professor at the Harvard Business School who applied psychoanalytic techniques to corporations, has argued that a primary reason that General Motors lost its market share was ''the internalization of ideals, values and corporate

Table 2.1
Executive Behavior: The Visionary and the Missionary

|  | Organization (Strategy) Fit | Characteristics of the Style |
|---|---|---|
| The Visionary | Organization in the entrepreneurial stage, developing and aggressive growth.<br><br>Also fits organization in the turn-around stage. | Intuitive, extrovert, optimistic, excitable, flair, analytical, calculated risk, dominant and flexible. |
| The Missionary | Organization in the maturity and stable stage.<br><br>Organization in the decline and retrenchment stage. | Bureaucratic, team player, conformist, systematic, mature, calm, friendly, specialized, priority oriented and conservative. |

structures and practices that can be traced back to the company's legendary chairman, Alfred P. Sloan Jr.'' In other words, General Motors' chief executives have been so overawed by Sloan's performance and by the radical way in which he redesigned the corporation that they are unable to adjust the image to meet the realities of present situations. Because these chief executives are well established in the power structure and enjoy a protected position, they develop certain narcissistic gains from belonging to the organization and they are very difficult to influence. However, since middle management and the workers are excluded from mythological structures that provide these narcissistic gains to the chief executive, it is often difficult for chief executives to persuade subordinates to put their plans into action or to receive the criticism that would be appropriate to deal with and adjust to realities.

And because, in General Motors, for example, the chairman has his eyes fixed on a mythological structure that is no longer appropriate, he finds it difficult to compete with the Japanese and German car manufacturers.

Consultants are often brought into organizations to help them to identify their culture and to look beyond the mythologies that are holding back the companies. As Zaleznick argues, it is important for chief executives to remain objective and to have the capacity to look at the world as it is.

### Failure for Chief Executives Means the Golden Parachute

Golden parachutes, that is, multimillion-dollar bail outs that make chief executives even richer when their companies are taken over, represent a form of insurance for top management. In the early days these parachutes were reserved only for a corporation's top two or three executives, but now they have become part of the fabric of compensation programs. For example, in 1983 William M. Agee, the chairman of Bendix Corporation, received $4 million after selling his company to Allied. Another example is Michael C. Bergerac, Revlon's former chairman, who received some $35 million after his company was taken over by Pantry Pride.

### Roger B. Smith and General Motors

Roger B. Smith, chief executive officer of General Motors, restructured the corporation in January 1984. Great hopes were expressed that the company was in fact going to achieve a turnaround. The idea was that it would have two supergroups (big cars and small cars) and that this would allow for a more effective method for designing, engineering, and manufacturing cars. Unfortunately, General Motors is now, in the early 1990s, going through a very difficult passage: its market share has shrunk considerably, profits are down, and Ford and Chrysler have moved more effectively into the market.

Smith's counter-argument is that General Motors' loss in market share is due to the company's need to switch from the manufacture of large rear-wheel-drive cars to mid-size front-wheel-drive models. The critics argue that General Motors' problems are much more serious and relate to their material, labor, and overhead costs for the cars. Unfortunately, Smith would not adjust to the idea that General Motors is going to have a much lower market share and that he ought to shift General Motors away from car making to other areas. Indeed, General Motors' acquisitions did include electronic data systems and Hughes Aircraft in an effort to achieve diversification, but with mixed results.

## REBUILDING THE AMERICAN CEO

Many effective American CEOs are adopting a new philosophy that puts corporate survival above all. These new style executives scorn loyalty in favor of market leadership, profits, and a high stock price.

Increasingly American CEOs are coming to recognize that corporate survival cannot be taken for granted. A good example of this new breed of CEO is David T. Kearns, chairman of Xerox Corporation, who set aside Xerox's time-honored philosophy of manufacturing and selling copiers in the United States. Now the Xerox line includes components and even whole machines that are manufactured in the Orient.

This is a new breed of chief executive officer. No longer preoccupied with a favorable trade balance or even manufacturing in America, the new CEO is preoccupied with ensuring the survival of the organization. The new view is that change is the only constant in society. This new view casts the chief executive officer as a global warrior, who is a proponent of joint ventures with other companies. Let us consider, for example, the recent joint venture effort by Apple and IBM. A good example of the old-style executive was Reginald H. Jones, chairman of General Electric in the 1970s, who was regarded by other CEOs as a statesman. He was very much involved in the pronouncing of public policy. Indeed, he was very much admired by the executives of his time. Now his successor, John S. Welch, Jr., is a representative of a new brand of CEO. Welch sits on no other corporate board, makes few public speeches, and concerns himself exclusively with the managing of GE, which has been transformed from a stodgy manufacturer into a real goal-getting company. CEOs are no longer involved in social concerns but are up to their eyeballs in the nitty-gritty of their businesses.

These new-style CEOs are learning to deal with paradox and uncertainty, are focusing on back-to-basics, and are vitally preoccupied with the market. To put this new style of CEO in context, it is necessary to reflect on the fact that American chief executives had it easy in the thirty years following World War II. Because the allied forces had destroyed German and Japanese industries, the latter could not compete effectively with the United States. In these circumstances marketing didn't matter so much, and Henry Ford's philosophy, "Give them any color they want as long as it's black," applied in many cases. Now with the boom markets of the 1960s gone, chief executives have to focus increasingly on customer demand. Beginning in the late 1970s after the gold standard had been abandoned and the U.S. dollar began its swings, the oil market caused inflation and interest rates to soar and business became a lot more difficult to manage. With the foreign onslaught, market position has taken precedence over all other considerations: maintaining market share has become synonymous with survival.

Unfortunately, most observational studies of chief executives have little to say about the context in which the managers actually operated. They focus on the idea of the managerial job being ad hoc, fragmented, and of brief duration (see Table 2.2). Most chief executives of the nineties would argue that they have an obsession or a preoccupation, and this preoccupation is in favor of market leadership, profits, and a high stock price. And as we know in 1993, the imperial CEO is dead. Gone is Robert C. Stempel from General Motors, dismissed by the board; departed is James D. Robinson III of American Express for failing to stop fleeing cardmembers; gone is John Akers of IBM. Going is the imperial CEO.

**Table 2.2**
**Chief Executives: Differing Pictures**

| Observational Studies | Newspaper Reports |
|---|---|
| 1. Unstructured: fragmented, adhoc, brief, unplanned | 1. Structured: full of "white knuckle" time awaiting data for quarterly report |
| 2. Devoid of emotion | 2. Emotionally charged: executives weakening at having to fire their boss |
| 3. Absence of drama | 3. Charged with drama: flamboyant moments in board meetings when the chairman declares "VICTORY" |
| 4. Superiors are courtly and accept "noise" and criticism from subordinates | 4. Subordinates don't speak back; in many cases they don't speak at all |
| 5. Nothing is said about telephone calls at home | 5. Much of the vital business is done by telephone after or out of hours |
| 6. Executives live in an "expletive deleted" environment - "A Gee Whiz, Oh" environment! | 6. The language of the executive suite sounds like a bunch of marines awaiting to go into battle |
| 7. An abstemions atmosphere. No sight of the liquor cabinet | 7. As our famous chairman used to ask "Where's the booze?" |

# 3

---

# The General Manager

The general manager of a company is the person who has prime responsibility for the performance of that particular company. In small businesses, the president is likely to be the only general manager; in large organizations, the term "general manager" encompasses people who range from the president to the manager who supervises the work of department managers. As the title suggests, a general manager has wide-ranging responsibilities, and his or her work includes complex, not easily defined tasks that are most difficult to achieve. Naturally, the rewards are large both in terms of salary and in fringe benefits; the greatest satisfaction, however, comes from managing an organization and being held responsible for overall goals. In many organizations the general manager will exercise complete authority over all aspects of production, sales, and finance. And now in the 1990s general managers are expected not only to manage existing businesses efficiently but also to exercise flair and entrepreneurial skills to create new businesses in line with the organization's mission. Many managers take up this position with a view to becoming directors of companies and eventually chief executives.

Here is the enigma of the general manager's job of reporting to the chief executive of the company. General managers are responsible for optimizing the company's potential and developing and improving production and marketing while at the same time achieving cost effectiveness and quality. To be effective, general managers have to develop a certain entrepreneurial flair that will enable them simultaneously to produce effectively and market through developing existing and new accounts. To be effective in their job requires exceptional negotiating skills and a real understanding of what customer service can deliver, together with a firm grasp, usually, of manufacturing, engineering, and marketing techniques.

Does this mean that the general manager truly understands all these different areas, including manufacturing, technology, and marketing? The answer is that to lead effectively general managers must be able to handle complexities that they cannot really understand. Thus as John Kotter points out in *The General Managers*, the general manager is put into a position where he or she is held accountable for a complex system that cannot be directly controlled or fully understood. All this means is that the general manager must have a certain managerial savoir-faire to identify problems and solutions in an environment that fits together in a way that's not totally clear. Hence, the importance of MBA case solving skills.

As Kotter has pointed out, the general manager (GM) has both responsibilities and relationships that must be integrated in a meaningful way. Turning first to the responsibilities, the GM is required to deal with both long-run goals, medium-term objectives, and short-run tasks. In terms of relationships, the GM has to be able to deal with an up-link, usually to the chief executive officer; laterally, the GM has to be able to relate to other general managers; in terms of down-link, the GM has to be able to relate to subordinates who typically are departmental managers.

## KOTTER'S EXISTENTIAL MANAGERS

Kotter's study focused on a group of successful general managers in a broad range of industries, including banking, consulting, television, and copiers. Kotter's work continues in the tradition of Sune Carlson and Henry Mintzberg. As Kotter points out in *General Managers*, this is "a study of a group of executives in generalist or general-management jobs: that is, individuals who hold positions with some multifunctional responsibility for a business (or businesses). Conducted between 1976 and 1981, this investigation employed multiple methods to look in depth at fifteen general managers from nine different corporations spread out across the United States. Although modest in scope by many standards, this is nevertheless the largest study of its kind ever conducted." The average salary of the GMs being studied was $150,000 per year.

Through personal interviews with the GMs and key colleagues, and by observing their daily routines, Kotter obtained information on the GMs' backgrounds, personalities, jobs, job contexts, behavior, and performance.

Kotter's study showed that GMs are specialists and team players. They do not slavishly follow channels, nor do they systematically set and follow formal plans. Instead, their lives are characterized by long hours (approximately sixty hours a week), fragmented episodes, and communication characterized by brief and disjointed conversations.

These GMs mobilize their personal resources, their drives, and organizational and technical savvy to get the job done in an incremental, largely informal process. Using an informal network of relations, doing favors, putting down and picking up markers, they get the job done.

They don't do the job by the management book. They don't POLE (plan, organize, lead, and evaluate) in a formal sense, but they do make good things happen, in an organizational sense. They rarely give orders, but they are out there influencing others.

Kotter's managers behave in an essentially existential way: They treat each day as a separate event to be lived out, where decision making is prime and moral issues of loyalty are basic.

### The Personalities of General Managers

In terms of personality, GMs seem to have a strong need for power and high achievement needs, and they are very ambitious. When Kotter asked about the high points in their lives, most of them spoke about personal incidents involving achievements of high business performance. They talked of going from a $1 million loss in one year to $3.5 million profit the following year. They talked constantly of achievements and, of course, status and power meant a great deal to these executives. In short, these GMs are highly motivated and ambitious. Temperamentally they are extremely stable. They seem to have the ability to keep their heads when everyone else is losing theirs. Interpersonally, they are personable and good at developing relationships with superiors, colleagues, and subordinates. They are also skilled at relating to functional specialists.

In terms of intelligence, they seem to be above average. They also seem to have an unusual combination of analytical and intuitive intelligence (see Figure 3.1).

### Technical Knowledge

One wonders whether a general manager is a generalist or a technical expert in his or her own field. Apparently, most of Kotter's managers were in fact technical experts who had worked in a particular area of their present company for some considerable time. Many of them had high-reaching contacts not only in their own companies but also in the industry to which their company belonged. The argument seems to be that GMs require an extensive technical and anecdotal knowledge of the business organization in which they find themselves. In terms of their backgrounds, most of the GMs were upwardly mobile, typically from lower-middle or middle class backgrounds. Most of Kotter's executives did not grow up in a household split by divorce, and almost all of them had at least one parent with a college education.

**Figure 3.1**
**The GM Personality as a System**

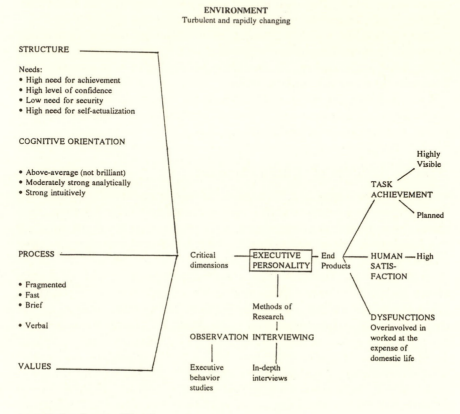

ENVIRONMENT
Turbulent and rapidly changing

STRUCTURE

Needs:
• High need for achievement
• High level of confidence
• Low need for security
• High need for self-actualization

COGNITIVE ORIENTATION

• Above-average (not brilliant)
• Moderately strong analytically
• Strong intuitively

Highly
Visible

TASK
ACHIEVEMENT

Planned

PROCESS

• Fragmented
• Fast
• Brief

• Verbal

Critical
dimensions

EXECUTIVE
PERSONALITY

End
Products

HUMAN — High
SATIS-
FACTION

Methods of
Research

OBSERVATION INTERVIEWING

DYSFUNCTIONS
Overinvolved in
worked at the
expense of
domestic life

VALUES

Executive
behavior
studies

In-depth
interviews

• a combination of career and life goals

## A Day in the Life of a General Manager

In "What Effective General Manager's Really Do" (1982), Kotter gives an account of a typical day of one of his managers, Michael Richardson. His is a busy day, work begins at 7:35 A.M. Coffee and conversation are the constants. There is also a constant flow of visitors who participate in a series of fragmented, disjointed episodes that help Richardson get the job done. In a busy day, Richardson touches on dozens of different topics. He seems to spend little time on planning, controlling, staffing, organizing, and directing in a formal sense, but these functions are achieved in an informal way. These activities are achieved through informal, almost casual meetings. People drop in; people drop out. But business gets done.

Twelve different events take place before nine o'clock. In this hectic schedule, Richardson has to maintain a steady course. Lunch, a relatively brief affair, is brought in and eaten in the conference room; it lasts from 12:20 until 1:15. It all sounds spartan. Having started at 7:35 A.M., the day finishes at 5:45 P.M. when Richardson leaves the office, but not before five people touch base with him on their way out.

According to Kotter, Richardson's day is typical for a general manager. GMs spend most of their time with others (75% with others, 25% alone, either at home or traveling). They meet superiors, peers, and subordinates. They also meet people who appear to be unimportant outsiders.

What do they talk about? Everything, apparently. GMs ask a lot of questions, literally hundreds, with a lot of joking and kidding. Non-work topics, such as golf, are also discussed. Orders are rarely given, but people get the idea and things get done. The rule is style over substance, which is hard to believe if you have never worked as a GM.

Is there a distinct personality for the GM? Apparently not. The job itself determines the behavior. They seem to be balanced, bright (but not brilliant) people who know what they are doing and who know their trade and how to trade with others.

All this means setting goals in a sea of uncertainty; operating with limited resources requires real judgement.

| Myths | Reality |
|---|---|
| Rational | Intuitive |
| Dispassionate Planner | Harried Improviser |
| Secluded | Highly Interactive |

### GM's Job Demands

1. Agenda setting
2. Network building
3. Getting networks to implement agenda

General managers use an informal network of relationships and doing favors to get the job done. Kotter's main finding was that managers were successful, not because of any MBA skill, but because they have detailed knowledge of the industry and technology. Also enormously important is the GM's large informal network.

### The Real Situation

Kotter's studies of executive behavior show in no uncertain fashion that successful managers operate in a manner very different from that suggested by the traditional view of management. The facts of behavior make it perfectly plain that the GM operates in a dynamic context where the simple mechanistic description is inappropriate. For a start, the GM operates in a much more iterative way than the certainties of scientific management would suggest. The manager who fails to recognize that the executive process is iterative may get into difficulties. This requires that any stand he or she takes must be flexible. The traditional idea that organizations can be characterized as networks of roles connected by single lines of authority is very far from being the case; it is a naive view. There is a multiplicity of relationships between managers in an organization. Much early work in this field oversimplified the issue by make a too rigid use of the terms "line" and "staff."

The most important thing a manager should know about decision making is that it requires the collection and analysis of information, all with a view to solving a problem that will enable the organization to achieve a goal. According to Kotter, managers collect a lot of soft information. Earlier approaches employed a model of rational decision-making that presumed that organizational goals could be made explicit, that problems could be arranged in their proper priority, that alternatives could be splayed out, and that correct alternatives could be selected on the basis of some science of utility. The modern approach to decision making was promulgated by H. A. Simon (1947), who has argued that managers are restricted by bounded rationality, engaged in directed research, use standard rules of thumb, and make a maximum use of established programmed procedures. In brief, managers employ strategies of satisficing rather than optimizing or maximizing. Kotter's managers do this by having hundreds of interactions each day.

All the GMs studied had, at least, a graduate education; three of them attended prestigious schools (Harvard, Yale, and Princeton). Many had MBAs. Not surprisingly, most of these GMs exhibited a kind of success-syndrome, that is, they did well in early assignments, which led to promotions, which then reinforced their self-esteem, which in turn led to improving other important relationships, which helped them to perform their jobs, and then led to another promotion. So the process went on until they arrived at the level of general manager.

## AGENDA SETTING AND NETWORKING

General managers have a detailed technical knowledge of the fields in which they work. They operate by setting up agendas and they continue to update these agendas as they move forward in achieving some of their goals. The agendas that they developed were made up of connected goals and plans, which addressed their various responsibilities. These agendas would include financial, product, market, and organizational goals. For example, a manager would set out to complete the installation of the new computer system or the development of a new performance appraisal system for the unit.

Although all but one of the organizations involved had a formal planning system, GMs' agendas always included goals, priorities, and strategies that were not in the written document. In addition to agenda setting, the GMs all allocated sufficient time and effort to developing a network of relationships to help them to achieve their tasks effectively. This network building is a major activity. GMs develop cooperative relationships with bosses, peers, and subordinates. GMs develop these relationships through a wide variety of face-to-face methods. They try to establish a set of obligations. As Kotter points out, "they acted in ways to encourage others to identify with them." They carefully nurtured their professional reputation in the eyes of others. They even maneuvered to make others feel particularly dependent on the GM for resources, career advancement, or other support.

## KOTTER'S PARADIGM—VULNERABLE POWER

These GMs took their jobs very seriously indeed. In many respects the GMs were in the hands of other people. In terms of behavior, they work excessive hours at a relentless pace, in activities that are characterized by brevity, variety, and discontinuity. They prefer action and avoid writing; they favor verbal media such as telephone calls and meetings. Priorities and schedules are what their lives are all about; their goal is to work smarter, not harder.

Kotter's paradigm reveals the fact that these managers seemed to be high on power, the need to achieve, and the ability to relate to a wide set of specialists. They seemed to be expert in agenda setting, especially in developing goals, priorities, strategies, and plans. They were quite skilled at blocking what they did not want. Managers exercising vulnerable power is the key Kotter paradigm.

The general manager's power base is a function of organizational factors. Explicitly, this means that the exercise of power requires recognition that managers are dependent on others, particularly others they do not directly control. Because GMs are so dependent, Kotter points out in "Power, Dependence, and Effective Management" (1977), they have become increasingly vulnerable. To operate effectively in this context of dependency, they need to develop skill in managing and using power effectively (see Figure 3.2).

The most important things to know about GMs' personalities is that they are highly motivated, they have a fixation about achieving, and they seek challenge in their work. As managers ascend the hierarchy, they display more self-confidence and pay less attention to security.

**Figure 3.2**
**Organizational Leadership of General Managers as a System**

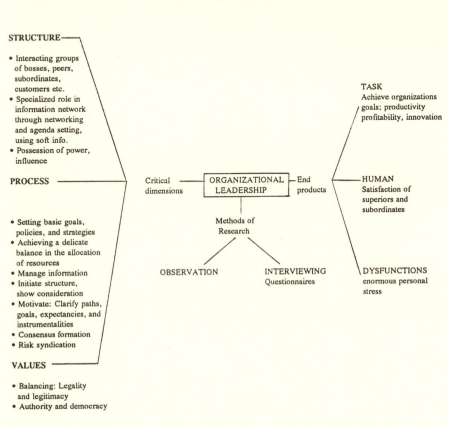

UNCERTAIN ENVIRONMENT

STRUCTURE

- Interacting groups of bosses, peers, subordinates, customers etc.
- Specialized role in information network through networking and agenda setting, using soft info.
- Possession of power, influence

PROCESS

- Setting basic goals, policies, and strategies
- Achieving a delicate balance in the allocation of resources
- Manage information
- Initiate structure, show consideration
- Motivate: Clarify paths, goals, expectancies, and instrumentalities
- Consensus formation
- Risk syndication

VALUES

- Balancing: Legality and legitimacy
- Authority and democracy

TASK
Achieve organizations goals; productivity profitability, innovation

Critical dimensions — ORGANIZATIONAL LEADERSHIP — End products

Methods of Research

HUMAN
Satisfaction of superiors and subordinates

OBSERVATION    INTERVIEWING
Questionnaires

DYSFUNCTIONS
enormous personal stress

## ROLES

Based on a sustained and thorough review of the literature, Mintzberg (1973) came up with an idea of ten working roles. These roles are interrelated and are performed by all general managers.

### Interpersonal Roles

- *Figurehead*—symbol. The figurehead's role is to provide subordinates with coaching, guidance, and rewards, with a view to clarifying paths to goals that achieve satisfaction or effectiveness. Consideration on the leader's part is more effective in structured situations.
- *Leader*—defines interpersonal relations. Charismatic leaders who display confidence, dominance, and purpose help to articulate goals,

which has the effect of developing devotion and unquestioning support among followers.

- *Liaison*—makes external contacts. Many liaisons had high-reaching contacts not only in their own companies but also in the industry.

## Informational Roles

- *Monitor*—searches out information. Monitors all allocated sufficient time and effort in their jobs to developing a network of relationships.
- *Disseminator*—transmits information. Disseminators typically ask a lot of questions.
- *Spokesperson*—represents firm to outsiders.

## Decisional Roles

- *Entrepreneur*—initiates. For example, an entrepreneur would set out to complete the installation of the new computer system or the development of a new performance appraisal system for his or her unit.
- *Disturbance handler*—manages conflict.
- *Resource allocator*—controls.
- *Negotiator*—sorts out. Negotiators influence other people by asking, cajoling, persuading, or intimidating.

# 4

---

# The Middle Manager

The term "middle manager" refers to those executives who report to general managers and have reporting to them junior managers and supervisors. Thus, in general, "middle manager" refers to all those managers who are in the middle to the top of the organization other than general managers. According to Rosemary Stewart in "Middle Managers: Their Job and Behaviors" (1987), the most important thing to note about middle managers is the diversity of their jobs. Based on her research, Stewart has shown that managerial jobs differ in the kind of contact that the manager has and in the type of relationships that he or she develops. Some middle manager jobs require frequent contact with the boss and other senior managers, but many middle manager jobs do not. These are primarily backroom desk jobs requiring less contact with bosses. Likewise, the amount of time that a middle manager spends with subordinates varies depending on the technology and the level of competence of subordinates.

In 1964 Leonard Sayles published a study of the lateral relations among middle managers in a large engineering company. Sayles distinguished among seven different types of lateral contact. These included workflow, trading, service, advisory, auditing, stabilization, and innovation. For a middle manager to be effective, he or she needs to be expertly skillful at several of these relationships.

Stewart came to the conclusion that some middle level jobs involve strategic decision making. For example, many middle level personnel and marketing people make decisions with long-term strategic consequences for their organizations; that type of decision is not too common for departmental heads of manufacturing units. An important point made by Stewart's study is the need for top management to recognize that the middle managers will often make choices that senior management does not respect or desire. The most famous study illustrating this point is by Melville Dalton (1959).

## MIDDLE MANAGERS: CLIQUES AND CABALS

Dalton, a sociologist at the University of California, Los Angeles, carried out a research project in an oil refinery to find out how the political system works among middle managers. What Dalton discovered was that the key group in this outfit was made up of people with Anglo-Saxon or German backgrounds. Although the company policy of promotion was based on merit, it also helped to be a Mason, an Anglo-Saxon, or a person of German descent. It was also useful to be a member of the local yacht club and a Republican. Dalton made a close study of these cliques and cabals and came up with a variety of different coalitions operating in vertical and horizontal directions. What Dalton spells out is that middle management is a political arena where there is real conflict between cliques and cabals. For example, production department managers blackmail the maintenance managers to avoid the constraints of the planned maintenance system. Furthermore, a major war was going on between line and staff middle management people. In general terms, staff innovations were opposed unless they had the backing of top line management.

## BURNS'S HORIZONTAL MIDDLE MANAGER

The task of the middle level manager is to translate top level directives into operational plans that can be effected by foremen and supervisors. What do these managers do and how do they communicate? These managers often have a difficult time trying to answer these questions. To try to answer some of these questions, an executive behavior study of the departmental manager was made by Tom Burns, a sociologist at Edinburgh University (1954). Using a classical study, Burns observed the behaviors and communications of a department manager interacting with two production engineers and a design manager.

These executives spent 80 percent of their time interacting, some on the telephone, a lot of it in meetings. Prior to the study, the researcher asked his managers being studied to estimate how they spent their time. Apparently managers overestimated time spent on production and underestimated the time spent on personnel. Most of the interaction took place within the department; a good deal of this interaction was in the horizontal dimension, between peers.

Reviewing the observational studies of middle managers, it is possible to reach certain general conclusions about Burns's paradigm of the "horizontal managers."

The idea that a manager should have only one boss has to be set aside. Managers have line and functional superiors. Managers spend a great deal of their time in horizontal communications with peers. Frequently, according to the research, when a manager thinks he or she is issuing instructions, the team members report receiving advice. Not too surprisingly, the manager does a great deal of the work oneself instead of delegating it. And for reason; authority and responsibility are rarely balanced.

The manager is highly involved in personnel work. The idea that a middle manager has a role that is clearly defined and demarcated also has to be set aside, as the work a manager does is a function of technology. Significant time is spent bypassing bureaucratic status circuits to reach the "movers and shakers." Attempts to describe a manager's behavior in systematic terms can turn out to be tricky because the manager spends so much time in an ad hoc mode.

Burns has also described how cliques and cabals emerge in the midlands of organizations. In his study, "The Reference of Conduct in Small Groups: Cliques and Cabals in Occupational Milieux" (1955), Burns described how cabals of middle managers recruit from "young turks" who are preoccupied with moving up in the system. These "young turks" are concerned with power, patronage, and prestige and try to capture the support of more powerful corporate oligarchs. Cliques, on the other hand, are made up of middle managers who are full of anger at being passed over. Understandably, these "oldies" tended to select comics who ridicule the antics of the "young turks."

Eugene E. Jennings made a special study of these middle managers who are on the way up in the organization (1970). Jennings calls these upwardly mobile executives the "mobicentric" managers and has argued that there is a close relationship between mobility and success. In arguing this, Jennings seems to be lending some support to the argument of Fred Luthans, who distinguishes between successful managers and effective managers (1988). Successful managers for Luthans are those who move through the organization rapidly. An interesting point to note about these mobicentric managers is that they move laterally once for every two moves up, and they also move outside their own technical area occasionally.

## GAMESMEN AND JUNGLE FIGHTERS

Michael Macoby has also investigated middle managers and has come up with a new type of manager called the "gamesman" who is essentially a flexible, competitive middle manager and glory seeker (1976). Macoby, who takes a psychoanalytical approach to his work, has become a kind of corporate anthropologist. Macoby actually identifies four different types of middle managers: the craftsman, the jungle fighter, and the companyman, as well as the gamesman. The craftsman is the sort of manager who holds traditional values, believes in the work ethic, and stands for quality and thrift. The jungle fighter lusts for power. The companyman sees the organization basically as a form of insurance. The gamesman, on the other hand, sees business in general, and his or her career in particular, as a series of choices and chances, as if playing a game. He or she likes to take calculated risks and is fast to find new management techniques and ideas.

In *The Gamesman* Macoby describes Jack Wakefield, a typical gamesman. Wakefield is an extremely likeable and charming type, but with Wakefield there is always the danger of being taken advantage of. Through his charm, he is seen as being very seductive. Wakefield is presented as a gregarious guy who is introverted and a little lonely. The management of his company saw him, at the age of thirty-two, as one of the young managers with the highest potential. Wakefield was perceived as being energetic, dynamic, and full of verve, and as a manager with great capacity to motivate others. Of course, Wakefield was deeply involved in his work. Away from work, understandably, he had difficulty connecting either with his wife or with other people who shared his professed ideals. Wakefield is contrasted with Ray Schultz, who is presented as a kind of jungle fighter, like a fanatical football coach who has to win. Schultz told the researchers, straight-faced, that the three persons he most admired were Vince Lombardi, Jesus Christ, and Harry Truman.

## MACGREGOR AND THE THURSDAY MAN

Arthur Elliot Carlisle (1976), who in the course of his research interviewed more than 100 managers, describes the modus operandi of a man named MacGregor, a manager in one of the largest refineries of an oil company. MacGregor is one of a hundred managers he interviewed in the course of his study. Carlisle was very surprised to discover that when he called MacGregor's office, MacGregor answered the phone himself. When Carlisle asked when he could have an appointment, MacGregor said anytime. Today, tomorrow, or anytime would be good, except Thursday. Apparently, MacGregor, who is an extremely effective manager, held only one regular staff meeting with his subordinates—once a week, on Thursday, between 10:00 A.M. and 12:00 noon. When asked what took place at these meetings, he answered that they dealt with problems, factual problems brought by subordinates. Asked if he believed in participative management, he said, "No." Asked why he held meetings, he replied that this staff meeting gave him the opportunity to appraise the technical and managerial qualities of his subordinates.

When Carlisle interviewed MacGregor's subordinates, he received a very favorable report on MacGregor's managerial style. Apparently what MacGregor did was to give the subordinates maximum discretion through delegation, and he told them to go ahead and solve their own problems. And it was only reluctantly, when they were really up against it, that he allowed them to bring their problems to him. What he would then do was ask the subordinates to state precisely what their problem was; MacGregor would write down exactly what this statement was. MacGregor then called for the conditions for a solution and he would invite the subordinates to come up with the solutions. Let's say the solution proposed was X, he would then ask: What are the consequences of applying X? Let's say it was A. Would A, in fact, solve the problem? The answer would be no. Then they would explore the possibilities with solution Y. Would it solve the problem? Partially, yes. And then they would look at Z. Would it solve the problem? Again, it would be seen as partially successful. MacGregor would then coach the subordinate on how to combine the elements of X, Y, and Z to find a solution that truly met the requirements of the situation.

In his discussions, MacGregor referred to the "Thursday man," apparently meaning the middle manager responsible for running the Thursday meetings. Using this technique MacGregor was able to provide his subordinates with maximum delegation, which created autonomy and encouraged their own problem-solving skills. When they ran up against a really tough problem, MacGregor showed them how to apply, through their subordinates, the case study method. Thus, the problem was properly diagnosed; the factors of the problem were spelled out; and some kind of model evolved to link these various factors. Once this process of diagnosis had been completed, subordinates were encouraged to develop a range of alternatives, and they were then coached as to how to put these alternatives together to find a solution to the problem. Implementation apparently was left to them as to how to develop a particular plan, how to sell it to their people, and how to build a control system.

## SUCCESSFUL VERSUS EFFECTIVE MANAGERS

What do successful managers have in common with effective ones? The answer, according to Fred Luthans, is surprisingly little. Successful managers have been promoted relatively swiftly. Luthans, who studied managers who were mostly in the mushrooming service industry in middle America (1988), points out that this finding essentially confirms the cliché that the successful are simply astute politicians, and effective managers are so busy doing their job that they are passed over.

The managers studied had titles such as department head, general manager, store manager, marketing manager, office manager, agency chief, and district manager, essentially from the middle levels of organizations. Trained observers were used to observe freely and record the behaviors and activities of forty-four managers, who came from retail stores, hospitals, corporate headquarters, a railroad, government agencies, insurance companies, a newspaper office, financial institutions, and a few manufacturing companies. Using the Delphi technique, which includes both interaction and sharing judgments, a panel helped to analyze the actual data; the data was reduced into twelve descriptive behavioral categories, which were then translated into role activities. Four role activities were noted: communication, traditional management, human resource management, and networking. Communication, of course, consisted basically of exchanging information and paperwork. Traditional management consists of planning, decision making, and controlling, or POLEing. Human resource management contains the most behavioral categories, including such activities as motivating, disciplining, conflict management, staffing, and training. Networking, a big activity, refers to interacting with outsiders, socializing, and politicking.

Luthans then set out to distinguish between the successful and the effective. A scale was developed to define exactly what was meant by a successful manager by calculating a manager's level in his or her organization by his or her tenure, that is, length of service there. For example, someone at the fifth level for three years was rated more successful than a manager at the fourth level who had been there for twenty-five years. Effectiveness was defined by getting the job done in quantity and quality and by generating satisfaction and commitment (i.e., task and human relations).

## WHAT DO SUCCESSFUL MANAGERS DO?

The main finding was that successful managers concentrated on networking, that is, interacting with outsiders, socializing, and politicking. Thus, apparently the main way to be successful is to go out and influence the big wheels, with the object being to discover "the movers and shakers" and to influence them. Correspondingly, successful managers pay less attention to POLEing and, for that matter, to paperwork or communications. Luthans quotes a successful manager: "I find the way get to ahead around here is to be friendly with the right people, both inside and outside the firm. They get tired of always talking shop, so I find a common interest—with some it's sports, with others it's our kids—and interact with them on that level. The other formal stuff around the office is important but I really work at this informal side and I found it pays off when promotion time comes around."

Communications and human resource management activities make up the major part of the effective managers' activities; POLEing and especially networking make the least contribution. Here is a comment of an effective manager: "Both how much and how well things get done around here, as well as keeping my people loyal and happy, has to do with keeping them informed and involved. If I make a change in procedure or the guys upstairs give us a new process or piece of equipment to work with, I get my people's input and give them the full story before I lay it on them. And I make sure they have the proper training and get their feedback on how they're doing. When they screw up, I let them know it, but when they do a good job, I let them know about that too." In short, this manager's effectiveness is derived both from communication and human resource management activities; there is little time spent in networking activity. This research discovered relatively few managers who were both successful and effective. These managers used a fairly balanced approach, a delicate balance between all four managerial activities.

## FAST TRACK MIDDLE MANAGERS

An increasing number of young, middle managers, especially MBAs, are looking for fast tracks through organizations. Many of these new fast-track middle managers are part of the "Me Generation." They are anxious, indeed impatient, for promotion and show little loyalty to the organizations for which they work. These fast-track managers like problems and challenges to give them high visibility. They are mobile; when they can't change the system, they change systems.

Many of these fast-track managers have an essentially hedonistic approach to life derived from the boom of booms in the 1970s when the economy kept expanding in an exponential manner. Unfortunately, a surprising number of these fast-track managers of the "Me Generation" have ended up burnt out. "Never having to say you're sorry" turned out to be a bad guide as many of these fast-track types in fact crashed.

These fast-track managers grew up with a different view of the world through television, air travel, and the sexual revolution. They arrived in corporate organizations with an expectation of instant gratification. And in the greedy 1980s many of them succeeded beyond all measure. Are they interested in tenure? "No." This new group is ready to trade commitment for power and autonomy.

These fast-track managers, many of them members of two-career marriages, have different ideas about how companies should operate. They are anxious to take risks, are optimistic and flexible, can be either male or female, tend to be workaholics, are comfortable with computers, and are ready to work long hours to make money. When they join an organization, they won't jump right in there and do routine work. The work has to be significant and meaningful. And of course there have been many clashes between the "young turks" who are upwardly mobile and their more established, and more establishment-oriented, superiors.

Theresa Carson and John A. Byrne, in an article entitled "Fast Track Kids" (1986), point out that this willingness to challenge authority is causing generational clashes. For example, they refer to a twenty-nine-year-old manager of General Motors who was in charge of the Corvette air bag program as typical of this new generation. This young manager believes older managers in the company are mainly interested in cranking out cars and don't pay special attention to people out on the line. Since they never got on with their shop floor workers in the past, they are uptight about dealing with them. What this young manager found out was that contact with people on the shop floor quickly helped solve production problems. Many of these fast-track managers acknowledged that they had to be careful with older workers.

These fast-track middle managers don't want to work in multilevel, highly centralized companies. Their managerial style is essentially looser, more informal, and less militant. These young managers dislike bureaucracies that will lead to leaner and possibly meaner corporate staffs. Unfortunately, many of them, while they have the hard technical skills such as planning and computer skills that enable them to be effective, lack the soft skills such as the ability to motivate people that enable them to be insightful into others' problems and generally to be empathetic.

## HOW THE MIDDLE MANAGER MOVES UP TO THE GENERAL MANAGER'S POSITION

A major issue to consider is what is the best way to take over a new department or group. John J. Gabarro, in "When a New Manager Takes Charge" (1985), has come up with a useful description of how this process works. Gabarro's research is based on studies of managerial transitions in fourteen management successions over three years. Gabarro describes the process as a sequence of five predictable stages of varying durations. The first, "taking hold," is typically an intense effort to adjust to new surroundings, as the middle manager assumes the reins of command. Change at this stage tends to be corrective rather than fundamental. The manager is trying to talk him- or herself into the job. The next stage, "exploration," involves searching out values. The third stage, Gabarro labels "reshaping." It is important that during this period the new manager learns to exercise his or her most important influence as he or she implements strategic plans. Reshaping is followed by "consolidation," which is devoted to building the changes into the organization. The final phase is, again, reshaping.

Gabarro's research has pinpointed the factors that determine success of newly promoted managers. The first is prior experience within their particular functional areas. The second is the ability to maintain a cordial atmosphere with subordinates. Gabarro also agrees with Kotter that "The all-purpose general manager who can parachute into any situation and succeed is a myth. Experience and special competencies do matter." The lack of the practice of "Fast-Tracking" promising executives is also cast in an unfavorable light: Clearly, the duration of the successful changeover is longer than is generally supposed. The argument seems to be that middle managers who are going to be promoted somehow have to be exposed selectively in their organization so that they can acquire the necessary experience. When they are promoted, therefore, they will be successful.

## DEVELOPING WORKING RELATIONSHIPS AMONG MANAGERS

The development of effective interpersonal relationships among managers is extremely important for middle managers. Gabarro has reviewed the literature of this matter of interpersonal relationships among managers and reported his findings in"The Development of Working Relationships" (1987). Since managers are dependent upon subordinates, peers, and superiors, it is therefore necessary to cultivate these relationships for their effectiveness. These interpersonal working relationships have many dimensions. The first is openness and self-disclosure, which allows individuals to include personally sensitive, private, and controversial topics in their conversational exchanges. The second dimension is knowledge of others, which requires a recognition that this knowledge is more complex and extends to aspects of values, attitudes, needs, and expectations. The third major dimension is predictability of actions. Of course, these relationships do not develop immediately or spontaneously. They have to be nourished and sustained, and usually begin on some sort of reciprocal basis and involve sampling, bargaining, commitment, and then, institutionalization. But these relationships, of course, will not develop unless they are based on mutuality. Most of the research in working relations shows clearly that openness in confrontation of differences is the key characteristic. The dilemma is that openness needs to be reciprocated, and it can be threatening. Therefore, it is necessary to develop a degree of trust before attempting openness.

Furthermore, these matters are complicated by the fact that both parties do not know in the beginning what will be the consequences of these working relationships. Therefore, for a relationship to develop it is necessary to develop what is called retrospective sense-making involving a reflective glance. Thus, much of the work developing and agreeing on mutual expectations is both metaphorical and figurative. Middle managers have to develop real skill at working at these relationships. To do this effectively, the managers have to develop certain managerial skills.

## MANAGERIAL SKILLS

In effect, the middle manager requires technical, human, and conceptual skills. Technical skills refers to specific technological information and ability to teach it to subordinates. Many managers are highly valued for their technical competence. Human relations skills are necessary for the manager to lead and motivate and still be empathetic with subordinates. High motivation and morale are necessary correlates of human relations skills. Conceptual skills enable managers to look at their problems in a larger context. Management education is seeking to enhance the skills of managers.

## MIDDLE MANAGERS ARE VULNERABLE

Middle managers will remember the start of the 1981–82 and the 1990–91 economic recessions as "Black Fridays" when they saw the time and energy they invested in their careers slip away. Some managers can look back with relief: They still have jobs. Others were not as lucky. As a cost-cutting measure, companies during both recessions thinned out their management ranks by clamping down on nonessential functions. In addition, an onslaught of takeovers, mergers, and leveraged buyouts reduced the number of available positions. Where two individuals had worked in different companies, only one was required. Middle managers were left out in the cold. The U.S. Bureau of Labor Statistics reports that unemployment for managers and administrators reached a peak of 4 percent in 1982. While this figure was still far below the national average, middle managers considered it much too high.

As Jeremy Main in "The Recovery Skips Middle Managers" (1984), points out, strangely enough, four successive quarters of economic recovery did not improve the job market for middle managers. Even three years after beginning their job search, members of the Forty Plus Club, located in Chicago, were still sending out resumés and banging corporate doorknockers. Unfortunately, they already have two strikes against them. First of all, they are older professionals, over forty, usually in their fifties. This is a handicap when companies are looking for young, fresh blood to rejuvenate corporate life. Second, these people have been out of the job market for years and are not familiar with job-hunting skills and techniques. Some managers will have an easier time finding a job because they have specialized in the right fields. Generally, managers whose specialties involve producing or selling products or services (e.g., data processing and health and financial services) will find the market has a lot more to offer than professionals with a background in corporate staff positions in finance, personnel, law, or public relations.

What does the future hold for these strife-stricken managers who have lost their security blankets? According to Main, even the experts disagree.

William S. Woodside, chairman of American Can, states that corporations are no longer going to maintain large corporate staffs: lean is here to stay. According to Alan R. Schonberg, president of Management Recruiters International Inc., companies will begin increasing their staffs in time with the beat of economic recovery. Eugene E. Jennings, professor of business administration at Michigan State University, claims that a fundamental change is taking place. He states that most organizational structures resemble lightbulbs rather than the academic pyramid structures, and the response to the recession and other factors has been to start trimming off the excess fat.

Main refers to McKinsey & Co., a consulting firm that developed a method of evaluating management functions. The first step is to eliminate functions that are superfluous and therefore unnecessary; the next step is to eliminate the people who perform these tasks. Companies cannot cut people and positions haphazardly. A systematic method of determining functions that are essential and those that are not must be used, otherwise a return of prosperity and growth will render the company incapable of handling increased business and will necessitate rehiring. Another method of reducing costs is to increase the span of control, that is, to increase the number of people each manager supervises. Xerox raised managerial spans of control to fifteen and claimed that many of their managers have their own assignments in addition to supervising others.

That reducing excess weight (middle managers) is a trend, as suggested by Jennings, is supported by statistics showing that, in addition to hard-hit companies and industries, relatively untouched service industries and companies with rapid growth and high profits are also cutting middle management positions.

Main concludes that the evidence shows corporations shrinking in terms of the number of employees, and therefore more managers are looking for jobs. On the other hand, those people who are not terminated find that they have to be flexible in order to deal with increased volumes of work and more varied assignments. For those who stay, the future offers fewer opportunities and less security. With fewer managers at each level, opportunities for promotion are reduced and interpromotion time increases. The alternative to keeping the manager in the same position is to offer lateral moves, ostensibly to gain a broader knowledge base. On the other hand, because numbers are reduced, visibility is increased; therefore, a manager who is good has a greater chance of moving ahead.

## MIDDLE MANAGERS AND ALIENATION

The contemporary middle level executive may well wonder why the ancient mariner of alienation has picked on him or her.

But before saying more about alienation, it might be useful to introduce our hero, the executive who appears in several guises and is known under a number of names. What do the names Tom Rath and Bob Slocum mean to you? Do you remember Tom Rath, *The Man in the Gray Flannel Suit*, created by Sloan Wilson?

We first get to know Tom in 1955, when he was making $7,000 a year as a minor functionary—not enough to get by in suburban Connecticut with a wife, three young kids, a car, and a home, of which the latter two were always breaking down. Remember how he got a break as a special assistant (and $2,000 more a year) to Ralph Hopkins, president of a well-known broadcasting company and a self-made millionaire, because he reminded Ralph of his son who was killed in the war? Tom had done well in the war. What happened to Tom Rath, ''the man in the gray flannel suit,'' who did so well in the war? What happened to the hero of classical organizational theory?

The trouble with organizational theory is that it has not caught up with *Catch-22*. In his novel *Catch-22* (1961), Joseph Heller set out to show the absurdity of modern organizations at war. What Heller showed was that in the crazy, impersonal world of war, heroism was a bad joke, and the only thing that made sense was looking after one's own survival.

In *Catch-22* Heller celebrated the black mass of manipulation and showed how behavioral technology was mobilized to keep people doing absurd things. One of the crazier things was the fact that the number of missions pilots were required to fly kept steadily rising, always just out of grasp. The technique of constantly raising the quota, which would never be tolerated among shop floor operatives, is widely used by those in charge of executives. This constant rising of quotas frustrates and maddens managers and makes their lives an existential hell.

## Executive Malaise

Inspired by the madness of modern managerial life, Heller wrote *Something Happened* (1974), which is essentially concerned with executive malaise. Bob Slocum, the narrator, is locked in an existential crisis of identity, trying desperately to find an answer to the question: ''What have I done with my life?''

Heller, who has been compared to the Marx Brothers, Kingsley Amis, and Al Capp, took thirteen years to write *Something Happened*, which draws on his experiences at *Time*, *Look*, and *McCalls*. His inspirational first sentence for *Something Happened* came to him while he was sitting on the deck of a house on Fire Island. Then it came: ''In the office in which I work, there are four people of whom I am afraid. Each of these four people is afraid of five people.'' And so Heller began his novel of Bob Slocum, the contemporary organization man.

Slocum is a well-groomed, sourly witty, middle-level executive who works in the communication business. He is restless, bored, and dying of sheer ennui in slow motion, spinning in the wind. The comparison can be made with the Syrian-American, Yossarian, the madly sane bombardier of *Catch-22* who was described by Heller in the following terms: "It was a vile and muddy war, and Yossarian could have lived without it—lived forever, perhaps." And what happened when he tried to live forever?

Slocum is the "man in the gray flannel suit" twenty years further on. What happened to the young lions? Something happened.

### Complex Overwhelming

Slocum is a husband, father of three, and a womanizer. In his domestic life, Slocum is a small dictator presiding over the nuclear family, first in a New York apartment and then a Connecticut house. Slocum describes his svelte wife in the following way: "My wife is a good person, really, or used to be, and sometimes I'm sorry for her. She drinks during the day and flirts, or tries to, at parties we go to in the evening, although she doesn't know how." He is beset by dreadful domestic problems: an aging mother in an institution and a retarded son at home. At work Slocum is an operator who defers to his superiors and is cavalier with his subordinates. Overwhelmed by the Cassandra complex, or a sense of doom, he is consumed with apathy, anxiety, alienation, and anomie while boredom serves him as a kind of aphrodisiac as he whiles away his life. Combatting the Cassandra complex is what top management faces today. How are they going to overcome this sense of despair, this loss of direction, this absence of trajectory?

Like Slocum, executives regret the missed opportunities of their youth. Slocum is a fairly good looking man in his forties, with a growing paunch. He has wavy hair, but with a bald patch that is also growing.

Slocum suffers endless boredom and anxiety. But, on the whole, he feels more comfortable at his office than at home. Like a great number of executives, he finds vacations a drag. He finds "close relationships suffocating." He suffers from a vague general sense of inferiority. "Something did happen to me somewhere that robbed me of confidence and courage."

Most middle-aged executives are going to find it hard to accept the total pessimism of *Something Happened*.

Heller's *Something Happened* is a portrait of "the man in the gray flannel suit" in his midlife melancholy as he struggles to find himself again before he suffocates in a kind of corporate claustrophobia. Few executives will finish Heller's relentless and exhausting anatomy and geography of executive melancholy, spoken as it is in a deliberately boring psychoanalytical monologue. To try to get further into evaluating this matter of executive ennui, it is necessary to have a quick peep at anxiety and a longer look at alienation, its dimensions, causes, and "cures."

An increasing number of executives have gotten "burned": bent, spindled, and mutilated. To pursue this managerial malaise properly, it is necessary to define the concept of alienation more precisely.

Alienation can be defined in psychological terms as a mode of experience in which a person experiences himself as estranged from himself. This essentially "that's not me" experience is frequently the first step on the road to existentialism. This feeling of being out of touch with one's self can be analyzed into a number of dimensions: powerlessness, meaning-lessness, normlessness, and isolation.

## TOP BRASS SURVIVE

Interviews with corporate godfathers confirm what David McClelland (1976), professor of Social Relations at Harvard, had already noted: people who get to the top in business give off strong odors of "nPow," a need for power; indeed, a compulsion to influence, control, and manipulate, in fact, to possess the people who work for them. In discussing executive alienation and unionization with such top dogs, who are highly articulate, competitive, and empathetic, one is continuously struck by their sense of "omniscience, omnipresence, omnicompetence," that is, their feeling of being on top of things and people. They can understand the problems of their capos, their capers, their coronaries, their crash programs, their sense of alienation, and their socked-out sensation of "not having made it."

## NAGGING ANXIETY

For the middle-level manager, there is the constant nagging anxiety that one may be sticking to a particular specific role too long. The emergence of the "mobicentric" manager who has made it (for whom career movement is life itself), the rapid development of computer firms with all their attractive offers, the mushrooming of consultancy, the slowing down of the aerospace and electronics businesses, the appearance on the executive scene of successful ethnic minorities, feminism, the pleasures of the existential culture, and a multitude of other social and corporate factors, make sticking to one's role dangerous.

Increasing numbers of America's millions of middle managers (from plant foremen up to top management) are seeking mid-career changes. A general feeling of obsolescence seems to overtake managers when they reach their late thirties. This makes for a critical problem for their bosses, the presidents, and vice presidents who must face the excruciating choice of either deciding to try to save these early flameouts by reinvigorating them or to fire them.

Research on executive careers suggests that early flameouts go through a mid-life crisis by the time they are thirty-five. With "too old at forty" just five years away, they get the first intimations of their mortality; are tempted into depression, drugs, debauchery, and drink; and generally peter out. Many have floated to their level of incompetence.

## WOMEN EXECUTIVES AND ALIENATION

Many young American women are becoming disillusioned with corporate America. A major concern is that many companies are treating women executives as either fast trackers or mommy trackers. The fast trackers follow an accelerated career trajectory that includes specially selected, elite, high-visibility jobs and more opportunities for executive training. Because the cost of employing women in executive positions is higher than for employing men, companies are putting some women on slower moving tracks, where their careers are more likely to plateau. Glass ceilings are created which block the upward progress of women executives. The company expectation is that the rate of turnover is much higher among women executives due to the fact that many women return late or not at all from maternity leaves.

While there was a dramatic increase in the number of women graduating from university business schools in the 1980s, rising to a third of all MBAs graduating in 1990, the number applying in the early 1990s is sharply diminishing. A major problem is that most business schools require applicants to have work experience and this requirement may delay admission for many young women to their late twenties. For many young women, this delay is unacceptable as it may interfere with their plans to have children. Many young women are switching to law school, or more often taking their chance in business with an undergraduate degree only.

In existential terms, the executive has become colonized. As Marcus G. Raskin, a founder for the Institute for Policy Studies in Washington, argues in *Being and Doing* (1971) that the new industrial state colonizes executives and turns them into dependent and subjugated persons: "In the pyramidal structure even if the individual has great latitude in his lifestyle and the appearance of choice (freedom for lust), he lives according to forces external to the relationships which he might otherwise freely seek. As the individual grows older, he comes to represent those forces in his life relationships."

Middle managers become convinced that they lack influence on corporate decision making, yet they must implement company policy—frequently without adequate authority or resources to see the job done.

If progress in combatting the Cassandra complex is to be made, then, instead of trying to change only the VANE (values, attitudes, needs, and expectations) of managers, it will be necessary also to make structural changes, that is, encourage the managers to participate in the process of deciding their own destiny; and this means some kind of industrial democracy. On this vector of managerial involvement in policy making, North Americans could learn much from their cousins on the other side of the Atlantic.

In Western Europe, a widespread effort is underway to beat the blues, not only among blue-collar but also white-collar workers, including managers. This effort goes well beyond the current North American efforts to combat administrative authoritarianism through MBO, T-groups, the managerial grid, OD, intervention strategy, and process consultancy. Such change strategies in Europe are part of a broad-based movement toward industrial democracy, which could involve managers as elected representatives and as an integral part of the policy-making process. Such elected managers, as well as pursuing their own interests, become a check-and-balance system that restrains the shop floor people from going too far.

In any case, "winning the hearts and minds" of middle managers involves not only changes in management attitudes but also structural changes. The role of the chief executive in orchestrating the structural and attitude changes is vital. Perhaps we need another ancient mariner in the form of an executive steward (or perhaps only a representative) to point out that the Cassandra complex is catching and to tell our Chief Executive "No man is an Island, entire of itself. . . . Any man's death diminishes me, because I am involved in Mankind; and therefore, never send to know for whom the bell tolls; it tolls for thee" (John Donne).

# 5

# The Supervisor

The supervisor is directly responsible for supervising shop floor operatives to ensure that work of the requisite quality is "got out of the gate" on schedule. Because the supervisor operates in the demilitarized zone between middle management and the shop floors, he or she experiences a certain degree of ambivalence. The literature of supervision is replete with terms indicative of this ambivalence, including the "man in the middle," "marginal man," and the "manager in no-man's land." Caught in a bind between the formal and informal systems, he or she is frequently forced to become the master and victim of "double talk."

The etymology of the term helps to explain why the supervisor is the most maligned and least understood of all management personnel. The term "supervise" is derived from *super* (over) and *videre* (to see) and is usually defined as "to oversee, to superintend, to inspect the work of others, to lead, motivate, direct, and control."

The duties of the production supervisor include:

1. Programing function: to find out what work is coming forward and to determine priorities
2. Technical function: to organize running repairs to the machines, to trouble-shoot; to ensure quality control; to ensure that the sociotechnical system is ticking overnight
3. Personnel function: to allocate the work and ensure that it gets done; to staff and manage the shop floor in a firm

In the 1990s the job of the supervisor is changing rapidly. These changes have been brought about because of smarter, that is, better educated, shop floor people, increasing automation in production lines, and the introduction of computers and visual display terminals in the workplace. The job of the supervisor, of course, varies from industry to industry, but generally supervisors are held responsible for getting the goods out of the gate. Contrary to what many outsiders believe, supervisors play little part in the hiring process. In the modern organization, there are management specialists who do a lot of the supervisor's job of yesteryear. These specialists, such as personnel, for example, have gradually assumed many of the responsibilities of supervisors, especially for hiring and training. Production engineers often assume responsibilities for the technological aspects of the job. Furthermore, computer-based technology is beginning to take control of the monitoring of the production line. On the shop floor, the effect of this action is to diminish the power of the supervisor. Furthermore, many young workers coming to work on the assembly line for the first time have a higher level of computer literacy than their supervisors.

Given these changes, first line supervisors inevitably experience sharp role and status conflicts, often reflected in such terms as "the man on the firing line" or "master and victim of double talk." In effect, the supervisors are trapped between management and the shop floor. They are neither one nor the other, and, thus hobbled, it is very difficult for them to operate in an impartial and clear manner. In many companies the supervisor is paid a salary but does not receive any additional payment for overtime. Supervisors generally feel they do not make decisions but that they simply implement decisions made upstairs. Observational research on the behavior of supervisors shows clearly that they spend a great deal of their time doing actual work, setting up machines, sorting out breakdowns, and generally acting as trouble-shooters. Much of this trouble-shooting activity involves them in actually sorting out work difficulties on the shop floor.

Various studies of foreman behavior are in broad agreement. Four different studies confirm that most of the foreman's work with other people is devoted to close details of work. Three areas—technical, programing, and personnel—account for the great majority of all the foreman's activities. Could it be that the task approach to management has enabled this increased emphasis on the details of work as reported here? In other words, in terms of old style supervisory training, "structure" and "consideration" are both important, but in that order.

## THE BEHAVIOR OF THE SECTION MANAGER

A picture of the section manager can be built from a study of first-line management in a plant making engine bearings (Kelly, 1964). Section managers spend two-thirds of their time with other persons; a fifth of their time with their bosses, the unit manager. It is worth noting that approximately one-third of their time is spent with colleagues and half with subordinates. The unit manager meets them mostly at the morning meeting. A great deal of informal rearranging takes place, especially at a rather extended coffee-break in the morning. They spend half of their time on the shop floor, a quarter in the production and engineering department, and the balance in other sections or outside the unit. Their work is mainly programing (one half), followed by technical (one quarter), and only a little personnel work (one tenth). Compared with others, they spend more time on the close details of work. In a phrase, they are "task specialists."

Going in a nonhierarchical direction, it may be observed that approximately one-third of the total interaction time is devoted to peers. Dubin (1962) has drawn attention to the lack of reference in the literature to "the horizontal dimension of organization and the volume of business that is transacted among peers to keep the organization going." Indeed, it is probably among organizational equals that much of the real coordination of work flow and operations takes place in what Dubin (1958) has called the "non-formal behavior system": "The non-formal behavior system is the arena in which the organization is made to work by supplementing the formal procedures, rules, etc."

Elliott Jacques (1951) has drawn attention to the need for informal activity "to make policy completely explicit. There remains always a residue of unrecognized and unidentified aspects of the culture of the concern." Much of this informal behavior takes place at the section managers' morning coffee-break, which is timed to follow the unit manager's meeting. Recognizing this need for informal contact, the unit manager allows the break to run well beyond its prescribed time. This time elasticity allows the managers to enter the world of "organizational Alice," peopled by existential executives.

### Communications

Studies of the interactions of supervisors show that they spend most of their time communicating in the vertical dimension. That is to say, they spend most of the time communicating with bosses and subordinates and little time communicating with peers such as other foremen, engineers, or functional management people. This research also shows that, in effect, supervisors spend little of their time outside their workplace. Effective supervisors spend time communicating with their superiors. Indeed, it is widely established that supervisors cannot have power with shop floor people unless they are seen as having power upstairs. As Steven Kerr and colleagues point out in "The First Line Supervisor: Phasing Out or Here to Stay?" (1986), the management style of supervisors differs significantly from the style of middle and top managers. First line supervisors are basically concerned with the nitty-gritty of internal work matters, which tend to be rather narrowly defined. Research has shown that time spent supervising others decreases and the time spent on planning increases as one moves up the hierarchy. First line supervisors "do" activities that produce results within a fairly short time period, for example, within a two week period. Middle and general managers have a longer time span to finish projects. A widely established finding is that effective supervisors show both "structure" and "consideration." Structure is the ability to "define the task," spell out in detail how it is to be done and "give clear indication of how performances are to be measured"; "consideration" is the ability of the foreman to take an interest in his or her people and to be supportive. In general, what happens is that where supervisors are high in structure and low in consideration, high levels of production are achieved but considerable grievances are generated. The reverse is true for the supervisor who is low in structure and high in consideration: there is low production and high satisfaction among subordinates. Training in the 1950s and 1960s for supervisors focused attention on the need to show both structure and consideration. More recently, research has shown that supervisors simply follow the cues given to them by their bosses.

## Initiating Structure and Consideration

Therefore, behavioral scientists have turned their attention to the structure and function of groups. Inevitably, whenever two or more people get together, one will dominate. But the form of the leadership depends on group members, the task, and the group ideology.

If leadership is the ability to influence others in the group, then all group members may exhibit a degree of leadership. The leader in the conventional sense is the one whose influence predominates.

## The Ohio State Studies

The Ohio State Leadership Studies (Stodgill and Coons, 1957), which began shortly after World War II, had as their objective the specification of how a given situation affects leadership behavior. The original research took place in military organizations.

The studies found that there are two basic types of group behavior: task behavior and human relations behavior. Task behavior stresses the importance of the objective, focuses attention on production, and reviews the quality of the work that has been done. Human relations behavior includes "keeping the group happy," "settling disputes," "providing encouragement," and "giving the minority a chance to be heard."

Corresponding to these functions are two dimensions: "initiating and directing" and "consideration." Initiators make sure not only that their role is understood but also that official procedures are followed; they also try out new ideas on members. They are most efficient when the group faces a task problem. Executives high in consideration are group oriented; they reward good work and invite participation in the setting of group goals.

Leaders who excel in initiating structure make specific work assignments, spell out deadlines, evaluate the quality of work, and establish well-defined work patterns and procedures. They were highly rated by their superiors and generated high performance in terms of productivity; they also reduced costs. But high-production supervisors had higher rates of grievance and labor turnover than their low-scoring colleagues.

Supervisors scoring high on consideration (who were supportive, willing to explain their actions, warm, and friendly) had more satisfied subordinates and lower levels of grievance and turnover. The essence of the problem appears to be that superiors and subordinates view the leadership behavior of supervisors from different perspectives. Production supervisors with abilities in both dimensions could get the production out without increasing either the rate of grievances or labor turnover. Figure 5.1 shows these concepts graphically.

### The Relationship

Human relations managers do not seek to formalize role relationships but prefer to deal with problems informally. At one level their behavior may ensure good relationships at the expense of efficiency. They prefer informal discussion with subordinates to regular staff meetings. They are inclined to select friends from within the firm. Given this desire for finding

**Figure 5.1**
**Ohio State Studies of "Structure" and "Consideration"**

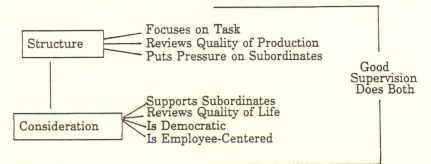

friends at work, they are frequently accused of trying to dominate and possess subordinates. According to research, they will delegate only relatively minor matters and insist on frequent individual consultation.

Their opposite, the task specialists, tend to formalize role relationships with both superiors and subordinates. They are somewhat more reserved and withdrawn in their relationships within the firm. They tend to take "calculated risks" and prefer formal staff consultation to seeking opinions informally. Their most striking characteristic is their acceptance or rejection of subordinates on the basis of performance. Oddly enough, though they are reserved, they still have the ability to ensure smooth interpersonal relationships. They do not develop deep friendships with colleagues. Being task specialists, they demand considerable freedom of action from "up top" and usually get it. Being realistic, they expect people to make mistakes, and plan accordingly. They prefer ambitious subordinates.

Steven Kerr and his coauthors prepared a list of supervisory behaviors that can lead to an improvement in performance and subordinate attitudes. In this list, the authors point to the importance of supervisors to be able to accept criticisms, to accept suggestions, and to let subordinates know what they think of their work; and to be ready, above all, to go to bat for their subordinates. But, on the other hand, this list also shows that supervisors are effective when they follow instructions, company policies, and the chain of command, and when they keep their bosses informed. Furthermore, displaying confidence in human relations and creating a favorable climate also helps to get work done. These lists show, quite clearly, that the demands placed on the supervisor in the modern environment are very pressing. He or she is expected both to show outstanding effort in terms of structure, and somehow to maintain consideration of relationships with subordinates. Kerr has argued that the first line supervisor in the future will face increasing difficulties mainly because there are major changes in management techniques, requiring self-managed autonomous work groups operating computer-driven automation equipment. Working in this environment is an increasing number of specialized staff managers, particularly in personnel and information management. Further, modern manufacturing techniques are such that most of the shop floor operators are located in widely separated work stations. This means that the supervisor has little opportunity to counsel work people as a group. Of course, in the autonomous work groups, the need for a supervisor diminishes rapidly. In self-governing work groups, members are meant to make their own decisions. This shift in decision making sharply changes the role of the supervisor who is now required to operate as a coach or a team manager. These autonomous work groups are widely established both in Europe and in Japan, and they are coming in North America. The argument seems to be that American workers are oversupervised. For example, in the Honda car plant the ratio of supervisors to production workers is 1:200, whereas in the U.S. car plants the ratio could be as low as 1:10.

## QUALITY AND THE SUPERVISOR

In "Quality on the Line" (1983), David A. Garvin analyzes American and Japanese quality management techniques in the air conditioner industry. His study includes nine of the ten US manufacturers and all seven Japanese producers. Sales per corporation range from $50 million to $200 million and the survey accounts for 90 percent of all shipments in the United States and 100 percent of Japanese production. "Each manufacturer uses a simple assembly line process," Garvin reported; "each uses much the same manufacturing equipment; each makes an essentially standardized product. . . . Both that industry's manufacturing process and its managers' range of approaches to product quality give these findings a more general applicability."

The author was shocked to find that the failure rate of the highest quality plant was "between 500 and 1,000 times less than those of products from the lowest." The rework time, scrap, and warranty costs were consistently lower at the higher quality producers. In general the worst Japanese plant had better quality ratings than the best US plant. The return on investment of inferior producers averaged 4.5 percent compared with 10.4 percent for average producers and 17.4 percent for superior manufacturers.

Although Garvin rejects the notion that Japanese workers are superior to their American counterparts, he emphasizes the importance of sound supervisory practices aimed at achieving high levels of performance. American industry requires a lasting approach to increasing the quality of its products and not a passing infatuation with Japanese management techniques.

What is needed is a long term commitment to the fundamentals—working with vendors to improve their performance, educating and training the work force, developing an accurate and responsive quality information system, setting targets for quality improvement, and demonstrating interest and commitment at the very highest levels of management. With their companies' futures on the line, managers can do no less.

## OVERCOMING RESISTANCE TO PARTICIPATION

In "Why Supervisors Resist Employee Involvement," Janice Klein (1984) probes the problems of supervisor resistance to employee involvement programs that seek to improve the quality of work life. Lack of support for these programs, on the part of first-line supervisors, springs from a perceived threat to their job security, job definition, and work load. Klein outlines five categories, each of which represents supervisors with unique reasons for opposing such programs. The article closes with a strategy for helping the supervisor feel like an integral part of the process.

This article is based on research conducted in 1981 and 1982, which studied the responses of supervisors to various types of employee involvement programs (e.g., quality circles, semi-autonomous work groups). Data was collected from eight US manufacturing plants.

The research reveals some enlightening statistics: While nearly three-quarters (72 percent) of the supervisors perceive the programs as being good for the companies, and more than half (60 percent) view them as being good for employees, only 31 percent felt they are of any personal benefit.

If supervisors do not actively encourage participation, neither do they voice their negative opinions, since they feel their jobs depend upon how well they carry through instructions. Generally managers hold that criticism comes from older foremen in senior positions, whose calcified disposition makes it difficult for them to adjust to changes. However, the study found no relationship between age or seniority and such resistance. Resistance is said to develop out of fear concerning job security (Will a system of participative management render supervisors superfluous?), job definition (What are they really expected to do?), and work load (Are they expected to assume administrative duties, as well as implementation, coordination, and follow-up?).

Klein presents a system for classifying sources of resistance; resistance may stem from a combination of sources.

1. Proponents of Theory X: the concept goes against their leadership style.
2. Status seekers: derive ego-stroking satisfaction from being in a position of control and cannot see themselves in an ancillary capacity.
3. Skeptics: hesitant to support a program not backed by a committed, sincere management team. It was found that "supervisors who rated their managers highly were significantly more positive (39 percent versus 25 percent) toward employee involvement programs than were those who gave their supervisors low marks" (p. 90).
4. Equality seekers: concerned "not that employees are finally getting recognition, but that they are getting it at the supervisors' expense" (p. 91). They want a more active role in such programs. The research shows that supervisors who perceive (a) their role in decision making as significant, and (b) their role in directing activities as important have a much more positive view toward employee involvement programs than those who did not (5 percent versus 25 percent, 39 percent versus 19 percent, respectively.)

5. Deal makers: resist employee involvement programs because they interfere with informal control they gain through making "deals" on a "one-to-one" basis.

The research indicates that objections were minimized when management also provided employee involvement for the foremen and recognition as well as a clear definition of supervisory duties and managerial expectations.

Klein suggests a strategy for overcoming resistance by appealing to their need for support and involvement.

*Support based training* involves two important elements that must be provided on a continuing basis: managers must demonstrate their commitment to the program and guarantee their long-term support.

*Supervisory involvement* is necessary in the development of employee participative programs and in the definition of their own roles.

*Responsibility with authority*—responsibility and decision-making powers should increase proportionately so that supervisors do not perceive a loss in power as their subordinates gain decision-making power.

*Supervisory networks* are necessary to encourage peer group support through informal mechanisms.

*Replacement*—if these measures are not successful in reducing objections, then the supervisor may have to be transferred to another position.

## THE FUTURE

Computers and automation both continue to change the nature of the actual workplace and will make the job of the supervisor much more difficult. In many plants today the assembly line operators receive their instructions and directions by computer through the use of video display tubes. In these computerized lines many supervisors will be phased out, certainly in terms of the traditional role. There will be fewer supervisors in the future, but they will be more highly selective and more highly trained. Tomorrow's first line supervisors will have to be proficient in human relations, and of course they will be highly paid. The effect of this will be to make the title of "supervisor" redundant, and these new roles will probably be known by the title of "section manager," or "project manager."

# Part II

---

# Executive Selection, Leadership, Communication, and Pay

# 6

---

# Executive Selection

Executive selection is essentially concerned with finding the right people, recruiting them, teaching them what they need to know, allowing them to progress through the organization, and rewarding them accordingly. And of course, at the end of their time, their return to society has to be facilitated.

The important thing about the selection system is that it socializes people to its ways; selection is a secondary consideration. For example, the interviewer starts with a stereotype of the ideal candidate and looks for a round peg to fit the round hole in this perceptual system. Thus, inevitably, the interviewer turns out to be somewhat inefficient. Nevertheless, the interview continues to be widely used because it helps to socialize the candidate into the organization.

## CEO SELECTION

The most important decision most boards make is selecting the CEO. As Richard Vancil points out in ''A Look at CEO Succession'' (1987):

Most executives know that the choice of the company's chief executive officer is the most important decision the board of directors and outgoing CEO will make—the decision that determines the future course and health of the company.

Excerpts reprinted, by permission of publisher, from *Organizational Dynamics*, Spring/1979 © 1979, American Management Association, New York. All rights reserved.

But they also know that this decision is one with which the people involved have little experience. A large U.S. company changes its CEO only about once every eight years. A bad choice can be costly, troublesome, and embarrassing.

The most common form of top management is the duo mode. There are two executives at the top, a chairman and a president, with one or the other carrying the additional title of CEO. Succession resembles a relay race: at some point, the chairman-CEO passes the baton—the CEO title—to the president while retaining the chairmanship.

When the chairman retires, the president-CEO usually becomes chairman-CEO, and a successor president is named who becomes the new heir apparent. A few years later, if all goes well, the president gets the CEO title. This is virtually a nonevent—a confirmation of everybody's expectations. No surprises. The two continue to work together a few more years before the chairman retires. Sometimes problems between the two surface during this period, but rarely.

The first event in the relay process, naming the heir apparent, is called selection. The second event, passing the CEO title to that person, is called validation. The interval between these two events is called transition. A formal period of transition is the hallmark—and the great virtue—of the relay process. [See Figure 6.1]

An increasing number of CEOs are being recruited from the outside. Insiders following John Kotter are better off in that they know business and industry, especially products, and they have established social networks.

As Kae H. Chung, Michael Lubatkin, Ronald C. Rogers, and James E. Owers argue,

Each year, 10%–15% of major U.S. corporations change their chief executive officers. The majority of these corporations (80%–85%) select their new CEOs from outside their organizations. Why do they prefer outsiders? Do insiders make better CEOs than do outsiders? Some of the nation's most respected companies—including GE,

**Figure 6.1**
**The Structures at the Top**

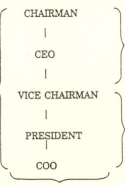

GM, IBM, and Coca-Cola—seem to think so. In his book *Theory Z*, William Ouchi asserts that promoting executives from inside is a characteristic of well managed companies in both Japan and the United States; the policy provides employees with opportunities to advance within the company and thus creates a sense of loyalty and stability. Thomas J. Peters and Robert H. Waterman, in *In Search of Excellence*, echo this sentiment. According to them, successful American companies motivate their employees by providing job security and creating a "feeling of family." These organizations rarely hire managers from the outside (1987, pp. 323–329).

## MANAGER SELECTION

### The Assessment Center

One of the most interesting and dramatic developments in executive selection has been the emergence of the assessment center, which employs a form of group selection. The assessment center was introduced early in World War II in Britain to choose candidates for officer training after the supply from the public schools such as Eton and Harrow had dried up. This selection procedure required a group of candidates to perform a variety of tasks together under observation. They were also required to take intelligence tests, to engage in group exercises including leaderless groups, to take part in case studies, and to be interviewed. The U.S. Office of Strategic Services, or OSS, a precursor of the Central Intelligence Agency, began using assessment centers in 1943. The OSS used the assessment center for selecting agents and saboteurs.

An assessment center in its civilian context is a standardized procedure that uses a variety of different techniques including tests, interviews, leaderless groups, and stress interviews to evaluate potential managers. Using this method, trained observers can objectively evaluate people in terms of their managerial potential. Nowadays the assessment center is also frequently used as a means of giving management trainees useful feedback about their performance and behavior. Assessment centers vary greatly in duration, cost, contents, and administration. They have also been used for determining management potential.

### Elements of the Assessment Centers

Assessment centers are widely used in North America and Europe as a means of selecting executives. Assessment centers usually begin in companies when top management feels that the present system of selection is not producing the executives that the company needs. To begin the process, the personnel director calls together the top managers of the firm to develop a personal profile of the managerial jobs to be filled. Usually what happens is a long list of traits is developed that characterizes the manager's job. After some discussion, this number is reduced from as many as thirty to perhaps fifteen. The object of the exercise now is to develop a set of test cases and exercises that will help to measure these traits.

Usually, the assessment center employs psychological tests to measure either intelligence or personality. Interviews are also used to ascertain how participants handle themselves in one-on-one situations and to get a more in-depth understanding of their managerial styles. Participants are frequently placed in a leaderless group problem-solving situation. The ''In'' basket exercise, for example, requires candidates to take over the office of a senior manager who has suddenly been called away. Peer evaluation is frequently used as a means of evaluating the candidate's standing with other members of the group.

All of these tests, cases, and exercises take a considerable amount of time, and this assessment process is usually held in the company training center, away from the hurly burly of work. It usually takes three or four days.

### Validity of the Assessment Center

Some managers use the assessment center to give difficult employees feedback about their performance, especially when such employees are not ready for promotion. What often happens in such circumstances is that the general manager sends the particular subordinate who thinks he or she is ready for promotion to the assessment center, hoping that he or she will get appropriate feedback about unacceptable leadership style and lack of managerial competence. Fortunately, in the assessment center this feedback is given in a form to which managers can respond.

In general terms, it is safe to assert that the validity of assessment centers is generally higher than other selection techniques available for assessing managers. One thing is certain, however: the assessment center has face validity (i.e., it looks like the real thing), but this is only achieved at a high cost. It has been estimated that it costs between $4,500 and $10,000 for each candidate to be assessed, but the cost of making an error in management selection is very high too. In some circumstances it may cost as much as $30,000 to $40,000 to terminate a ''bad'' management appointment.

A growing number of companies are having success with assessment centers in identifying suitable people for promotion. Assessment centers are now used in hundreds of businesses, government agencies, and educational institutions. They are widely used not only in the United States and Canada but also in the United Kingdom, Japan, Australia, Brazil, and elsewhere. In the United States, assessment centers are used by AT&T,

Sears, IBM, Sohiyo, the IRS, Universal Oil Products, and many other organizations.

Probably the best known assessment center effort is the AT&T program that began in 1956. The typical assessment center deals with approximately a dozen candidates per week, and each group of candidates spends three days at the center. After the candidates leave, the staff gets together to write competency reports and to make ratings. A candidate's potential success in a specific position is recorded in a three or four page report that spells out in considerable detail both strengths and weaknesses. These reports can be used with current performance data to select and develop the candidates with the best chance of success in their organizations.

## The Assessment Center Process

The whole assessment process is invalid unless the company is prepared to act on the decisions made at the assessment center. In this regard, it is extremely important to ensure that top management is on board and that they in fact believe in the assessment process. In spite of all these efforts at objectivity, some candidates come away from the center feeling they are being unfairly treated. For example, many candidates regard it as a kind of knife-and-fork test, a sort of test of middle class values. In other words, they believe they are being brought to the assessment center to have their table manners assessed. Or to see whether they can take a drink without getting drunk, or whether they can conduct themselves properly in informal settings. And indeed there may be some truth in these allegations because the observers and the candidates, of course, mix socially and they are bound to form impressions about each other.

A significant way of making the system somewhat more fair is to allow failed candidates to go through the assessment process again. In addition, the assessment center must be kept under some degree of statistical control to ensure the system maintains a level of validity.

The validity of the assessment center is reasonably high. Research carried out by Douglas Bray at AT&T for the selection of new salesmen shows quite clearly that the assessment center led to improvements in the actual selections. Longitudinal studies of the center reveal that this method is much more accurate than traditional appraisal procedures. The reason for this is that the exercises are designed to bring out specific skills and aptitudes required in those particular jobs. Furthermore, since the assessors do not know the candidates personally, there tends to be an increase in objectivity.

The assessment center is particularly important for identifying management potential among women and minority group employees. For example, the Michigan Bell Telephone Company employed the assessment center for selecting white and black females who were then promoted to supervisory positions. The assessment center technique was found to be predictive of subsequent behavioral ratings made by their superiors. Therefore, given the present civil rights legislation and increasing public and corporate concern, it is highly probable that the assessment centers will be more useful for selecting suitable managers among minorities and women.

When the candidates have completed their part of the exercise, the selectors remain for a further two days to discuss each candidate's contribution and to form a judgment about his or her suitability for a management position. Three kinds of decision are possible: ready for promotion immediately; requires further training; and not suitable for promotion. Assessment centers have been found to be relatively effective but perhaps not as effective as many of their proponents believe. Nevertheless, these centers are becoming increasingly popular, mainly because they are high in face validity, that is, they look like the real thing. Both the selectors and the candidates feel that the actual selection experience is meaningful.

## Training and Development Aspects

Nevertheless, assessment centers are coming under increasing criticism mainly because top corporate management places too much faith in the results of such exercises. Another major problem arises from employees who flunk the process and feel that the selection system is loaded against them. Many of the people who flunk the assessment center are highly promising young accountants, engineers, and scientists who have little experience of the managerial ambiance that successful candidates seem to be able to manifest. In such circumstances, morale of the executives can be lowered, which can have a negative impact on their performance.

To overcome some of these difficulties it is increasingly being argued that assessment centers should be used more for development and less for selection. Gary L. Hart and Paul H. Thompson (1979) have come up with the idea of development-oriented centers. How do participants respond to this type of center?

Tom was a scientist who was technically outstanding and who also appeared to possess many leadership skills. He was under great pressure from his management to accept a managerial assignment but had successfully resisted for more than a year. When he was invited to attend a workshop, he accepted because he was curious, but he made it clear that if this was another ploy to get him to be a manager he would be unhappy. By the evening of the first day of the workshop he had decided to go home, but he was persuaded by the director to stick it out. At the conclusion of the workshop, the staff had considerable difficulty writing Tom's report. The strengths he had displayed were considerable, but so were his limitations. He had been rude, offensive, arrogant, and selfish at the workshop, but the staff was uncertain as to how candid they should be. What's more, since he had expressed such reluctance to be a manager, the typical rationale to change ("if you want to be an effective manager") was inappropriate. But the report was very candid. And because Tom had expressed a considerable desire to be active and effective in community affairs, the entire report was written to that end, making no mention of company management.

During the postworkshop interview, Tom said that the report described a person he would detest. However, he discussed the feedback with his wife, and she agreed with points contained in the report. He later indicated that the workshop experience had a profound impact upon him. His eyes were opened to the challenges in leadership positions and the limitations he would have to overcome before he could perform satisfactorily as a manager. After considerable introspection he decided to accept a management position. He worked hard to overcome his limitations as a manager and has since been promoted to a senior manager position. He has also returned to the workshop as a staff member

If the Assessment Center is to prosper, then this development approach will have to be more carefully exploited.

## INTERVIEWING: SEARCHING FOR THE STEREOTYPE

The most important thing to know about the selection system is that its main purpose is to socialize, not select. A careful reading of the research literature reveals that both interviewing and group selection procedures are largely dramatic encounters with the starring roles going to the selectors and the candidates left in supporting roles.

There are two main characters in the interviewing drama. Taking the most important first, the interviewer starts off with a stereotype of the ideal candidate and seeks to match an individual with the stereotype. A typical and fairly useful stereotype for a junior manager would be "aggressive but clubbable." A bias is established early in the interview and tends to be followed by a favorable or unfavorable decision. A typical bias would be to assume that people who wear glasses are more intelligent than those who don't. Interviewers set out to collect information that will refute or confirm their hypotheses of their stereotypes. They are more influenced by negative information, and after they have it the interview for all practical purposes is over. In unstructured interviews, the interviewer talks more than the interviewee.

On the actual interview itself, the scientific evidence is decidedly negative. The interview is, in general terms, somewhat reliable (two interviewers rank candidates in somewhat similar but usually somewhat wrong order), and thus, rather low in validity (a measure of how good the interviewer was in picking the right person for the job). In a great number of cases, where tests are used, the interviewer will attempt to improve the efficiency of the test scores by inputting his or her own judgment, which generally has the effect of worsening the prediction.

## The Interview

Personnel managers have spent a great deal of time and energy improving the effectiveness of the interview, but unfortunately most interviews are still unplanned and are conducted by untrained interviewers. Nevertheless the interview continues to be used for selection for a wide variety of reasons. One major reason is that psychological testing is expensive and usually requires the use of psychologists to ensure that the tests are reliable and valid. Second, the interview itself is relatively inexpensive, is easy to use, and enables the personnel manager to assess the candidate on a large number of different characteristics. Third, the interview can also be used both for recruitment and negotiatory functions.

Unfortunately, there is no certain formula for conducting the interview that will ensure that the right candidate is selected. However, interviewing has developed to a point where it can be properly described as an art. But before looking at the interview as an art, perhaps it would be useful to list some of the weaknesses of the interviewing method that have not yet been overcome. First of all, there is the problem of objectivity. This varies among interviewers and will probably never be completely overcome. Second, many personnel managers fail to recognize the limitations of the interview. Third, most interviewers have not been properly trained.

There are three basic types of interview: the structured interview, the nondirected interview, and the stress interview. The structured interview uses a set of standardized questions that are asked of all applicants. Its purpose is to develop a set of data on all applicants that will enable comparisons to be made. The supreme beauty of the structured interview is that it allows the personnel manager to prepare a set of questions in advance that are related to the job and it includes the completion of a standardized evaluation form. But the structured interview should not be conducted in too rigid a fashion. It is useful to begin with a set of questions that deal with routine information such as the candidate's full name, address, educational background, and work history. When all these details have been gained, it is then possible to explore the more general aspects of the candidate's personality. At this later stage in the interview it is useful to ask questions such as: What is your principal asset/liability? What type of supervisor do you enjoy working with?

All this means employing a nondirective approach where the objective is to approach the candidate in a more general or tangential way. But unfortunately unstructured interviews are more likely to be unreliable. The reason for this is that biases and selected perceptions are more likely to creep into this type of interview. The stress interview is a special type of encounter designed to create anxiety and pressure and to see how the applicant responds. The stress interview is sometimes used in assessment centers.

### Some Characteristics of the Interview Process

Based on research carried out by Webster (1964) and Carlson (1967) of the Life Insurance Marketing and Research Association, it is possible to make certain comments on the interview process.

1. Interviewers develop stereotypes about a good applicant and seek information to confirm or disconfirm this stereotype. Probably the best approach is to write up the behavioral science terms and require the interviewers to make predictions about job behavior.
2. Unfavorable information about a candidate is more influential on interviewers' decisions than favorable information. For example, a management trainee applicant who has an MBA but who failed to get a commission in the military is seen as having failed in a significant organizational context rather than being an educational success.
3. An interviewer, having a quota to fill, behaves differently than an interviewer without a quota. For example, when "bodies" are needed, standards are lowered; that is, the "average" candidate is rated higher.
4. If the interviewer does not follow a structured process (asking a carefully prepared set of questions), he or she is likely to make a global judgment accepting or rejecting the applicant.
5. Only structured interviews generate information that enables interviewers to agree with each other. The important point is to use a standardized, highly structured interview schedule, take extensive notes, and concentrate on answers of factual material.
6. Experienced interviewers who follow the above procedures can agree on the rankings of candidates. To make all this happen, interviewers need feedback on their performance.

G. W. Allport has identified some interesting stereotypes:

Faces with wrinkles at the eye corners are seen as friendly, humorous and easy-going. People wearing spectacles are perceived as studious and industrious ("they have strained their eyes through study"). Those with high foreheads are seen as more intelligent and dependable ("they have more room for brains"). Women with thicker than average lips are considered sexy, those with thin lips asexual. Facial expression, gesture, posture in sitting and standing, and even the firmness or flabbiness of a handshake convey information from which judges make broad generalizations. Long faces are considered sad; smiling faces are considered intelligent. (1961)

### The Interviewer's Strategy

A number of vital preliminary steps must be taken to prepare for the interview. First, the personnel manager must develop an appropriate role description and then design a selection process to ensure a suitable person is found for this role. Second, an application form must be developed. When the candidate is invited to the interview, the invitation should include a short job description and a map as to how to get to the actual place of the interview. The receptionist should have a list of candidates coming for interviews.

The interview form should contain a list of appropriate questions, such as:

- How did you get your last job?
- Why did you choose that particular job?
- What were your qualifications for the job?
- What were your principal functions?
- What kind of decision-making powers did you have?
- Describe the managerial style of your superior.
- What promotions and merit awards did you receive?
- Why did you leave that particular job?
- What can this company offer you that you can't get in your present place of employment?

Certain questions have to be avoided. For example, it is pointless asking questions that rarely produce a true answer, such as: How did you get along with your fellow workers? Nearly everyone responds to this question with "Just great!" Also, it is somewhat wasteful to ask leading questions such as: "You seem to be a kind of humorous person, are you not?" Answer: "Of course!" There are also certain no-no questions that relate to race, creed, sex, national origin, and so on. It is also a mistake to get involved in questions that probe into the sexual life of the applicant. For example, it is wrong to ask the candidate whether he or she is dating, if in fact he or she can get away for weekends, how his or her sex life is working out, and so on. Asking such questions often leads to situations where the interviewer is accused of sexual harassment, and rightly so.

Well-informed applicants, of course, are ready for appropriate questions and are also ready to answer such general questions as: "Tell me what you learned in college"; "What is your principal asset?"; and, of course, they are not fazed in the least by such questions as: "Where do you expect to be in ten years?" and "What kind of car will you be driving?" The experienced interviewer always saves such open-ended questions until the end of the encounter.

### Establishing the Right Relationship

In the interview it is necessary to establish a relationship that will facilitate the flow of communications between the interviewer and the interviewee. Good interviewers are highly skilled at establishing the right kind of rapport, allowing a depth and relevance of information to be communicated. This flow of relevant information at a meaningful level can be impeded by a number of barriers. Usually the applicant experiences the stress of being in a context in which he or she experiences a superior/inferior relationship. The candidate typically perceives the interviewer as the "insider" and him- or herself as the "outsider." More importantly, he or she feels that the interviewer has the authority to make or break his or her career. All this, of course, is very disturbing to the interviewee.

To overcome some of these difficulties, the interviewer should lay out the room in a way that does not accentuate this superior/inferior relationship. Interviewers should not huddle down, hidden behind the desk. They should place themselves in a position where they appear to be somewhat accessible to the candidate. It is not unheard of for interviewers to have purposely selected chairs that require the candidate to sit at a lower level, which should, of course, be discouraged. The interviewer should try to avoid using words or phrases that have a strong emotional connotation for the candidate, such as "fired," "poor record," "flunked out," "welfare," "ghetto," and so on.

### Be Nice

The interviewer uses effective listening responses such as nodding, pausing, introducing casual remarks, echoing, and mellowing. Listening responses are an essential part of everyday, normal conversation and they can be used very effectively in the interview. Facial expressions, voice inflections, and gestures play a crucial role in establishing the right atmosphere at the interview and in guiding the interviewee. It is sometimes suggested that the eyebrows should be raised frequently, particularly when asking a question, as this helps in indicating an interest and gets the interviewee to open up. Many interviewers behave in a way that gives the impression of agreeing with everything the candidate says. This is usually achieved by nodding one's head and by making short comments such as: "I see," or "I can understand that," or "uh-huh." Unfortunately, many hardnosed books on interviewing take the view that such responses are a waste of time and merely prolong the interview without improving its efficiency.

However, it is useful to begin the interview with some small talk, often about the candidate's journey. As the experienced personnel manager knows, the interviewer can often soften the effect of the question by careful phrasing. Here, timing is extremely important. Questions that the candidate could take in his or her stride at one point in the interview may be entirely inappropriate at another time. Again, the way in which the questions are asked rather than their content can create emotional barriers. For example, a question that is too direct would be: "Why were you fired from your last job?" The less direct form would be "What are your reasons for considering other employment at this time?"

### Nonverbal Communication

When inexperienced interviewers first see themselves on a videotape replay, they are often quite surprised. What surprises them is their body language, their facial expressions, and their distracting body movements. If the interviewer's nonverbal behavior sends a signal—"I'm bored," or "You turn me off"—the candidate will pick up these cues and react accordingly. One of the most important aspects of nonverbal behavior is the establishment of eye contact.

Occasionally, but not often, interviewers gaze too long and continuously at the candidate, which can be distracting. In general, most interviewers are unable or unwilling to look directly at the candidate with an accompanying thoughtful or pleasant facial expression. Interviewers who sit too stiffly throughout the interview may induce an air of formality that is upsetting to the applicant. On the other hand, candidates may also be upset if the interviewer sits too far forward.

Some actions have a definite meaning in the minds of most candidates. For example, if the interviewer glances at his watch, it means "hurry up" or "I'm getting bored." If the interviewer offers the candidate a cigarette, it means "relax, take your time." If the interviewer puts her notes aside, it means "this is off the record." If the candidate says something and the interviewer suddenly notes down exactly what it is, looks at the candidate piercingly, and asks the candidate to repeat it, this can be very disturbing. Unfortunately, many interviewers have distracting habits including playing with their pens, shuffling papers, drumming their fingers on the desk top, scratching or rubbing their hands, popping knuckles, and constantly looking at the ceiling.

## Listening Skills

It is necessary for the interviewer to develop listening skills. Sometimes the interviewer is so busy formulating questions that he or she is unable to hear the answers that are being given. Since the average person speaks at a rate of 100 to 125 words per minute, it is sometimes very difficult to pick up everything being said. But it is necessary to keep in mind that listening is far more than just allowing the candidate to speak. Real listening is not a passive function but something the interviewer must do actively if it is to be effective. All this means listening for voice inflections and key words that are clues to hidden meanings, and so on. Once the candidate has completed his or her response, the interviewer must digest, analyze, and evaluate what he or she has heard.

The interviewer must also be able to face up to personal biases. A bias is a preference or inclination that inhibits impartial judgment. Biases or prejudices clearly hinder the process of objective evaluation during the interview. A good example of bias is the perception that career-oriented women are promiscuous or disorganized and unlikely to be able to maintain proper work schedules. Frequently, women in the workplace are seen as aggressive, ambitious, and difficult to work with.

The interview also has a significant effect on the interviewer. For example, candidates wearing glasses are often rated as being significantly higher in intelligence, dependability, initiative, and honesty than those without. Overweight people are frequently perceived as being not only funny and amusing characters but also as inefficient. Interviewers have to be particularly on guard against the "halo effect," which is the tendency to assume that almost everything about a person is good because we like that person. Interviewers also have to be careful about stereotyping.

Good interviewers are able to establish rapport, have a thorough knowledge of the job, are emotionally stable, and are not easily shocked. It is also useful to have a reputation among previous applicants for sincerity, sympathy, and sensitiveness. Unfortunately, there is abundant evidence to support the proposition that interviewers frequently make mistakes in recording. In general terms, it is safe to assume that mature people make better interviewers, that is, mature in the sense that they are people who have come to terms with life.

## The Interviewee's Strategy

We know from research that of the fourteen factors that most often lead to rejection, seven are interview-related. The main pitfalls are inability to show self-confidence, enthusiasm, and clearly set goals. To get ready for the interview, it is necessary for the candidate to research the company's background by checking either the company's annual general report or by browsing through Standard and Poors News Reports. From this data, a candidate should be able to build up some idea of the company's age, products, growth patterns, and competition. On the day of the interview, the best advice is to dress conservatively. For men, this means a dark suit, white shirt, and a simple tie that can be removed if the situation calls for it. Women should avoid dressing too flamboyantly. A dress or a skirt and blouse should be worn rather than jeans. For both, shoes should be polished and hair neat and clean. It pays to find out both the name and its pronunciation of the person who is going to conduct the interview. Many manuals on interviewing recommend that you dry your hand on your jacket before going in so that you can offer the interviewer a dry, firm handshake. Good eye contact should be established. The abilities to listen attentively and to be ready to speak clearly when spoken to should be evinced. Strangely enough, research on the interview shows that the candidate needn't do too much speaking, as the interviewer talks up to 90 percent of the time. Don't slouch; best of all, angle your chair at 45° so you can lean towards the interviewer without adapting a confrontational mode.

The key to success in the interview resides in your ability to present a positive ambiance about yourself and your career. Body language is extremely important; try to avoid crossing your arms or tightening your fists. Today especially, smoking is a no-no, unless, of course, you're invited by the interviewer to light up.

There are certain questions you should be ready to answer. You may remember that famous scene in Sloan Wilson's *The Man in the Gray Flannel Suit* where the job-hunting hero was invited to go next door where he found a typewriter on which he was to write the story of his life. The story had to begin with the following words: ''The most important thing to know about me is . . .'' Like the man in the gray flannel suit, you have to be ready to answer such questions as ''Tell me about yourself,'' ''Why did you pick this company?'' ''What are your most important strengths and weaknesses?'', and ''Where do you expect to be in five years?'' The purpose of all these questions usually is to ascertain what talents you are bringing to the company. Thus, in formulating your answers, you should try to reveal your personal objectives and your desire to learn, and how you can help your targeted company to improve its effectiveness. When you are asked about your weaknesses, it's usual to give answers like, ''I try too hard; I find it very difficult to give up; my problem is I'm a workaholic,'' or, ''I get overinvolved with the technical aspects of the job.''

Inevitably, at the end of the interview, you're going to be asked if you have any questions. This is a good opportunity to ask whether the company has developed career planning and what is a likely career trajectory for you. It is usually wise to avoid asking questions about salary, vacations, and benefits too early in the interview. Finally, as the interview closes, it is important to thank the interviewer for taking the time to see you and to ascertain when a decision will be reached.

To do all this effectively, it is necessary to develop specific job hunting skills early in your career. This can be best achieved by formulating a set of ranked job goals that should include specific job titles, a place where you want to work, and specific job skills. Next you should set out to get informed feedback about how realistic these objectives are. All this means practice. The best way to practice is by continually hunting for jobs. Then, following John Kotter, you should immerse yourself in your field and develop a file of appropriate articles and job advertisements. Last but not least, you should develop a contact network that will keep you advised about job contacts that might be of interest to you.

However, it would be a mistake to imagine that job opportunities are going to come up in any linear or logical fashion. The thing to do is to explore the real world around you and talk to people who work in the areas that interest you. The worst possible thing is to be looking for an *actual* job; this tends to ruin relations from the word "go." Inevitably you'll discover that most jobs are not advertised in newspapers. In general terms, in our turbulent environment, you can't really expect to work in the same field forever.

Specialization can mean getting to know more and more about less and less until you know absolutely everything about nothing. When this happens, people discover that they are trapped in a specialty. In spite of the current argument to the contrary, a solid liberal arts education can stand you in good stead provided you have the flexibility to get the right entry-level position, but a person studying liberal arts would be wise to include a little science and some mathematics. A good liberal arts program will help to develop a person's analytical skills as well as teaching him or her how to put things together; hence the much publicized move to the core curriculum in which Harvard University will require students to select a quarter of undergraduate courses from specific academic areas. Harvard students will also be expected to learn how to work computers, demonstrate their capacity for writing, and acquire some diligence in both mathematical reasoning and a foreign language.

## FIRING: DESELECTING EXECUTIVES

### The Sting and the Hit Men

The point is that an executive can learn more about the perverse process called firing (letting go, making redundant, separation, the shake-out—a variety of titles are in use) from reading the book or seeing the film "The Sting." Even a quick glance at the chapter headings of "The Sting" alerts the reader to the different stages of the process: "the setup, the hook, the take, the shutout, the sting." There are many similar cons in business that are nearly as elaborate and certainly as dramatic. "The Sting" shows blow-for-blow how to take the other guy, take him for all he's worth, for his shirt. My point is that most successful managers know this.

### What Every Manager Should Know about Firing

The most important thing the manager should know about firing is that it is a dramatic art form with its own particular scenario, plot and script. The main actors, of course, are the firer and the firee (see Figure 6.2). But the firer can do a much better job if he or she has an accomplice. The main role of the accomplice is to "cool out the mark."

What is being argued is that corporate life is a succession of dramas, each with its own particular structure of actors and process of plots and scripts and theatrical values. If the manager needs to fire someone, there are certain rules that ought to be followed. He or she ought to think carefully about the victim and his or her likely reaction. The manager should develop a plot and a script and make sure the right props are available. On the other hand, if you are the victim, you are in a different kettle of fish. You face loneliness, withdrawal, and isolation. The odd thing about being fired is that the victim is always taken by surprise. Coping with the experience of being fired is existentially very demanding but perhaps the only thing a fired executive can do is to make it into something existentially meaningful.

Nevertheless, there are certain things an executive can do to protect oneself. The main thing is to keep cool and try to figure out what stage the plot has got to and what the firer's plan of action is. If the victim can identify the strategy of the firer, then he or she should be able to formulate a set of alternatives.

The purpose of this section is not only to introduce the student to firing as a dramatic art but also to show the importance that existentialism plays in an executive's life. Remember that the existential executive wants to be able to stand up and be counted, to be somebody. And of course most executives are desperately engaged in a search for sanity in a corporate world that is frequently insane. What existentialism is arguing for is an environment in which people can exercise choice, act in good faith, and make their lives meaningful.

**Figure 6.2**
**Listening to Top Dog Chief Executives Talk**

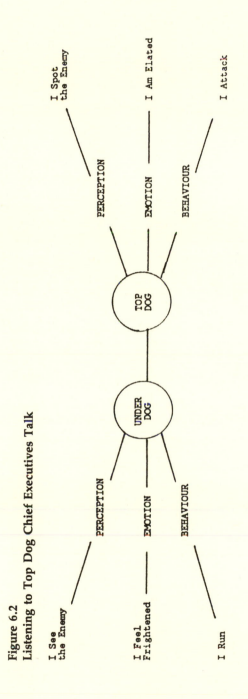

# 7

---

# Leadership: Linking the Strategic Vision to Operations

To be effective as a leader, whether you are the president of the company or a junior manager, you have to be good at defining strategic visions. To revitalize your team you need to transform organizational realities by developing a vision of what can be and by mobilizing resources and energies. To get there, something new has to be created. But somehow the innovative style of strategic vision has to match up with consumers' needs. Hence Chrysler's and Iacocca's failure; they ignored customers who wanted better engineering. In addition, short-term solutions such as firing experienced middle managers won't work; you can't eat your feedstock.

In 1991 the media was talking about William H. Gates being "too big for his boots" and how Microsoft would crash. But Bill Gates held onto his vision that Microsoft, the largest software company with revenue of $1.8 billion, would come through. And it did, and its value on the NYSE is greater than General Motors'. Microsoft in 1991 fell into conflict with its old mentor IBM. But by 1992 IBM was going along with Microsoft. What his enemies called ego turned out to be vision for Gates, who stuck with his vision, NT (new technology), and more particularly Windows. If Gates succeeds in his strategy, he will become the wealthiest (he is already the third wealthiest in the United States), most powerful person in the history of mankind, so says Paul Grayson, chairman of Micrografix.

Chief executives have to be ethical. Hence John Gutfreund, chairman of Salomon Brothers, was forced to resign for allowing his company to bid for US Treasury notes illegally. Gutfreund, known as the king of Wall Street, whiled away his time playing Liar's Poker with John Meriwether, a Salomon VP.

It was to Meriwether that Gutfreund is said to have offered a single bet of $1M on Liar's Poker, a game involving guessing the serial numbers on dollar bills.

Gutfreund's one-liner: "One hand, one million dollars, no tears" has become part of Wall Street folklore.

Meriwether's reply was no less dramatic: "No, John. If we're going to play for those kind of numbers, I'd rather play for real money. Ten million dollars. No tears." Gutfreund did not accept. (*London* (Sunday) *Times*, 18 August, 1991)

To be effective, according to David Ulrich, in *Organizational Capability: Competing from the Inside Out* (1991), an executive has to link the strategic vision to operations by being a social architect to create structure within which his or her team can self-actualize by achieving a high level of performance. Their jobs become a challenge (they do not park their minds along with their cars in the parking lot); middle managers can link vision to practice; they can make conflict work for them while maintaining trust; they can maintain and ensure that the basic systems are congruent with organizational objectives (see Figure 7.1). And above all they see to it that the cultural dynamics are right.

## STRATEGIC LEADERSHIP

Leading, taking the initiative, making the first move, directing, acting as a resource person—call it what you may—is an integral part of organizational life. And the odd thing about it all is that behavioral science has so little to say about leadership setting. We know a great deal about leadership from two sources: the lives of great men and our own personal experiences. While executives are inclined to laugh when informed that Richard Nixon, when the going got rough, was given to watching reruns of the movie "Patton" to screw his courage to the sticking place, such larger-than-life heroic figures can be a source of inspiration, metaphor,

**Figure 7.1**
**Leadership Style and Managerial Level**

| | | |
|---|---|---|
| President | → | Strategic Vision |
| ↓ | | ↓ |
| Vice President | → | Wrestles with Participative Jelly Fish |
| ↓ | | ↓ |
| General Manager | → | Agenda Setting, Networking |
| ↓ | | ↓ |
| Middle Manager | → | Human Resource Planning |
| ↓ | | ↓ |
| Supervisors | → | Structure and Consideration |
| ↓ | | ↓ |
| Shop Floor Operative | → | Human Relations or Alienation |

and moxie. Even Steven Jobs was looking for a video of "Patton" the night he got fired. Many American executives got a tremendous kick out of George Patton, both as an ambitious old-fashioned patrician and as a profane, patriotic psychopath who made it almost in spite of himself. What Patton had to say about other contemporary historical figures makes good reading that no behavioral science book could possibly equal. For example, as Martin Blumenson in *The Patton Paper* (1974) quotes Patton on his arch rival Field Marshal Montgomery: "War requires the taking of risks and he won't take them." From great men such as Patton, Winston Churchill, Charles De Gaulle, Franklin Roosevelt, Joseph Stalin, and John Kennedy, executives appear to be able to draw inspiring insights that apparently invoke analogues in their experience.

## TOP MANAGEMENT STYLE

### CEO as Charismatic Visionary

Putting one's experience together is an essentially existential exercise, and if the process is carried through in a perceptive way it can be a revealing self-encounter.

Great managers are charismatic visionaries who have made it back from the desert of despair to issue the clarion call to their people in response to the crisis of crises. They have an acute sense of history and see themselves as "saintly soldiers" trying to ride the coattails of history to meet their own personal destinies. Lee Iacocca, like Louis XIV, believes "Chrysler, *c'est moi.*" In other words, great managers consider themselves the personal embodiment of their institutions, organizations, or states. In brief, great managers are charismatic visionary frontiersmen or ideologues who want to leave their mark on history even if it means rewriting the book, page by page. Their every act is a letter, a word, or a line in their obituaries that they would like to write themselves. Hence Iacocca's terrific success with his autobiography. Listen to what Jack Welch has to say about what makes a good manager (see Figure 7.2):

I prefer the term business leader. Good business leaders create a vision, articulate the vision, passionately own the vision, and relentlessly drive it to completion. Above all else, though, good leaders are open. They go up, down, and around their organization to reach people. They don't stick to the established channels. They're informal. They're straight with people. They make a religion out of being accessible. They never get bored telling their story. Real communication takes countless hours of eyeball to eyeball, back and forth. It means more listening than talking. It's not pronouncements on a videotape, it's not announcements in a newspaper. It is human beings coming to see and accept things through a constant interactive process aimed at consensus. And it must be absolutely relentless. That's a real challenge for us. There's still not enough candor in this company. (Quoted in Tichy-Charan, 1989)

**Figure 7.2**
**Welch in Action**

| Strategic Vision | Vision | |
| | ↓ | |
| | Overall Objectives | |
| | ↓ | |
| | Long Term Strategic Plan | L |
| | ↓ | E |
| | | A |
| | Middle Term Operational Plan | D |
| | ↓ | E |
| | | R |
| Operations | Short Term Tectical Plan     ← | S |
| | ↓ | H |
| | | I |
| | Specific Goals | P |
| | ↓ | |
| | Action | |
| | ↓ | |
| Action | Etc. | |

## MOVING FROM STRATEGIC VISION TO OPERATIONS

### Images of Leadership: The CEO

In research for their article "The Person of the CEO: Understanding the Executive Experience" (1989), Harry S. Jones, III, Ronald E. Fry, and Suresh Srivastva asked executives to tell their stories, reflect on their lives in progress, and describe their approach to managing. Who of us, for example, has not heard a version of this story, recounted by the chairman of a major banking and financial service corporation:

In high school I worked on an affluent farm harvesting corn and putting up hay. One day in the cornfield—a hot, dusty, miserable day—I saw a big air-conditioned Cadillac go by and inside was a man wearing a white shirt and tie. I said to myself, "I'm out of this corn field." I think you must have had that kind of experience.

A recently retired CEO of a multibillion-dollar capital goods manufacturer recounted an early search for mastery:

One of the smartest things I ever did was probably the most mundane thing I ever did. That was to go take the Dale Carnegie course in New York. I got so wrapped up in it that I took an advanced course with Dale Carnegie himself—he was alive then—and they asked me to teach the course after that.

The chairman of a mining company spoke poignantly of facing personal challenges:

I had to face a personal crisis in my own life. One was the realization that I was an alcoholic, and I'd better do something about it, which I did. I went through treatment, and joined Alcoholics Anonymous. It made a big impact on me. The second thing was I become a widower. I lost a wife and I had six kids. So there were two things which were traumatic, but it tested you a bit too.

Personal tests of character may also come in the form of challenges from authorities, either individuals or institutions:

I learned about time management at the Harvard Business School. I was there in the first class after the War and we were absolutely convinced they used us as guinea pigs to experiment with the work load. We had three suicides in the class. It got so bad that a group almost went to the administration to complain but we said, that's not gonna do it. So you have to know how to choose what's most important.

The chairman of a large insurance company revealed:

I'm a leader [and] I'm becoming a legend. I see it. It's the most remarkable experience because I don't perceive myself that way. I mean, I've been coming to this office, the same office, for 32 years. I was a schlepper doing the most menial work. It's been a very gradual process.

Finally, the flamboyant chairman of a large insurance firm, himself a major art collector, underscored the importance of creativity in his minitheory:

Management is a very creative process. Most people don't understand it. You hear analogies to a football team to describe management, but it's a lot different when you have 3,000 people on the team. . . . Progress is doing things differently. The reason for the art [prominently display in the corporate offices] is to keep people aware that craziness is what life is all about: new thoughts, new perceptions, new techniques.

These few examples suggest that executives choose words and phrases in a way that is consistent with and expressive of their own characters. Again, we are not sure how such language actually impacts on members of the organization. However, we may hypothesize that to the extent that the specific language chosen by CEOs to articulate their image of leadership is seen as consistent with the overall perceptions of the CEO's character by organizational members, such language will be seen as more effective and meaningful by members.

## Transformational Leadership

James MacGregor Burns divides leadership into two types, transactional and transforming. In transactional terms the manager makes a practical deal with his or her people, and in transforming terms the manager existentially helps people to help themselves in self-actualizing terms, to accept the vision.

Burns's message is that the manager has to avoid "narrow, egocentric self-actualization" and must try to create an environment in which executives can grow and develop. Executives would be wise to examine their own styles to ascertain which type of leader they are.

A scenario of how leadership required by a situation emerges, operates, and is then rejected helps to flesh out the story line of such changes in leadership flavor as the replacement of the agonizingly self-critical Jimmy Carter with Marlborough man Ronald Reagan.

Iacocca's type of leadership is a nonoptional extra; you don't need it until you haven't got it. Leadership begins with a vision of success, the potentiality of snatching victory from disaster. Existentially, a manager frequently has been rejected by both peer and the hack. They are strengthened immeasurably by adversity. Existential managers like Iacocca have a vision of the future, a sense of impending apocalypse, and the courage to ride the coattails of history. They are not too far out front, where no one can see and follow, and not too far back, which would create a vacuum at the front. Leaders must also have a sharp sense of the ridiculous.

Noel N. Tichy and David O. Ulrich argue in *The Leadership Challenge: A Call for the Transformational Leader* (1984) that "an identifiable program of activity associated with the transformational leadership is the creation of a vision." The transformational leader must provide the organization with a vision of a desired future state. While this task must be shared with other key members of the organization, the vision remains the core responsibility of the transformational leader. The leader needs to integrate analytic, creative, intuitive, and deductive thinking. "At Chrysler, Lee Iacocca developed a vision without committee work or heavy staff involvement. Instead, he relied more on his intuitive and direct leadership, philosophy, and style. Both GM and Chrysler ended up with a new vision because of transformational elders proactively shaping a new organization mission and vision" (Tichy and Ulrich, 1984).

## A VICE PRESIDENT: WRESTLING WITH THIS PARTICIPATIVE JELLYFISH

In the 1990s, an increasing number of firms are moving toward a more participative form of management, but becoming a participative manager is a slippery business. Honeywell, in its Defense and Marine Systems Group in Minneapolis, has moved from a "steely, no-nonsense" type of executive to a more relaxed sort of executive. As Richard J. Boyle, a vice-president of Honeywell, points out in "Wrestling with Jellyfish" (1984):

When I began my career at Honeywell in the late 1950s and as I advanced to more senior positions, steely, no-nonsense executives were the norm. Many examples of their autocratic management are permanently blazed in corporate legend. One "productivity initiative" from those days (long since reversed) was the removal of bathroom stall doors to discourage reading on company time. Today's middle and upper managers were trained during that period, and getting them to commit themselves to a new management style was no simple matter. After all, why should they trade their pearl-handled revolvers for a copy of *The One Minute Manager* when a swift, Patton-like kick took only a few seconds?

To try to develop a new management style, Honeywell structured a task group—a sort of tight-loose organization. To integrate this somewhat democratic task group, the company came up with the idea of a parallel organization of the task group led by a steering committee, which acted as a coupling mechanism between the formal hierarchy and the flattened democracy of the task group.

But to get democracy into action, the vice president in charge had to take some action himself.

I found that making ostensibly trivial adjustments to organizational life could have major repercussions. For example, soon after my arrival at the group, an issue was made of assigned parking spaces. The reorganization of which I was part increased the ranks of management. An unanticipated result was that we ended up with more managers than could be accommodated in our parking garage. When I learned that two members of my staff had flipped a coin to see who won the last available spot, I told the loser that he could have mine. Now, indoor parking may have symbolic importance in many companies, but in Minnesota in January, the symbol carries more than the usual weight.

My action sent a ripple through the executive ranks—Boyle had given up his garage space! By failing to exercise my executive prerogative, I put people on notice that we would not be operating business as usual. (Later, when a garage space did open up, I took it. But even then I did not take the number-one stall next to the door. This was another chance to send a signal that power was being used differently).

Another manifestation of our company way was our dress habits. Although Honeywell had no strict policy on dress, house rules regarding office attire, including "mandatory" neckties, were in force throughout the organization. In the summer of 1982 I issued a memo to employees announcing a "relaxed" policy on neckties during the summer. Although I really did nothing more than restate the existing Honeywell policy, an editorial in the employee newsletter poked fun at the memo. Nonetheless, the editorial agreed that exercising common sense over arbitrary rules could be healthy for the organization in many areas. But only when I actually showed up at the office without a tie did people begin to believe that the new dress code was really OK.

But participation does not always work. In "The Case for Directive Leadership" (1987), Jan P. Muczyk and Bernard C. Reimann of Cleveland State University argue that "many managers have been forced to face the harsh reality that participative management simply may not work in some situations. Leadership is a two-way street, so a democratic style will be effective only if followers are both willing and able to participate actively in the decision-making process. If they are not, the leader cannot be democratic without also being 'directive' and following up very closely to see that directives are being carried out properly."

### Motivation of Top Managers

The findings on motivation of top managers can be summarized as follows:

1. Motivation is highest among top managers.
2. Highly motivated managers prefer open-minded, approachable bosses.
3. Money provides positive motivation for managers.
4. Executives overestimate the pay of their subordinates, underestimate the pay of their bosses, and generally feel underpaid.
5. Managers are more dominant than others, interested in directing others, and prefer independent activities.
6. All managers do not have the same utility function.
7. Managers score higher on initiative tests than the general population.
8. Managers place a high value on self-actualization, autonomy needs, and opportunities for personal growth.

### The General Manager Leads through Networking and Agenda Setting

The general manager (GM) is the person who has overall responsibility for performance. The GM's work includes complex, not easily defined tasks, and he or she is held responsible for overall goals, production, sales, and finance. General managers are expected to exercise flair and entrepreneurial leadership. As Kotter points out, a general manager is held accountable for complex systems not fully understandable.

- They mobilize their energies, drives, and managerial savvy to get things done using an informal network of relations: they get the job done, but not by going by the book. They don't POLE.
- They act in an essentially existential way. Like members of AA, they treat each day as a separate event to be gotten through.
- They have a strong need for power and achievement.
- They are highly motivated, ambitious, and extremely stable emotionally.
- They are analytical and intuitive.
- They have extensive knowledge.
- They manage by agenda setting and networking, the agendas including financial, product, market, and organizational goals.

Network building is a major activity, and includes relationships with bosses, peers, and subordinates.

### The General Manager's Style

General managers are perceived as having a very high task orientation, a perception made effective by virtue of the fact that they avoid the traditional managerial skills of planning, directing, controlling, and POLEing but engage in agenda setting. They are seen as managers who set very high standards of expectations for their subordinates; this demands considerable skill in delegating. All this agenda setting, networking, and task structuring has to be tempered by certain moral considerations, which make considerable demands on their personal integrity. Technological competence is an obvious must, as Kotter points out, though apparently not all senior managers appear to have the necessary technical "know how" to carry out their present assignments. Great emphasis is placed on the capacity to make decisions on the basis of inadequate information.

To weld these agenda setting and networking skills together, the senior manager has to have considerable leadership skills, especially the ability to treat subordinates as autonomous individuals. As we already noted, top managers defining the vision appear to employ an "optimal" organizational style; middle level managers expect to be used within a framework of human resources planning; presumably, first level managers would have a greater expectation of more traditional human relations style leadership.

## Working for a GM Can be a Problem

Analysis of the operating problems turned up the difficulties generated for this high level of task orientation. Tremendous pressure is being placed on subordinates who are receiving a signal to generate a high level of excellence, with the general manager having insufficient time to brief them fully on how to achieve this excellence. This leads to one of the basic dilemmas in managerial leadership. Thus if you are too structuring down the way, how can you be sure that your subordinates have sufficient autonomy? This difficulty is further compounded by the fact that general managers are highly dependent upon the subordinates for technical guidance, due to their lack of familiarity with the technical process. This basic antithesis of "structure versus autonomy" has become even more difficult in the 1990s because of the uncertainty in the environment and a need to develop new business areas. All this leads to personality conflicts and problems in communication. Furthermore, this problem of communications is bedeviled by the fact that managers are not fully aware of what other departments are doing. This inability to grasp "the whole scene" makes the highly structured and task-oriented approach of some general managers even more inappropriate.

Somehow the tension has to be overcome. Middle level managers cannot function in a constant state of paranoia that totally immobolizes them. Somehow the tension in the situation has to be released.

One solution to this problem has been presented by Jay A. Conger of McGill University. In an article entitled "Leadership: The Art of Empowering Others" (1989), Conger studied eight executive officers and executive vice presidents of Fortune 500 companies and successful entrepreneurial firms, representing industries as diverse as telecommunications, office automation, retail banking, beverages, packaged foods, and management consulting.

One of the subjects of the study, Bill Jackson, was appointed the head of a troubled division. Demand had outstripped the division's ability to maintain adequate inventories, and product quality had slipped. Jackson's predecessors were authoritarian managers, and subordinates were demoralized as well as paranoid about keeping their jobs. As one told me, "You never knew who would be shot next." Jackson felt that he had to break the tension in a way that would allow his staff to regain their sense of control and power. He wanted to remove the stiffness and paranoia and turn what subordinates perceived as an impossible task into something more fun and manageable.

So, I was told, at the end of his first staff meeting, Jackson quietly pulled out a squirt-gun and blasted one of his managers with water. At first, there was a moment of stunned silence, and then suddenly the room was flooded with laughter. He remarked with a smile, "You got to have fun in this business. It's not worth having your stomach in ulcers." This began a month of squirt-gun fights between Jackson and his managers.

The end result? A senior manager's comment is representative: "He wanted people to feel comfortable, to feel in control. He used waterguns to do that. It was a game. It took the stiffness out of the business, allowed people to play in a safe environment—as the boss says, 'to have fun.'" This play restored rapport and morale. But Jackson also knew when to stop. A senior manager told me, "We haven't used waterguns in nine months. It has served its purpose. The waterfights were like being accepted into a club. Once it achieved its purpose, it would have been overdone."

## MIDDLE MANAGERS MOVING BEYOND HUMAN RELATIONS TO HUMAN RESOURCES

There is increasing evidence that middle managers are moving beyond human relations to human resources. A series of studies conducted by Raymond E. Miles, a behavioral scientist at the University of California at Berkeley, revealed that managers espoused Theory Y positions, as did McGregor. But as Miles's research continued he found that it became more difficult to fit managers' views into these models. Managers appear to endorse participative management concepts as advocated in Theory Y, while at the same time expressing considerable reservations about the subordinate's capability to do the job.

On the basis of his research Miles developed the idea of the human resources model. He saw people as typically underutilized as resources. In fact, their full capabilities were seldom exploited. In this approach participation was viewed as a necessary means of helping the organization achieve immediate gains by improving decision making. The argument appeared to be that managers use a human relations model for subordinates while believing their own superiors should follow the human resources theory. In short, the human resources model exploits the idea that managers want challenging but rewarding work.

In other words, as you ascend the hierarchy, the actual style of relating to people changes. Employees on the shop floor expect to be treated in a benevolent and supportive way. Managers in the middle of the organization treat their subordinates through human relations, whereas they expect to be treated as human resources. The typical senior manager prefers an environment that makes the best use of resources, stretches him or her to the limit, and ensures he or she is properly rewarded for this effort even though some conflict or stress may be raised in the process.

Effective management in the upper echelons of business—the executive sphere—is a sought-after quality. Taking into account the types of tasks involved and also the group ideology, the ultimate leadership ability is to influence the group in the desired way, whether the aim is the achievement of a particular goal or sustaining effectiveness in the existing group. Comparison of two methods of management—the psychologically distant manager who maintains a formal relationship with employees versus the psychologically closer manager, the buddy type—comes up with some initially surprising conclusions.

## FINDING THAT ELUSIVE LEADERSHIP QUALITY

The efficiency of the executive is probably the single most important factor influencing organizational productivity. In spite of this, very little is known about the effective executive. Informed managers realize that psychologists have failed to provide a description of the effective leader in terms of personality traits.

Many studies have been undertaken to ascertain the personality traits of the leader. The leader tends to be bigger and brighter than the rest of the group but only marginally so. When personnel managers are discussing with other executives the kind of person who can fill a management vacancy, certain terms, irrespective of function or level, keep cropping up with monotonous regularity, for example: analytical.

As Shelley A. Kirkpatrick and Edwin A. Locke of the University of Maryland point out in "Leadership: Do Traits Matter?" (1991),

the study of leader traits has a long and controversial history. While research shows that the possession of certain traits alone does not guarantee leadership success, there is evidence that effective leaders are different from other people in certain key respects. Key leader traits include: drive (a broad term that includes achievement, motivation, ambition, energy, tenacity, and initiative); leadership motivation (the desire to lead but not to seek power as an end in itself); honesty and integrity; self-confidence (which is associated with emotional stability); cognitive ability; and knowledge of the business. There is less clear evidence for traits such as charisma, creativity, and flexibility. We believe that the key leader traits help the leader acquire necessary skills; formulate an organizational vision and an effective plan for pursuing it; and take the necessary steps to implement the vision in reality.

But it appears that the personality-trait approach has failed.

Following this failure, social psychologists turned hopefully to examine the structure and function of groups.

The crux of the matter is that leadership in these circumstances may be performed by one or many members of the group; leadership is regarded as a quantitative variable not as something found in some people and not in others.

Inevitably, whenever two or more people get together, one will dominate, and leadership emerges. But the form of leadership in a group depends on group members, the task, and the group ideology.

A very simple but extremely useful definition of leadership is "the ability to influence others in the group." The supreme virtue of this apparently simple definition is that it allows the possibility that all group members may exhibit a degree of leadership; the leader in the conventional sense is the one whose influence predominates. In this context, leadership is regarded as an interpersonal behavioral event; this means, for example, that by communicating their fears, anxieties, and so on to the leader, followers can influence him or her. For that matter, the official leader of a group may have no influence; formal leadership need not coincide with informal.

## LEADERSHIP FUNCTIONS, TASKS, AND ACHIEVEMENTS

There are two basic types of group functions. The first, the task function, is concerned with the achievement of some specific goal. The second, the human function, is concerned with the maintenance and strengthening of the group itself. Examples of task behavior are "stressing the importance of goals, production and quality of the work." Examples of human relations behavior are "keeping people happy, avoiding disputes, and giving encouragement" (Halpin and Winer, 1957).

Halpin and Winer, who studied leadership in air crews, found it useful to analyze leaders' behavior according to two dimensions: initiating and directing and consideration. Leaders high in initiating and directing make sure not only that their role is understood by their group but they also ensure that official procedures are followed; they try out new ideas on members. This type of structuring leadership is of special value when the group faces a task problem. On the other hand, leaders who are high in consideration are group oriented; they ·eward good work and invite participation. These two kinds of leadership correspond to task and human relations specialization.

Of course, in many cases, social behavior cannot be classified under either the task or the human relations heading, but there is a tendency for specialists in these functions to emerge. For example, experiments in group dynamics concerned with analysis of discussion-leading procedures show that there almost always appears in any group the "task specialist" and the "human relations specialist." In families the father is usually the "task specialist" and the mother the "human relations specialist."

## SOCIOLOGICAL CHANGES: PERFORMANCE VERSUS HUMAN RELATIONS

Can it be that research in social science is always a reflection of the problems of the society it studies? How are studies of the 1930s and 1940s, with their emphasis on good human relations, to be reconciled with the studies of the 1970s and 1980s, with their emphasis on psychologically distant leaders and formal role relations, and their concentration on developing organizational structures that will maximize the enterprise's economic efficiency? Society and its institutions—such as its educational system, army, industry, social science, and research—tend to keep in step more or less. A certain feeling appears to be abroad; a feeling that the old permissive arrangements, which insisted that everything must be made acceptable to subordinates, that nothing must be done to disrupt the human relations "set up," and that, above all, you must be seen as "one of the boys," are in the process of being replaced. Instead there is a concern for organizations that will maximize economic efficiency and within which a more remote and reserved leader can concentrate on productive returns.

## THE FAILURE OF LEADERSHIP THEORY

While examining the process of managing, and in particular that of leading, it might be useful to consider our unsuccessful search for a leader. The demand, "take me to your leader," would turn most executives in our contemporary corporate world upside down. Yet people are still looking for leadership; and, of course, behavioral scientists have a compulsive interest in the leader as a kind of behavioral missing link.

Indeed, *"cherchez le leader"* was a major obsession of psychologists in the 1930s, 1940s, and even the 1950s. The trait approach, an exhaustive and exhausting attempt to find a list of adjectives that separate the leader from the led, was fully examined and found to be wanting. However, despite scientific evidence to the contrary, most executives still believe that they have such a list at their fingertips.

The effort to identify these traits is of considerable interest because it reveals a preoccupation with a world of fixed talents that can be spotted, measured, developed, and deployed. Most behavioral scientists in the forties and fifties thought in these psychometric terms, and I was not an exception. For example, in the early 1950s I conducted an investigation, typical of its time, to identify the traits that distinguished leaders in a middle class school. The procedure is relatively simple. You give a leadership test: "Whom would you like to work with?" and correlate the scores with measures of height, weight, IQ, academic success, personality, and neuroticism. But when I looked at the correlations and saw they were nearly all zeroes (indicating no relation between the variables), my heart sank and I thought something must have gone wrong. Ten years later, when I was preparing the material for publication, the answer began to dawn on me. There was no relation. Leadership is not a bunch of traits. The moral of the exercise is that "negative findings are hard to recognize." The complete absence of relation between leadership and various traits is an important finding.

Meanwhile in the United States, careful work by Kahn and Katz in 1960 had shown that effective supervisors were perceived by subordinates to be employee centered, supportive, and democratic. In 1967, F. E. Fiedler, now with the University of Washington, came up with the alarming finding, based on equally careful work, that effective managers rate themselves as being psychologically distant from subordinates, particularly those subordinates who are least productive. How was this dilemma to be resolved? One answer is that managers as subordinates look up to their superiors for support and autonomy, and, as subordinates, look down on their own subordinates as those to be kept at a distance.

But as Fiedler progressed further into his thesis that the manager was psychologically distant, his data forced him to modify his approach and develop a contingency theory that presumed that style was a function of the situation (power, task structure, and group atmosphere).

In brief, leadership theory failed. At least it failed if one tried to explain the behavioral thing called "leading scientifically." For leading cannot be understood in completely rational terms. Some peculiar mix of system and existentialism is needed to meet the reality of corporate life.

## IMPLICATIONS FOR LEADERSHIP THEORY

Leadership has turned out to be of less importance as an explanation for performance. There are an increasing number of academics in the field of organizational behavior who are arguing that the concept of leadership is too ambiguous and is difficult to separate from other causes in regard to determining what produces performance. Thus a swift review of literature on organizational performance reveals the fact that more interest is being placed on topics like authority and power in structured organizations in terms of explaining organizational performance.

At one time it was presumed that leadership was just a question of getting the right mix of directing structure and employee consideration. Now, we're not quite so sure.

One problem is that leaders are not selected only on the basis of competence. Second, managers often seem to select people like themselves; whereas the findings of group dynamics research argue for having two different types working together, for example a task force specialist and human relations specialist. Jeffrey Pfeffer (1977) has argued that leadership is a relatively minor factor in explaining performance. Leaders become expert in separating themselves from failures. In short, leaders have positive genius for reconstructing reality so they always come out smelling like a rose even if the whole system collapses. As Pfeffer points out, for instance, if a manager knows the business in his or her division is about to improve because of the economic cycle, the manager may, nevertheless, write recommendations and undertake actions and changes that are highly visible and that will tend to identify his or her behavior closely with the division. A manager who perceives impending failure will attempt to associate the division and its policies and decisions with others, particularly persons in higher organizational positions, and to disassociate him- or herself from the division's performance, occasionally even transferring or moving to another organization.

## MOVING IN AN EXISTENTIAL DIRECTION

Faced with paradox and uncertainty, the existential executive is trying to supplement and find an alternative to his or her analytic skills. The executive is trying to get in sync with the "intuitive-synthetic" cognitive approach, which has an inventive mode (using metaphors like "Monte Carlo Random Walk of the Drunk Man" or "$E = mc^2$"), an integrative mode (using Zen aphorisms such as "Don't let the good become an enemy of the best").

A major reason why existentialism provides such a compulsive interest for executives is the fact that it is a philosophy for people in crisis. Existentialism in modern times has its renaissance in times of crisis.

## QUANTUM LEAPS IN MANAGEMENT STYLE

What is being argued is that a difference of style is required as a manager moves from the middle level in the company to take up a GM post. What it amounts to is that first level managers respond better to human resources planning where the emphasis is on role clarification and task decisions and human relations are not considered so important. Corporate level senior managers need to display strategic vision using an "optimal" organizational style of management.

| Level of Management | Style of Management |
| --- | --- |
| CEO | Strategic Vision |
| Corporate Level | Optimal Organization |
| Middle Level | Human Resources Planning |
| First Level | Human Relations |

The optimal organizational styles place emphasis not only on high-risk orientation but also technological competence and traditional conceptual management skills. All this is integrated into the capacity to make decisions in an environment where uncertainty is the order of the day and risk syndication and consensus management are sine qua nons.

# 8

---

# The Political Theater of Action

## THE DOGS OF EXECUTIVE WAR AND THE YUMMIE

As we know from the study of animal behavior, aggression, hierarchy, and sexual behavior are linked. Actual physical combat leading to serious injury or death is not common among animals because of the existence of fairly stable pecking orders. To ensure that the pecking hierarchy is still in position, the lesser animal defers to the higher by presenting its hindquarters, as a symbol of both sexual availability and as a token of respect.

Hierarchy imposes a necessary strain between the Top Dog and the managerial hired help such as the Yummie (young upwardly mobile manager into entrepreneurship and existentialism) who are not lesser people to themselves but only further down the totem. This produces a "winner takes all" syndrome in business. The problem is that the CEO Top Dogs are not only articulate, aggressive, and persuasive but they love creating "win-lose" competition among the under-dog Yummies. All this aggressive strutting causes problems in the vertical dimension.

CEOs are not unaware of the amount of this static but they creatively exploit it. All these dog fights are dominated by executives who have a strong sense of the jugular and who like to dominate their turf or territory and who love movies like *The Godfather*. But it would be naive to believe that such dog fights are relatively easy to deal with. The reality of the matter is quite different. Conflict is often expressed in subtle and elusive ways that defy simple and logical explanations.

## THE YUMMIES

A new player, the Yummie, has joined the game. The "new" young upwardly mobile manager into entrepreneurship and existentialism has been brought on board of corporate realpolitik (see Figure 8.1).

My aim is to strip back for a moment, only a moment, dear reader, the surface innocence of conventional corporate *"toujours la politesse,"* which allows the deceiver to deceive the deceived. "And oh what a tangled web we weave [in modern times] when first we practice to deceive."

To untangle this web the drama of management tries to deal with the ancient art of deception, sly sophistry, and useful manipulations that make up the infrastructures of executive life.

Perhaps we have come far enough in our discussion to introduce an executive-play to show how it progresses from the beginning, through the middle to the end (or if you like, exploitation, through complication, to resolution or dénouement). Management frequently happens at great speed and involves the manipulation of fictions. This incident deals with a CEO firing a COO and involves a widely used routine or ritual that has to be highly structured, practiced, and carried out with great gusto to be effective.

## THE DRAMA OF AN EXECUTIVE EXECUTION

Robert Johns, who is chief operating officer of New York Management Consulting Services, is sitting in his office gazing out the window and thinking about his friend who went through the Harvard Business School with him in the early sixties. He's just seen a note in the *Wall Street Journal* saying that his friend has "decided to pursue private interests." A cold shiver goes up and down his spine and he begins to wonder what in fact is going on in business. Suddenly the phone rings. He is being summoned to a meeting in Chicago to attend a board meeting of his company.

Robert Johns feels pretty good about himself and the performance of the consultancy operations under his control. The only "fly in the ointment" is that the chief executive officer and chairman of the board has asked him to syphon off his most effective product line, which deals with company reorganizations, and turn it over to the control of the CEO's son. Johns refused and tried to raise his issue at a previous board meeting.

Johns flies to Chicago and is no sooner installed in his hotel than he receives a call from the chairman who advises him that he'd like to talk to him before the board meeting. Johns suggests that he'll come a half hour before the actual board meeting so that any difficulties can be ironed out. The CEO tells Johns that won't be necessary since he's on his way over to the hotel right now to meet Johns. The CEO arrives with the three most powerful people on the board in attendance and the following conversation ensues:

**Figure 8.1**
**The Relation between Formal Structure and Organizational Power**

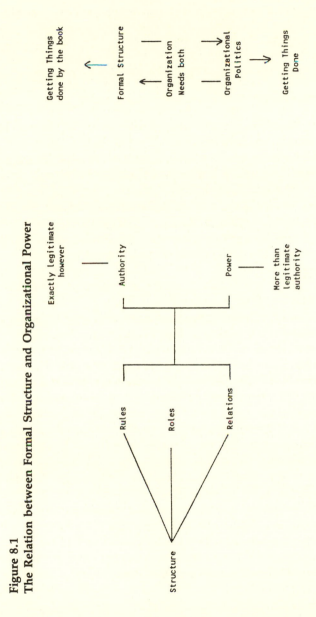

*CEO:* Robert, I've got some news for you which I think you ought to have before tomorrow's meeting.

*Robert:* What exactly is that?

*CEO:* We on the board have decided that we're going to dispense with your services.

*Robert:* Why is that? I want an answer now.

*CEO:* I want to make it clear to you that we have a legal opinion. The by-laws of the company charter do not require us to give reasons for such an action. But what I will say to you is I feel I've no choice but to either ask you to resign or to face the unnecessary embarrassment of being fired.

What this case illustrates is that the firing rate of chief executives is presently sharply accelerating in the United States. What it amounts to is that when performance pauses for a moment, boards move in and fire, which all helps to give the impression the board is biting the bullet and doing something savage to sort things out.

A question may be raised as to what is the cause of all these boardroom trauma. According to Douglas Bauer in "Why Big Business Is Firing the Boss" (1981), when American business began to decentralize in the 1950s and 1960s it created a group of "fast-track" executives. These fast-track men compressed fifteen years of training and experience into five, moved all over the world, and ended up as chief executives; when firms began to falter, however, they were the first to fall.

To keep pace with these managerial massacres, there is a great increase in the use of executive recruiters. Apparently what happens in these top executive confrontations is an encounter of egos; for example, according to Bauer, when Liman Hamilton was brought in as chief operating officer and president of ITT, he couldn't get along with Harold S. Geneen, who had built up ITT. Apparently, Hamilton would go to Geneen and say "Here's what I'd like to do," and Geneen would say, "No, I want to do it this way." As Geneen was CEO, Hamilton would go along with him, but when Hamilton became the CEO, and Geneen objected to his plans, Hamilton would say, "O.K., I hear you but until we take it up at the board, we're going to go ahead and do it my way." Liman Hamilton lasted eighteen months before he was fired by Geneen.

Dealing in deceptions and constructive manipulations gives the whole subject a conspiratorial ring that is about right, for when the theatrical is driven out you are left with a lifeless and sterile set of structures, processes, and values. To get the show on the road, let's look over the case of actors who make up the political structure.

## THE POLITICAL STRUCTURE OF CONFLICT DRAMA

This structural view presupposes that conflict arises from the anatomy of the organization. Conflict arises from two structures, two sets of rules, roles, and relations that cannot be fitted together and cannot be easily synchronized. In the contemporary organization the rules are unclear, inchoate, and ill defined; the roles create demarcation disputes; and the relations are confused because managers and the subordinates send the wrong signals.

Why do executives play these roles? To entertain others? Yes, but only in the full sense in which an effective actor entertains: reaching out to his audience, establishing rapport, focusing their attention, stopping them from nervous diversions such as coughing and fidgeting, and passing a "message" to them. But as the old show biz line goes, "If you're going to send a message, use Western Union." So it is not an ordinary telegraphic message you get from Edward Albee or Harold Pinter. It is a message like an artistic Rorschach ink blot—full of promises, but promises that vary from optic to optic.

### Enter and Exit on Cue

Executives set out to entertain in the same way as do actors. Their entrances are carefully timed; they choose their dialogue with care; they exit on cue. They capture and captivate the audience and they have too much to do to send all their messages by Western Union. So they must signal, some of the time, by ink blot. All of this can't be learned from a textbook on management; so the fledgling manager grasps every clue on how to "make like an executive." Constant practice and careful imitation, coupled with brilliant imagination—and reinforced by trips to the right movies and plays—can produce virtuoso performances (see Figure 8.2).

Reciprocity is one purpose of all this role playing. Each person must play his or her role fully to allow other persons to play theirs. The executive must transmit signals that reflect both the objectives he or she is shooting for and the inevitable conflicts between them.

### Recognize the Actors in the Executive Suite

If you want to play your part, you have to recognize not only the script but also the other actors. Your first problem is to separate the stars from the bit players, the principals from the supporting players, and both from the extras who are just along for the ride.

Failure to make this distinction can be fatal. In an OD exercise with an internationally famous energy company, the OD consultant made the error on day one, hour one, of mentioning that every time Eric, the CEO, spoke, there was no further discussion of that topic. The Exemplar had spoken, Eric took little or no part in further proceedings of the OD exercise, that is until the wrap-up or debriefing on day three. Evaluations were moderately favorable or neutral until Eric took a hand and accused his colleagues

**Figure 8.2**
**Getting Off and On Stage**

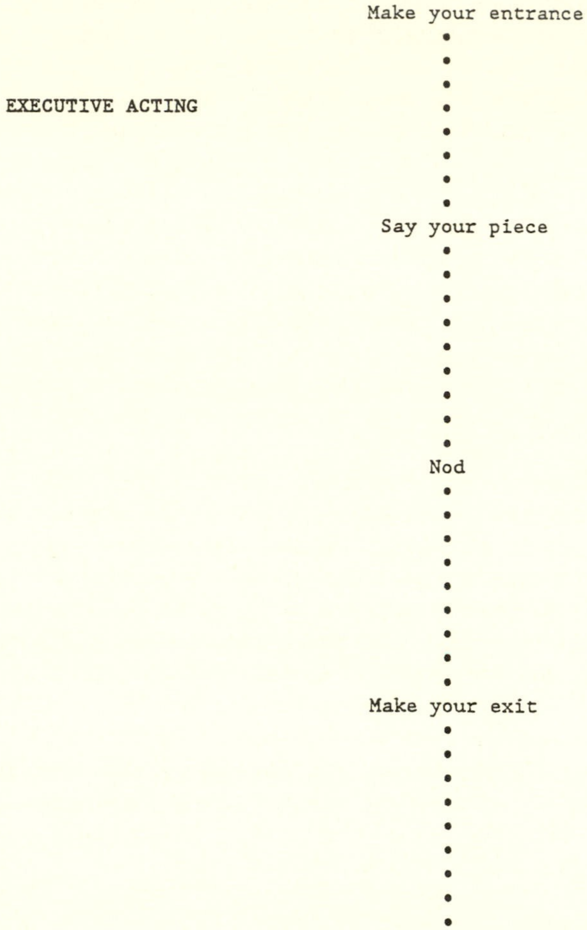

```
                                    Make your entrance
                                           •
                                           •
                                           •
         EXECUTIVE ACTING                  •
                                           •
                                           •
                                           •
                                           •
                                    Say your piece
                                           •
                                           •
                                           •
                                           •
                                           •
                                           •
                                           •
                                           •
                                         Nod
                                           •
                                           •
                                           •
                                           •
                                           •
                                           •
                                           •
                                    Make your exit
                                           •
                                           •
                                           •
                                           •
                                           •
                                           •
                                           •
                                           •
```

of being dishonest in not expressing their true assessments. Soon the participants were vying with one another to denounce the exercise. And this exercise was on video, for everyone to see. Somebody had failed to recognize a principal.

### Keep Track of the Plot

If you want to keep your place, you have to keep track of the plot. The worst thing you can do is come in once the "Big Picture," the main feature, has started. In other words, timing is extremely important, in case you miss the meaning of the story.

Managing the meaning is simply the exercise of the power of persuasion in interpersonal relations. But power has to be exercised in a meaningful way to get change, to overcome organizational inertia. Legitimacy may have to be broken by nonlegitimate means.

So far we have dealt with the structure or cast or dramatis personae of executive conflict. Now we must turn to the process, the plot, the scenario.

### The Process: From Overture to Dénouement

The process is essentially concerned with the sequencing of events, the plot of "acts, scenes, lines." The plot has its own pattern of momentum. A story, even a prosaic corporate operation, must have a beginning, a middle, and an end. Or putting the process in more dramatic terms, there must be an overture, openers, rising action, a climax, falling action, a conclusion, and then dénouement. All these events are on an interlock.

The essence of the matter is that episode one generates episode two. There are many historical parallels. For example, the Allies imposed such a harsh settlement on Germany at Versailles in 1919 that World War II became an inevitable consequence. The German nation experienced the frustration of economic ruin and developed the conceptualization that they were being victimized by Bolsheviks and the Allies. They decided to rearm, which led to the outcome of occupying or reoccupying the Rhineland, Austria, Czechoslovakia, and Poland, and thus led to World War II. But now let's look at a business example and see how interlocked the different episodes are.

- *Episode 1.* Discovery in corporate HQ in New York that a plant manager in L.A. is shipping out defective PCs to maintain production.
- *Episode 2.* Decision in New York to make an example of this case.
- *Episode 3.* Valuable plant manager is slapped on the wrist, dispensable MBA is fired *"pour encourager les autres."*
- *Episode 4.* . . . Your move?

Thus a conflict that broke out in episode 1 cannot be resolved until episode 3, only with the blackmailing of a weaker party. More typically these conflicts are not individual issues but involve in-fighting between cliques and cabals who fight according to certain rules organized in a model or metaphor that the players grasp intuitively.

### "THE GAME IS THE THING"

The drama metaphor of the firm sees the organization as a great bureaucratic arena in which executives and their hangers-on are players in the great game of realpolitik—a sort of non-stop business version of American football. The supreme advantage of the metaphor of game playing is that by reducing personal responsibility, it frees individuals to make decisions. But, of course, this "Dallas Cowboys metaphor" of the game of business, like the use of any other model, can lead to disastrous consequences.

These gamesmen have power, understand the drama of power, and use it. They use the "Executive Guard" maneuver and manipulate in order to get a job done and, in many cases, to strengthen and enhance their own positions. They are political actors.

## MANAGING THE MEANING IS THE POWER OF PERSUADING

The basic underlying proposition behind such efforts is the belief that there is no management without drama, that every executive act involves an imposition of meaning—my meaning. What it amounts to is you can't get action without imposing your meaning on a situation.

But strangely enough, today's values often reflect a sense of meaninglessness together with a post-Freudian emphasis on sickness rather than wrong-doing, which may have weakened the executive's sense of responsibility for his or her actions. So the contemporary corporate theater is at first sight either eventless or full of nonevents, pathetic rather than tragic. Hence the interest in the violence and conspiracy of *The Godfather* and Don Watergate, which many executives believe are not atypical case studies but are in fact descriptive of organizational actualities. They simplify life. A don whispers in the ear of his consigliori, and enemies are blown away.

## THE CONSPIRACY THEORY OF ORGANIZATIONS

Thus the conspiracy theory of organizations has captured the popular imagination. Therefore, it is not surprising that a number of contemporary movies, including *The Verdict* and *Chinatown*, have dealt explicitly with organizational intrigue. And executives find the conspiracy theory comforting because it provides a rational explanation for many bewildering corporate experiences.

Jan Kott, a Polish drama critic, who lived through both the Nazi tyranny and the Stalinist occupation of Poland, has persuasively argued that the power politics, Machiavellianism, down-right chicanery, low cunning, and violence of twentieth-century corporate life have their counterparts in Shakespeare's tragedies, particularly *Macbeth*.

And Shakespeare, especially in *Macbeth*, has provided us with what Jan Kott has called the "grand mechanism," the bloodstained struggle for power with all its terrible consequences, which can be so usefully invoked to explain corporate conspiracies.

In *Macbeth* Shakespeare provides a brilliant panoramic view of the struggle for power as relevant today as it was when it was written in 1606. Most executives who have made it even a little bit up the corporate ladder know the real meaning of anguish and guilt and can recognize

> Is this a dagger which I see before me
> the handle towards my hand?

It is a short step to the world of the existentialist via

> A dagger of the mind, a false creation
> Proceeding from the heat oppressed brain.

For the existential view of perception that "You describe what you see and you see what you describe" is but an echo of "There is nothing either good or bad, but thinking makes it so."

"Thinking makes it so" underscores man's ability to move effortlessly between drama and real life.

## SOME PRACTICAL ADVICE: THE TACTICAL DOCTRINE OF EXECUTIVE DRAMA

Now comes the moment of agonizing truth. "So what?" you may say. "What's the big deal? All very funny! But I'm not an actor." And your ever obedient retainer, as always at your elbow, will reply, "You might never have made it on Broadway, but boy-o-boy, Sir, when you play the simpleton at those international meetings in Brussels, a deadly hush falls over the house. And then they stop alibiing."

"You are having me on. You are the one who always says just before that moment of simplicity, 'Our chairman is just too much of a gentleman to ask this question but I feel I have to. . . .' It's not that I'm not a gentleman, I just haven't done my homework."

"With all due respect, Sir, I know you are dissembling when you peer over those half moon specs."

All good clean fun, part of the inevitable aftermath of any executive encounter. But you may be wondering if there are any sort of ground rules or tactical doctrine that can be drawn up on the drama of executive conflict. To try to answer that question, it is necessary to look at four things, the actual drama, the structure of the dramatis personae, the process or plot, and the values or atmosphere or climate.

### Recognize the Drama of the Moment

The show cannot begin until somebody recognizes the drama of the moment. You would be amazed how quickly innocent bystanders learn their parts in bank robberies and get down on the floor with their eyes tightly shut. And as you know there are only a few basic plots that everybody knows, but nobody can tell you what they are. You see them in the movies, but they do not always work out in practice.

For example, it was great fun watching Edward G. Robinson, playing the warden, go down alone into the penitentiary yard to challenge Humphrey Bogart as the leader of the rioting prisoners—and pulling it off. But when it happens in real life, it is a different kettle of fish. In a similar incident during the Korean War the rioting Communist POWs kidnapped the American general playing Edward G. Robinson. University presidents in the mysterious 1960s were more often than not caught playing the wrong movie at the wrong time, in the wrong house!

The answer is to stay in touch with contemporary theater, movies, novels, and music. Your answer may well be, "I'm too busy—working." Some thirty years ago Sune Carlson established the same point in the first observational study of chief executives. In his classic "Executive Behavior" he found that his CEOs were just so busy working that they did not have time for cultural activities. Therefore, before the show can begin it is necessary to recognize the drama.

### Set the Stage Carefully

Next, the stage has to be set with some care. The setting is extremely important. A geography of conflict could be written about stage setting: the Germans in 1940 bringing out the famous rail car from the museum at Compiegne to humiliate the French at the signing of the armistice; Douglas MacArthur in 1945 in the famous scene on the "Missouri" that ended the war in the Pacific; MacArthur on the receiving end at Wake Island being forced to receive Commander-in-Chief Harry Truman before he got his comeuppance; another president, LBJ, receiving high officers when seated on "the throne." And so on.

Many of the same capers are to be witnessed in the executive suite, with the same deadly effect. A good example of effective scene setting was provided recently by a president of a large telecommunications company who had been brought on board to trim the fat by cleaning house, which he proceeded to do with some abandon. He established for himself a formidable reputation, and the company began to prosper again. To get the show on the road he required each production and functional unit head to make a presentation before the board of its accomplishments and, most important, of its plans. The VP for personnel, being an internationally acclaimed expert in the field, made the presentation on OD and then asked for questions. The president had established the procedure that he would ask the first and, as it turned out on this occasion, the only question.

"Is that all there is?" Our distinguished OD man was soon on the big jets working as a consultant.

## HIGH PROFILE: A SUCCESS IMAGE

The most important thing managers should know about the political dramas of conflict is that they are important, interesting, and ubiquitous, and they must learn to love the game. Learning to love the game means they have to develop not only a successful style, but also a commitment to sure-fire and visible success. All of this means projecting the right image, high profiling visible success, and acting with distinction and great force. Managers with a dramatic sense produce superior performance and morale. This capacity can be developed.

Basically, it is a capacity to grasp, develop, and impose meaning on relatively unstructured situations. To manage meaning effectively managers must take their part in the *structure*, take their place in the *process* or plot, and have what it takes in terms of *values*.

## TAKING YOUR PART: GET UPSTAGE—THE EXECUTIVE AS ENTERTAINER

When thinking about how to develop this capacity, it is useful to keep in mind such theatrical ideas as the script (let's see how we are going to play this one), the size of parts (stars, supporting cast, walk-on parts), props, how to get off and on stage, how to get the drama in and out, and so on.

### Structure the Succession

The scene is a meeting of the top management of a well known automobile accessory company that operates along the Eastern seaboard from Maine to Florida, through two main divisions, North and South. The CEO, who is about to retire, has called his five senior executives together, ostensibly to work on the strategic plan—but in fact to plan the succession. Two of the less senior executives are members of his family, one by marriage. The most senior VP fears that he is going to be "excluded"—amputated.

The senior executives, dressed in their cardigans, open neck sports shirts, double knit stretch pants, and tennis shoes look like extras for a Pinter play. These ancient Laurence Oliviers and John Gielguds look dried up, spent forces as they shuffle about their business. They appear incompetent, incontinent, indeed insignificant. The meeting, which is in the company motel in Vermont, has been going for two hours. Nothing much is happening as the VP for planning runs through the upcoming five-year strategic plan. Suddenly there is an intervention from the senior VP executive.

*Senior VP:* Look, this has gone on long enough. Let's get down to business. Let's get this problem out on the table.

*CEO:* What have you got on your mind? I didn't spend twenty years building a successful 10 billion a year business through cutting off criticism.

*Senior VP* [lighting his pipe]: It's your job to spell out the future objectives and structure of the company, so that we can solve the problem of succession.

*CEO* [getting really annoyed and puffing on his cigar]: I could spend the rest of these days reading from the company policy documents on our objectives and policies.

This exchange continues acrimoniously for about thirty minutes.

*VP Planning:* This discussion is getting out of hand . . . it is counterproductive. Nothing good will come from attacking the CEO. . .

*CEO:* No, no, no. I think. . . .

*VP Executive* [interrupting]: Look. Let's go round the room and get each person to present an idea of this structure.

The meeting carries on like a bunch of MBAs solving a Harvard Business School case. The blackboard is covered with organization charts. One moment it is metaphysical; suddenly it is all light.

*VP Executive:* So what I am proposing is that we should have a chairman's cabinet made up of the new CEO and the two more senior VPs in this room.

A few minutes later.

*CEO:* This has been a most useful and productive discussion. I accept your proposal and I will accept total responsibility for its implementation.

What our CEO is showing is his genius for total delegation, picking winners (and dumping losers), and above all his genius for "accepting total responsibility."

One of the most potent myths, almost a sacrament of classical management, is the "acceptance of total responsibility." Like the old priestly vows of charity and chastity, the classical manager is expected to accept complete and personal responsibility for everything that happens in his or her bailiwick.

Classical managers can do this trick of "accepting total responsibility," which frees up their subordinates (to in turn accept total responsibility).

This kind of organizational power prayer is how iron commitment is established in any organization. But only if everybody is praying to the same God.

Only this kind of corporate "going for broke" is sufficient to mobilize the moral energies needed to get things done in the real world. And its utilization is a major dramatic skill, involving the use of body language.

## BODY LANGUAGE AND NONVERBAL COMMUNICATION

People not only communicate through what they say but they also send a message through their behavior, particularly their body language. As is well known, where you sit in a meeting gives a direct signal as to what role you wish to play in the meeting. Correspondingly, where the interviewer and interviewee sit relative to each other indicates whether the relationship is cooperative or competitive.

You can show your interest in someone by pointing your body at that person. How you interpret these nonverbal cues will tell a great deal about your personality. For example, if the person you are talking with or trying to get something from leans back in his or her chair and eyeballs the ceiling, you should follow suit without giving the appearance of being a complete sycophant. On the other hand, if you persist in leaning forward and staring intently at the interviewer, you've had your chips, as they say in England. All is lost. How you lay yourself out, the angle of your head, the way you place your feet, your breathing, your repetitive gestures, and tone of voice are all dead give-aways of your intentions.

The important thing is not only to know all this but to have some idea of how flexible your choices are and what effect each of these patterns has on other people. To be effective with people, it is necessary to establish rapport through body language; to do this effectively you must be able to read the other person's cues by listening carefully.

### Surrender the Stage, Occasionally, and Listen

There is some evidence to support the proposition that the managers who are most effective are somewhat androgynous, that is to say, they have the "proper mixture" of masculine and feminine qualities. Michael Billington in the "Modern Actor" has argued that no male actor ever made more creative positive use of his femininity than Sir Laurence Olivier. This particular point was raised with Olivier in an interview conducted by C. W. Pepper in *The New York Times Magazine* (1979).

"Of course," replied Olivier. "A man who is entirely masculine isn't really normal, is he? I'm not saying he has to be as queer as a three dollar bill. Ha! I mean if he hasn't a certain amount of absolute feminine in him—feminine, mind you, *not* femininity—I doubt he'd be very interesting.''

Executives, apparently, are very like actors. They have to have sufficient masculinity to allow them to structure the task, to define objectives, to set schedules, and to have sufficient gonzo to get there. But they also have to have sufficient feminine qualities to be able to hear what other people are saying, to be passive at least some of the time, to be able to let their intuition work for them, and so on. And, of course, in the development they have to learn to make like an executive, which means they have to be able to imitate the superior performance of their superior, which means the executive has to be ready to surrender some autonomy—until recently only a feminine requirement.

## THE SHOW MUST GO ON

Inevitably, such demanding role playing leaves the system somewhat unbalanced, and odd games have to be invented to dispel the anxieties generated. A great variety of games and subroutines can be observed in any workplace. Many executives greet with hoots of derision the fact that in the Hawthorne Studies some of the workers whiled away their time ''shutting the window the other guy had just opened.'' In ice hockey, the player who scores a goal receives a tap on the bottom from the sticks of his teammates, presumably to show not only that there are no hard feelings at his triumph, but also to calm his euphoria and remind him that he is still on the team.

Organizational life is suffused with games and pranks that are calculated to clean up some of the tensions and anxieties generated by the difficult role work required to keep the organization operational. Psychologists have had a field day looking at the bizarre behavior of participants as they wander off and on stage, upstaging others, and so on. The metaphor of the theater is never far away, but the problem of finding a part, guessing the game, learning your lines, and making your exit remains a constant problem as the scene shifters and playwrights are always changing the plot. Anyway, ''the show must go on'' is the cardinal rule. ''Anyone for tennis?''

# 9

# Make Conflict Work for You

Contrary to conventional wisdom, the most important single thing about conflict is that it is good for you. While this is not a scientific statement of fact, it reflects a basic and unprecedented shift of emphasis—a move away from the old human relations point of view where all conflict was basically seen as bad.

The modern organizational revolution has been characterized by an acceleration of healthy subversive tendencies that gathered force and speed in the 1960s in protest against the brittle iron law of corporate oligarchy; a protest against the presumption that, in organizations, policies and instructions flow down the hierarchy and reports flow up. It is a protest against the cozy paternalistic world of classical management theory where top management carries total responsibility. It is a protest exemplified by the success of *The Peter Principle* by L. J. Peter and R. Hull (1969), which was on the best seller lists for many months. It is increasingly a middle-class protest by executives and professionals, and decreasingly a protest from a diminishing shop floor. It is a protest with its own particular diabolism; some of the games played in executive suites make Edward Albee's ''Get the Guests'' and ''Bring Up the Baby,'' as portrayed in *Who's Afraid of Virginia Woolf?*, seem like nursery pastimes.

Briefly put, in our new frontier environment conflict is the order of the day.

The new look is so radical that many top managers wonder just how this change came about. Not that most knowing managers have not adopted a different posture to conflict management; most have mastered the new argot that includes such choice phrases as "structure me a meeting," "let's go for confrontation," "they're definitely going to escalate this one," "minimize our maximum losses," "let's introduce a little uncertainty into the situation," and so on. Most experienced executives recognize the script and know they have learned new parts, but are curious to discover how it all came about. This is not only intellectual curiosity as to what happened in the past; it also conceals a deep and pervasive need to try to guess the practical implications of "conflict nouveau."

In this chapter, I argue that the old concept of human relations view of conflict fails to acknowledge its importance as a creative force in today's society. What is needed, in my judgment, is a new look or realistic reassessment of conflict that, if properly handled, can make conflict work for you in your role as a business manager.

## REALISTIC REASSESSMENT

The emerging new view of conflict, as shown in Table 9.1, reverses many of the cozy nostrums of human relations management, which had its intellectual origins in the famous Hawthorne studies of the 1920s. These studies "proved" the then startling proposition that interpersonal relations counted more for productivity than the quality of the physical environment, such as the level of illumination. An entire school of management grew up around the notion that if people were well treated, they would produce. Conflict, by definition, was harmful and should be avoided. Those who generated conflict were troublemakers and were bad for the organization.

**Table 9.1**
**Human Relations and Realistic Models of Conflict**

| Old View | New Look |
| --- | --- |
| Conflict is by definition avoidable. | Conflict is inevitable. |
| Conflict is caused by troublemakers, boat rockers, and prima donnas. | Conflict is determined by structural factors such as the physical shape of a building, the design of a career structure, or the nature of a class system. |
| Legalistic forms of authority such as "going through channels" or "sticking to the book" are emphasized. | Conflict is integral to the nature of change. |
| Scapegoats are accepted as inevitable. | A minimal level of conflict is optimal. |

It is easy to take a somewhat superior if not jaundiced view of human relations as a management philosophy, but this is to pluck it out of its historical context. In its time, it was quite apposite, essentially part of the New Deal of the 1930s. It might be appropriate to regard human relations as the infrastructure change in the primary work group to correspond with Franklin Roosevelt's statement, "We have nothing to fear, but fear itself," which helped to get America's depression-ridden economy going again. The philosophy of human relations helped to ease Western society into a post-Marxist era in which the robber barons and the sweatshop capitalists all but disappeared.

But the old concept of human relations does not fit today's facts. It no longer describes the managerial thinking of those men who run enterprises that are a mixture of public and private investment, and who have learned that while they must strive for private profit, they must defer to public welfare. These epoch-making organizational changes have come so quickly and pervasively that the entrepreneurs who have managed through the actual phases of human change are somewhat bewildered by it all.

In brief, the human relations school fails ultimately because it does not have a proper frame of reference; it fails both to acknowledge the importance of sociological forces and to recognize the importance of conflict as a creative force in society. In particular, the idea that conflict is always bad warrants closer examination. Perfect organizational health does not mean freedom from conflict. On the contrary, if properly handled, conflict can lead to more effective and appropriate adjustments.

## OPTIMAL ANXIETY

There is a curious link between conflict management and anxiety. At one time, psychologists believed rather naively that anxiety, in any form or level, must by its nature be bad. But studies of both soldiers in combat and patients after surgery strongly suggest that a moderate level of anxiety may be adaptive and facilitate survival.

Other researchers reinforce this point by arguing that an environment devoid of novelty can be unbearable to human subjects. In other words, there seems to be an optimal level of uncertainty for effective functioning.

Anxiety (in small quantities) facilitates adjustment, for people need some uncertainty. Ethologists like Konrad Lorenz are bringing forward persuasive evidence that controlled aggression has survival value and that although dominance ultimately depends on force, it leads to law and order. Lorenz has argued that aggression is a function of normal selection and produces an increased expectation of survival; further aggression brings about a dispersal of individuals. Lorenz, who has observed animals in their natural habitats, believes that fighting may generate a stable "pecking order." Much the same discussion can be repeated about our own society, which is learning to allow dissent but not unlimited dissent.

Aggression, apparently an essential characteristic of executives, makes many managers miserable with guilt. Adopting an "attack ethos" usually stands an executive in good stead, but it is aggression moderated by a need to maintain social acceptability.

Conflict management recognizes that executives have aggression to expend, can withstand a fair amount of anxiety, and welcome uncertainty as an opportunity to restructure their environment. Hence the way conflict is managed—rather than suppressed, ignored, or avoided—contributes significantly to a company's effectiveness.

## DISSENSUS AND CONSENSUS

In this section, let us turn our attention to the intellectual origins of this new approach to conflict management. Some executives, perhaps jaundiced by the disturbing skill that social psychologists have shown in managing and eventually dissipating conflict in laboratory situations, have blamed the behavioral scientists.

But the more mathematically oriented executive might be tempted to think it all began with game theory that refers to a mathematical technique that finds an optimal strategy for a player, taking into consideration all options open to an opponent. Reflection suggests, however, that its mathematical assumptions are too abstruse and abstract to have much organizational relevance.

Nevertheless, many executives have found the language of game theory, such as zero-sum or mini-max strategy, easy to incorporate into their argot. Other executives blame the Cold War and quote Thomas C. Schelling, who has pointed out:

The precarious strategy of cold war and nuclear stalemate has often been expressed in game-type analogies: two enemies within reach of each other's poison arrows on opposite sides of a canyon, the poison so slow that either could shoot the other before he died; a shepherd who has chased a wolf into a corner where it has no choice but to fight, the shepherd unwilling to turn his back on the beast; a pursuer armed only with a hand grenade who inadvertently gets too close to his victim and dares not use his weapon; two neighbours, each controlling dynamite in the other's basement, trying to find mutual security through some arrangement of electric switches and detonators. (1966)

A more fundamental reason has been the demise of human relations as a management philosophy and the emergence of the task approach to conflict management where the emphasis has been on developing the optimal organization by considering both the task to be done and the resources available. In the task approach, the exploitation of crisis becomes a major avenue of development.

For example, in the Apollo Project, the capsule fire that took the lives of three astronauts in 1967 was seized as an opportunity to change relations between NASA officials and executives of contracting companies. Whereas before the fire two parties had met in a negotiating context, after the fire they got together to solve problems. The result was not only increased effectiveness, but also the beginning of a change in the role of the liaison executives; their companies began to question to whom they owed their allegiance—NASA or the contractors.

## CRISIS: USE AND MISUSE

In the creative use of crisis, the effective executive welcomes uncertainty and plans for its exploitation, if not its creation. An example of this is provided by the experience of a British manufacturing company that reacted to the government's introduction of a payroll tax by grasping the chance to reorganize and rationalize its product lines, so that each factory was charged with the making of one component instead of two.

What is significant about this case is not only that the company subsequently had the tax and a bit more refunded to it, but also that the chief executive grabbed the chance to make dramatic organizational changes he had been mulling over for some time. In other, more tranquil, circumstances, such changes would have been subject to considerable and sustained negotiations in both the front office and the work councils.

## CREATIVE TENSION

In the turbulent environment of contemporary business suffused with ambiguity, the hard-headed executive with strong nerves and a feel for the moment of drama that a crisis affords has the chance to restructure the organizational scene in a way that at once may well meet his or her needs for self-fulfillment as well as the interests of the institution.

Moreover, the social science "angels" would be on the side of this hard-headed but imaginative executive. Research evidence suggests that tension needs to be reappraised and that the exploitation of healthy tension can stimulate learning, serve to "internalize" the problems of other managers, increase critical vigilance and self-appraisal, and induce decision makers to examine conflicting values (including their own) more discerningly when they are making decisions.

There is also considerable and growing evidence from the study of creative tension and scientific performance that research scientists, if they are going to function effectively and achieve excellence, require an intellectual and social environment made up of two sets of apparently inconsistent factors: one set related to stability, confidence, or security; and the other pertaining to an optimal level of disruption, intellectual conflict, or "challenge."

To illustrate, the most effective researchers are those who control their product mix of personal interaction in such a way that they get sufficient critical feedback from competitive colleagues; they also have a steady supply of "generally supportive" human backup they can use as a form of "psychic heavy water" to keep the fissions and fusions of intellectual ferment from becoming critical and detonating.

In brief, at the risk of oversimplification, what the social scientists are saying is that there is an optimal level of anxiety, arousal, and conflict for humans to function effectively. Fortunately, this intelligence is coming to business leaders at an appropriate moment because, both at home and abroad, conflict is manifesting itself in ways that challenge conventional wisdom in management theory.

To make this point of theory meaningful, it is necessary to distinguish between structure and process. We seem to know a lot about the structure, in terms of organization shapes, definitions, and roles; but we seem to know very little about the process, in terms of what actually happens within or without the structure. The student revolution, with its emphasis on confrontation, conflict, and crisis, is but one vivid example of the organizational process bursting the conventional structure of bureaucracy.

## ORGANIZATIONAL ATTRITION

Conflict is endemic, inevitable, and necessary to organizational life; it always involves some testing of the power situation. A typical example of organizational conflict is revealed in this case based on an actual corporate situation (see Figure 9.1).

Bill Jones, a department manager, was sent to a management course, and on his return found that his auxiliary but highly valued position of assistant general manager was apparently up for grabs. Before his departure, his name had appeared on the organization chart set aside for assistant general manager. On his return, he found that a new organization chart had been issued, but that this particular box had been left empty.

Jones was thus faced with a dilemma: Had it been done deliberately? The decision he had to make at this stage was whether he ought to keep silent and bide his time, or to raise this matter with the general manager, John Fulton, to try to have his name put back in this box.

As it happened, he decided to follow a policy of "wait and see." But when he returned from his annual vacation, he discovered that the name of a rival department manager, Ned Carter, was in the assistant general manager's box.

**Figure 9.1**
**Typical Example of Organizational Attrition**

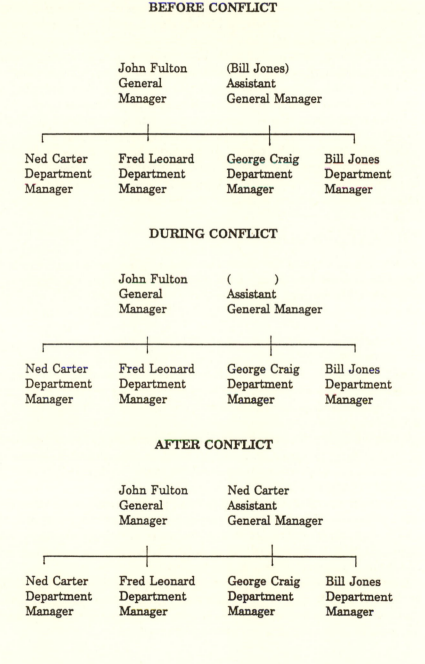

### BEFORE CONFLICT

John Fulton
General
Manager

(Bill Jones)
Assistant
General Manager

| Ned Carter | Fred Leonard | George Craig | Bill Jones |
|---|---|---|---|
| Department | Department | Department | Department |
| Manager | Manager | Manager | Manager |

### DURING CONFLICT

John Fulton
General
Manager

(        )
Assistant
General Manager

| Ned Carter | Fred Leonard | George Craig | Bill Jones |
|---|---|---|---|
| Department | Department | Department | Department |
| Manager | Manager | Manager | Manager |

### AFTER CONFLICT

John Fulton
General
Manager

Ned Carter
Assistant
General Manager

| Ned Carter | Fred Leonard | George Craig | Bill Jones |
|---|---|---|---|
| Department | Department | Department | Department |
| Manager | Manager | Manager | Manager |

Taken with other signs, Jones realized he was getting the treatment. His boss was using the technique of "nonlosing hazard," which put Jones at a considerable disadvantage, and describes a strategy that can produce a win but not a loss for the general manager. In other words, if Jones had reacted to the first move of "leaving the box empty," then the general manager might have acquiesced but accused him of being paranoid and generally oversensitive.

In fact, Fulton continued the squeezing process, circumscribing Jones's role by establishing very close standards of performance for his department and leaving him without much organizational slack. Fulton, in his inspection tours, freely criticized the department's performance.

Jones experienced a good deal of stress and anxiety, and he had to exercise considerable restraint to ensure that he did not transmit his anxiety to his subordinates, who were already under enough pressure from the more exacting performance standards required by the general manager. In view of this level of conflict, Jones had understandably begun to search for a more secure niche elsewhere in the corporation.

## DILEMMA AND DEFENSE

The type of organizational conflict we have just seen starts in a very low key. The first move of "omitting the name" faces the department manager with alternate choices, neither of which is particularly attractive, to accept or to protest. With the latter strategy, it might be possible to go over the general manager's head to the divisional vice president. Most department managers would likely regard this move as a strategy of last resort. If Jones had protested to the general manager, Fulton might well have acquiesced, with bad grace, and allowed the name to be reinserted; or, alternatively, "suggested" a postponement of decision, say, for three months, when a new organization chart would be issued in any case.

Once this first strike had been successfully launched, the way was open for the general manager gradually to escalate the conflict. The ensuing anxiety and vagaries of organizational life make it difficult for the target victim to function effectively.

In such circumstances, various defensive postures are usually invoked—from depersonalization ("try to imagine it's happening to somebody else"), adaptive segregation ("keep out of direct contact"), or rationalization ("man is made to suffer"), to the formation of new coalitions, placatory behavior, and so forth.

One of the most depressing features of this type of organizational conflict is the fact that it may well be incomprehensible to nonorganizational members, such as the wife of the victim, who may well wonder about his anxiety when matters of pay are not involved.

But let us look at the problem from the viewpoint of the general manager. The sophisticated manager has a great interest both in breaking traditional modes that are no longer appropriate, that bind the business to conditions no longer appropriate, and that bind the business to conditions no longer existent, and also in establishing a new consensus defined by the emerging legitimacy.

## COMMITTEE CONSENSUS

Perhaps the most misunderstood word in executive parlance is "consensus." Before attempting to define such an elusive yet serviceable concept as consensus, however, it might be useful to review changes emerging from research on executive meetings.

In my opinion, the most brilliant research on what happens in discussion groups was conducted by R. F. Bales, a professor of social relations at Harvard (1954), who made two extremely telling points: one regarding process ("What actually happens at meetings?") and the other about structure ("Who does what in meetings?").

Briefly, on the first point, groups work through three phases: clarification ("What is it?"), evaluation ("How do we feel about it?"), and decision ("What are we going to do about it?"). Second, to work through this process, the group selects two people to fill two roles: the task specialist who talks in terms of "Let's zero in on the problem," and the human relations specialist who is usually warm and receptive and acts as a "first-aid" person to help alleviate group tension without diverting it too much from its primary task.

The response of an executive who has done his or her homework on group dynamics might be that there is nothing excitingly new in all this; it has presumably been going on for some time. But executive meetings have not stood still. A dramatic change in tone and content has become more obvious in the last five years. The significant difference is the emergence of naked conflict in managerial meetings, conflict that is so common and visible that executives have been compelled to find both a rationale and a ritual for it.

One such ritual is the "Hawks versus Doves syndrome" that gained considerable currency after its creation during the 1962 Cuban missile crisis. One of the most curious conclusions suggested by a careful reading of Robert F. Kennedy's account of this confrontation is that the dialectic of the situation had to be polarized in this way. Thus, even if the Hawks had not existed, they would have had to be invented so as to give the Kennedy–McNamara axis an opposition and perspective against which to test and present their ideas, and to give President John F. Kennedy an alternative, which he might need. Such are the complexities and complications of the new-style executive meetings.

Within the foregoing context, it is possible to define consensus. No longer are chief executives prepared to be guided by simple majorities; nor, for that matter, are they prepared to wait for unanimity. They shoot for the consensus that implies two conditions, one positive and the other negative.

On the positive side, the presumption is that the significant authorities endorse, or at least tolerate, the proposed solution. On the negative side, sufficient feedback is available to indicate that a vociferous minority will not emerge that will make the solution inoperable.

Such is the nature of the modern management process; risks are high, stakes are high, and the risks must be syndicated among the executives.

## ROLE INTERDEPENDENCE

The principle invoked in this section is one of deadly simplicity, capable of wide application, but difficult to understand and even more difficult to apply. It is the proposition that in an organization executive action must take cognizance of interdependence of roles.

If this statement seems simplistic, invite someone in your peer group to define his or her role. The answer usually involves a list of functions and decisions emphasizing responsibility to the person's superior. Such a "worm's eye" response reveals an underlying organizational philosophy where the emphasis is on the exclusively vertical dimension of bureaucracy and where a person can be held "totally responsible" for something.

A more intelligent answer, emphasizing the concept of interdependence, would be, "You define your role and then I shall try to define mine." More briefly, a role can only be delineated by defining a set of roles. Consider this illustrative scene:

The time is late Friday afternoon and the focus is the general manager's office of a medium-sized engineering firm that makes components for the aerospace industry. The general manager, G. B. Macdonald, is in the process of firing his personnel manager, Bill Murray.

*Macdonald:* You're all washed up, Murray. You're through.

*Murray:* I'm sorry, but I didn't quite catch that.

*Macdonald:* Look, I'm telling you that you've done your last job around here. The way you really botched up that negotiation with the shop stewards on the new contract is unforgivable. Besides, I'm sick of the way you keep coming back to me for policy decisions. If I hear you say, "Could I have your policy input?" once more, I'd go right out of my skull.

The one-sided tirade continues for some minutes with Murray, his back to the wall, silently waiting for his chance. Abruptly and unexpectedly, the general manager begins to fumble for feedback.

*Macdonald:* Well, Murray, isn't it valid? You keep coming back to me, then botching it?

*Murray:* Sir, could I ask you to cast your mind back to when you invited me to become your personnel manager? Your very words were, "As general manager, I shall retain the executive function, whether it is programming, technical, or personnel. You are merely the personnel extension of my role." I accepted the job on those terms. With all due respect, in firing me, you are really firing yourself.

*Macdonald:* What are you driving at?

*Murray:* I'm merely saying that as the "personnel executive," you are unjustifiably blaming me for living up to your own prescribed terms.

*Macdonald:* Wait a minute, Bill. I'll get the sherry bottle from my liquor cabinet. . . .

What is significant about this incident is the exploitation by Bill Murray, the acting personnel manager, and perhaps more important, the general manager's acceptance of a line of argument that ten years ago would have been unthinkable.

What I am arguing in more general terms is that conflict is always moral conflict. Where there is a dispute, values, norms, roles, and statuses will be involved. What this means for the hard-pressed executive is that he or she must dig beneath such clichés as, "It's a problem in communication." Searching behind such gadget words for their value orientation makes the latter-day executive a thoughtful person who understands semantics.

## NEW PERSPECTIVE

An excellent test of a graduate business administration student's understanding of the new behavioral approach to management would be to ask that he or she "reconcile the psychologically distant, task-oriented executive of the 1960s with the human relations directed, democratic manager of the 1940s." It would be impossible to respond properly without getting involved in a discussion of the new morality.

Traditional morality is dead. It is a victim of the new technology exemplified by the "pill," organ transplants, instant communication, and zero privacy (generated by electronic bugging devices). In addition, it is aided and abetted by a new organizational logic that somehow resolves the dilemma of trying to integrate self-fulfillment and loyalty with the traditional institution, whether it be the corporation, the church, or the crack combat unit. The mobicentric manager has considered the permissiveness of Sigmund Freud, worried with Jean-Paul Sartre about the futility of "choosing to act unfree," knows something about game theory, and feels a diminishing loyalty to traditional forms of organization. In the manager's view, "Everything is up for grabs; the next move is yours."

## A CASE EXAMPLE

Now let us turn to a case illustration of how conflict technology can be used as a means of improving corporate effectiveness. This will serve to set up the ground rules for the several roles the executive may have to play in a conflict situation.

In the past, an independent social science research institution had achieved considerable success and growth by creating a democratic work atmosphere in which some of the best social scientists in North America had done research, mainly for the government but also for large corporations. All major decisions were agreed on by the heads of the various departments, and this executive consensus was then pumped through a corporate research council that met every month.

The director, who was younger than any of her department heads, and who had managed the institution to its present dynamic position by a combination of aggressiveness, political acumen, and administrative know-how rather than research excellence, was dissatisfied with the institution's present performance. She had made up her mind to do something about it, and she planned her moves most carefully.

In the evolution of this research institution, three large departments had evolved, each of which was run by a department head who was distinguished in his or her own field.

One of the many anomalies in the institutional structure was that the "behavioral science group" handled marketing projects. The rationale for this was never fully explicated. One view was that when the company got into marketing, much of the work had been concerned with exploring consumer attitudes to new products; thus a psychologist had been nominated for this function and located in the behavioral science group.

Starting at a lower level, the director decided she was going to transfer the marketing function to the "computer science group." She began her strategic ploy at a private meeting in her office with the department head of the behavioral science group. After some general discussion of the group's performance, the director began her attack on the specific situation.

*Director:* I am going to initiate a major change of policy; in fact, a large reorganization of our existing structure. I am going to move marketing from your behavioral science group. I want this out in the open. I am not going behind your back in this. I want the discussion to be all above board.

*Department head:* I have no strong views on this either way, but I would like to consult with my group.

*Director:* Marketing is not functioning well at the moment because we can't get the people we need who can do forecasting using mathematical models; that type of person would be more at home in the computer science group.

Ten days after this meeting, at which no decision had been made, the director launched her second strike at the situation at the weekly meeting of the department heads; she invited the head of the behavioral science group to raise the question of the location of marketing in his department. This the department head did. Opinions among his subordinates had varied, he reported, but the majority had agreed that for political purposes they wished to hang on to marketing.

The director made her move. She first asked for the documentation of the decision and then asked for and received permission to attend the next meeting of the department.

At that subsequent meeting, the director presented her plans for how the marketing function would have to be developed, and she challenged the department to reveal its plans (if any) for marketing. Considerable uncertainty had been aroused that had focused on how the company got research contracts in the first place and, second, on how they were processed. But still no agreement was reached to release marketing.

The director then decided to change direction. At the next meeting of the department heads, she put forward the proposal that an organizational analyst spend sufficient time with the company to thoroughly assess the entire situation. This was agreed on, and some six weeks later the analyst came up with this proposition:

> The company is a "gourmet" organization that specializes in finding interesting problems and then solving them. In such a context, the conventional form of organization is quite inappropriate and an organic rather than mechanistic model is needed.
>
> In a task-oriented business, R&D can be defined and therefore managed; objectives are specified; programs are produced and policed. Research standards are of necessity less detailed, but both modern behavioral science investigation and executive experience confirm that social scientists are able and willing to work within such constraints.
>
> The conventional departments should be abolished and the task-force concept used—with interdisciplinary task groups set up to handle the specific problems that arise; further, these groups should be headed by the person most expert in that problem.

A special weekend meeting of the corporate research council was called, and over a period of three days the researchers debated their future and presented position papers. The proposal to dissolve the departments and replace them with task forces was regarded as too radical; but it was acceptable that task forces would be created from department members who would still be part of their respective departments for "pay and rations."

What does examination of this case tell us about conflict management? The most significant point to emerge is that it is not always necessary to have a clearly stated set of operational objectives in mind before you initiate change. It is necessary, of course, to have a set of criteria to judge the efficiency of the change (e.g., return on investment, share of the market, and so on).

The director started from a vague but strong hunch that performance could be improved. Instead of issuing an order to move marketing from the behavioral group to the computing group (which she legitimately could have done), she opted for a more general revision that led to a major change in policy: the use of the concept of task forces. That was a concept not imposed by fiat, but one that the whole organization had a chance to look at and debate.

In brief, what the director did was to work systematically through a well-conceived plan for achieving change by initiating conflict. Because she understood the inevitable process of conflict, she was able to maintain a balance between creating uncertainty and maintaining a data base, and getting people to participate and keeping direction.

## GROUND RULES

To this point in the discussion, we have been looking at theories of conflict. Next, let us turn our attention to specific guidelines that may help the hard-pressed executive to apply these theories in such a way that conflict can be meaningfully exploited. The important thing is that the objective must be to achieve, at all times, a creative, acceptable, and realistic resolution of conflict.

One of the most effective means of formulating ground rules for executive conflict is to consider the three roles that an executive might play in a conflict situation. He or she can be: (1) the initiator, (2) the defendant, or (3) the conciliator. At one time or another, most executives are called on to play each of these roles.

*The Initiator Should . . .*

- start at a low level and advance on a narrow front on one or two related issues, following a well-documented route;
- maintain second-strike capability;
- pick the terrain with care; where and when the case is heard is vital;
- be prepared to escalate, either to a higher level in the organization or to a meeting of peers;
- make it objective, private, and routine; above all, keep it formal;
- search for reaction; remember that you may have to settle for token conformity in the first instance;

- reinforce success and abandon failure.

*The Defendant Should . . .*

- not overreact; keep your cool; let the initiator state his or her case; listen carefully and neutrally;
- ascertain scale of the strike; try to build a decision tree with "go/no go" decision rules;
- ask for the name of the game (e.g., Is it a courtroom? If yes, ask for the counsel of the defense);
- ask not only for an exact definition of the charge, but also for the evidence with, if possible, identification of the source;
- if it is a "minor crime," be prepared to plead guilty;
- ascertain the various lines of appeal;
- consider the option "Waiting Brief" and be prepared to reserve your defense; take notes; above all, let the initiator score somewhere, and then try for informality.

*The Conciliator Should . . .*

- get the parties of the dispute to realize that conflict is not only universal but a necessary requisite of change;
- break down the attitudinal consistency of each disputant (belief that his or her attitudes do not contain contradictory elements);
- after breaking down frozen but antithetical attitudes of the disputants, minimize their individual "loss of face";
- break the conflict into fractional workable components;
- consider common enemy, high interaction, shared subordinate goal strategies;
- remember, nobody loves a go-between.

## CONCLUSION

For the contemporary manager, one of the most exciting organizational developments may well be in the efforts of behavioral scientists to approach conflict as a subject whose structure and process can be properly exploited as a means of promoting effective change. Guided by a realistic model that recognizes the importance of conflict as a creative force, scientists are now searching for hypotheses about conflict to test both in the laboratory and in the executive suite.

Even such subjects as ethology (the study of animal behavior) have been relevant. The new attitude toward aggression, while admitting that it may be triggered by environmental stimuli, also recognizes its hereditary basis. Furthermore, it is now recognized that humans, like all other animals, have some kind of pool of aggression that, when properly mobilized, facilitates the emergence of stable social structures.

The works of Konrad Lorenz, Robert Ardrey, and Desmond Morris fascinate many managers who recognize the truth of linking conflict and social space and who derive some satisfaction from the proposition that "zoos drive apes psycho." But these same managers appear to forget that "the corporate zoo drives people anomic." When applied in an organizational context, the social space (i.e., "elbow room") and the territorial imperatives of the ethologists refer not only to physical things but, more importantly, relate to matters of rules, roles, and relations. An organization consists of a network of roles, structured in a particular way to achieve a particular purpose.

What the systems concept of management teaches the contemporary manager is that if one of the interlocking elements in this network is changed, then some or all of the other elements will be affected. Inevitably change will be resisted and conflict generated. The modern theory of conflict emphasizes the importance of structural factors in predetermining how conflict will develop; the structure of an organization is largely determined by how authority and power are distributed.

What causes conflict is the fact that the organization exists in a social environment that may be thought of as turbulent. In a state of turbulence, the rate of change in the environment inevitably outstrips the rate of change in the organization, thus leaving the organization in a maladapted state.

Change is endemic to any organization due to the fact that the less powerful members in it have a vested interest in recognizing that the organization is a phase behind its environment, while the more powerful members have a vested interest in denying this phase lag. This introduces an element of inevitability into organizational conflict and change.

Of course, sometimes the conflict may be the unintended result of poor coordination. In a positive sense, conflict may be deliberately created to compel the organization to define goals, change processes, and reallocate resources. But conflict is only likely to produce constructive change when there is a rough balance of power between the parties of the dispute.

### Predictable Pattern

Conflict usually follows a particular pattern and is frequently quite predictable. For example, the pattern of wage negotiations is well established, although a change in economic conditions, such as the government's fiscal policy defining its reaction to inflation, can affect the ritual.

Most, but not all, organizations have evolved procedures that deal with such contingencies. The university administrators in the late 1960s discovered to their horror that they had no procedures for dealing with conflict and no properly constituted lines of appeal.

In fact, even a cursory examination of the student revolution emphasizes that the pattern is predictable: (1) *crisis*, the establishment commits a "crime," (2) *escalation*, occupation of administrative offices, (3) *confrontation*, show-down with officials, and (4) *further crisis*, challenging of the legitimacy of the committee appointed to investigate the original charge. And when the immediate fight is over, the organization is left to build not only a new hierarchy of an appeals system but also a new code of ethics.

None of these processes will work, however, unless executives fully understand the concept of good faith. Good faith demands that in communication one party does not deliberately control the flow of information in such a way as to manipulate the interests of the other party. In the new approach to organizational behavior, which is based on information science concepts, authority is defined in terms of three factors: location, function, and reference. *Location* refers to a particular node in the matrix of information processes; *function* describes the requirement that the manager has to search, collect, process, and disseminate particular kinds of information; and *reference* defines the constituency he or she represents.

To the information scientist, a measure of the amount of information that a message contains is the degree of surprise it induces, but a breach of good faith also produces a surprise. The offended party invariably presumes that he or she has the necessary information to participate in the exchange.

Even the way the information is sequenced may well induce this feeling of bad faith. A great number of managers have experienced this sensation, which they usually describe as a manipulation. Knowledge of the management of conflict may give one party in a dispute a significant advantage over his or her opponent, and the use of such knowledge may in itself be seen as an act of bad faith.

Thus the need for more managers to familiarize themselves with the structure and processes of conflict becomes more pressing. How to make conflict work for you is going to be an increasingly crucial management issue in our rapidly changing industrial society.

# 10

## Surviving and Thriving in Top Management Meetings

### IACOCCA'S CHRYSLER: "DALLAS" WITHOUT THE SEX

Watching the CEO in action on video can provide some useful insights and things to think about. For example, an NBC/Tom Brokaw program on Lee Iacocca ("Report: Iacocca—An American Profile," 1984) opens with Chrysler's CEO chewing out Hal Sperlich on some sports car program that is six months behind. He spouts some boss spiel that includes phrases like "All I know was I woke up one morning . . . and we were six months behind. . . . That's crap!" All this is achieved with the pointed finger while Sperlich is chewing on his glasses, visibly wilting.

When Sperlich starts answering with, "I'll give you a brief answer . . .," Iacocca drags on his cigar and gives a flicker of triumph at the camera. As he talks, Sperlich waves his hands, palms toward Iacocca in a placatory gesture and Iacocca edits his comments by flicking his eyes to the ceiling indicating a credibility gap at the choice moment. Also, interestingly enough, Iacocca cuts into a space in Sperlich's answer to say, "Incidentally, the cars look good." What can one make of all this Iacocca charisma? Some executives appear to love it, in a twisted sort of way. In the next video clip, Sperlich begins, "No way this guy can lose." All the world loves a winner. Nothing succeeds like success. Iacocca has a lot of idiosyncratic credit.

## THE STRUCTURE

### Sometimes a Cigar Is a Panzerfaust

Certain nonverbal things are really noticeable. For example, some executives smoke. They tap their cigarettes on the table to achieve a certain effect. They won't knock the ash of their cigarette into the ashtray until their opponent is finished speaking so that the surveillance, the tension of the unbroken gaze, cannot be cut. And, of course, there is the ultimate smoking gun of meetings: the cigar. In the NBC video on Iacocca we see the chairman of Chrysler flourish his giant cigar like a smoking panzerfaust as he rams home point after point. Iacocca is building the structure (see Figure 10.1). But as a modern Freud might have said, "Sometimes a cigar is just a banana." But subordinates can win.

### The Structure Is a Web of Rules, Roles, and Relations

Of committees, Sune Carlson observed that they (1) tended to grow regardless of considerations of efficiency, (2) found difficulty in limiting the duration of individual meetings, (3) needed to explore other means of communication such as staff officers and reports, (4) found difficulty in following up decisions taken (this pointed to a need for staff assistants), and (5) were composed of overworked executives who as committee members were loaded with still more work.

**Figure 10.1**
**The Structure**

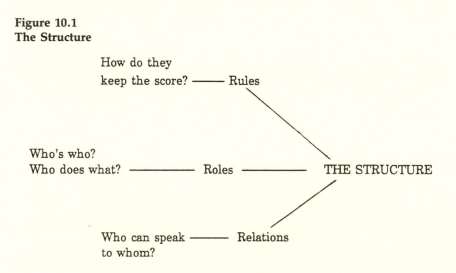

We know from behavioral studies that managers spend up to 80 percent of their time talking. A fair proportion of this interaction time is spent with more than one other person. Some critics argue that managers spend too much time in committee. Complaints often take such forms as "The committee is a meeting called to design a racehorse, but it ends up producing a camel"; "Minutes are kept and hours thrown away"; "The ideal number for a committee is three with two in absentia"; "Meetings should be held only at 5:00 P.M. in a room with no table or chairs."

If you want to be a chief executive officer, you have to act like one, especially in executive committee meetings. These are the meetings in which you will probably be coolly appraised by reigning members of the management group who are deciding whether to let you in. They will be watching vigilantly to see whether you are going to become a member of the inner circle or just another vice president of human resources.

Surviving in this environment requires a fairly cool understanding of what makes a top management meeting different from a middle management meeting. When middle managers get together, they usually analyze computer printouts, drawings, and other materials in an earnest search for feasible options to sell to the next level up. Differences of technical opinion may arise and tempers may soar, but nearly all involved are anxious to find and support an optimum solution.

On the other hand, video studies reveal that a top management meeting is more likely to be an adversarial proceeding—not necessarily an open clash of wills, but a group of opposing viewpoints in a struggle to achieve dominance. Such a meeting will usually be conducted in a courteous, formal, almost legalistic atmosphere, but it's nevertheless a game of getting the upper hand. If you want to survive in this paradoxical environment, you must learn how the players interrelate, what roles they play, and what weapons they consider acceptable.

### What Happens in Meetings . . . and Why

Sometimes the video camera catches participants off guard as they are milling around waiting to begin the meeting. The scene is reminiscent of an infantry platoon trying to organize itself before heading for the front. Everybody is nervous but trying to be genial; nobody really knows what is happening. The first minute of the meeting is everything; the video shows conclusively that more things happen in that first minute than any person can rationally absorb. To see this, you need only advance the video one frame at a time and watch carefully.

Researchers in one project, who studied a meeting in a large, international telecommunications company, observed several striking things after a number of careful viewings of their video. The meeting consisted of four executives in a data-processing group; the two leaders were assistant vice presidents, one from Montreal and the other from Toronto. As the meeting was about to begin, the assistant vice president from Montreal asked, "Are any of you people going to the operations research meeting at lunchtime?" As it turned out, nobody was going except the assistant vice president from Montreal. He then said, "Okay, that's fine, but I want to get there on time, so I'll give a signal fifteen minutes before the presentation starts." Thus he began the meeting by structuring the time frame to show that his time was important.

Sitting to the left of the assistant vice president from Montreal was his colleague from Toronto. The Montreal assistant vice president next asked one of his staff to make a presentation on a technical computer subject. As his staffer began, the Montreal man leaned forward so that he blocked the line of vision between the assistant vice president from Toronto and the speaker, thus "protecting" the speaker, in a sense, until he had picked up momentum and was off to a good start. Once the speaker was in stride, the Montreal assistant vice president put his feet on the desk and pushed his chair back from the table so that he was behind his colleague from Toronto. It seemed from the outset of the meeting that the man from Toronto had been cast in an adversarial relationship.

One explanation for such behavior is that the nonlinear part of a manager's brain is involved in the process of running meetings. This process apparently involves a kind of nonverbal communication; it requires an executive to have a sense of where his body should be and how he should respond to a particular situation. In such cases, the right hemisphere of the brain—the hemisphere responsible for intuitive spatial relations and creative thinking required in many artistic pursuits—is supplementing the usual analytical skills that an executive brings to a meeting. Managers are apparently able to balance the functions of both hemispheres in order to achieve what they want. All this interaction seems to reflect the ideas expressed by George A. Miller in his book *Spontaneous Apprentices: Children and Language* (1977) when he speaks of the "left hand of subjective accidents, odd metaphors, wild guesses, happy hunches, and chance permutation of ideas that come from who knows where." Managers are apparently very skillful in utilizing this left side of the brain—in other words, in developing their intuitive skill in nonlinear logic. Much of this skill is revealed in their unconscious ability to make a spontaneous physical intervention in a meeting.

A brilliant new model of decision making has been developed that presumes that businesses are organized anarchies with three things floating around: problems, decision makers, and solutions. The reality of the matter is that, since organizations are so technically complex today, the right problems are never in the right room with the right people who can in fact come up with the right solution. What this means is that executives have to be ready to travel through organizational space hoping to arrive eventually in the right context with the right problem, people, and solution. James G. March and his colleagues, who have played a decisive part in the "garbage can" model of decision making, have argued that organized anarchies are a characteristic of organizations, particularly conspicuous in public, educational, and illegitimate organizations like the mafia.

### Role Playing in Meetings

What these videos reveal, then, is that sophisticated role playing is a major part of the drama of managerial life. Playing a role is like playing a hand in poker; things are happening at a number of different levels. Since roles, rules, and relations are socially ordained, behavior conforms to probabilities and perceptions. "Play it as it lays" and "Play it by ear" are expressions that describe the subtle double-dealing of role playing.

A video may show a chief executive using psychological gamesmanship to throw a scare into opponents even though his or her aboveboard behavior is impeccable. For many managers, a meeting is psychological warfare waged at nerve-wracking intensity. Sometimes these psychological games are elevated to the level of a debate. These managerial debates have a certain entertainment value; moreover, they can sometimes help clarify a political situation. The ultimate aim of the exercise is to make the opponent appear ridiculous. Because executives are frequently quite skilled in debating techniques, they will often give a real display of verbal pyrotechnics.

The aim of the debating game is not necessarily to be right; rather, one must sound convincing and denigrate one's opponent as coolly and elegantly as possible. Body language and facial expressions are tremendously important in this context; smiling subtly while your opponent delivers his or her main point can often be as telling as coming up with an objective rejoinder. The need, above all else, is to give a good performance.

In trying to find a suitable role model for developing this performance, one can examine the John F. Kennedy–Richard M. Nixon presidential debate of 1960. Kennedy scored points by adopting a certain patrician aloofness that made Nixon look shifty by comparison. The truly effective executive debater has an uncanny knack for improvising effects and verbal ploys that make an opponent look gauche.

Perhaps the most important thing to keep in mind about executive encounters is that the format can shift very quickly. There is no guarantee that an orders-giving session will not degenerate into a debate in which logic and loyalty give way to a mere display of wit.

## Meetings as Drama

Running a meeting is an exciting activity, but from a scientific point of view it consists of long, boring lists of things to do. When you consider the manager who actually has to run the meeting, you soon realize the need for myth, magic, and meaning. Producing and directing meetings become the art of transforming inputs into outputs with the addition of value. This "two plus two equals five" aspect of meetings demands a certain *savoir faire* that owes more to theater than it does to science.

This new approach to meetings assumes an imaginative integration of structure (the cast of characters) and values (myth, magic, and meaning). If the meeting is seen from this perspective, it is transformed into a powerful theatrical experience.

All groups work through three phases: clarification ("What is it?"), evaluation ("How do we feel about it?"), and decision ("What are we going to do about it?"). To work through this process, the group selects two individuals: the task specialist (who "zeroes in on the problem") and the human relations specialist (who offers first aid to help alleviate group tension).

The executive who has studied group dynamics might find nothing particularly new in all this. Nevertheless, executive meetings have undergone a dramatic change in tone and content. Naked conflict has begun to emerge, conflict so common and visible that executives have been forced to find both a rationale and a ritual to contain it.

The executive as entertainer can learn much from the playwright about how to figure out the scenario, interpret the script, and enter and exit on cue. He or she must grasp the meaning of the phrase, "We will entertain this motion," that is, "We will fool around with it, pummel it, and see generally what it is made of." Like a good chess player, the successful top manager is a sportsman in a meeting. He or she never squirms while losing, never crows when winning. Like the chess player, he or she merely concentrates on trying to outwit and outpsych the opponent.

However, this entire process cannot work unless the right kind of values are involved. The conflict between democratic values and task-oriented values can create dilemmas at executive meetings. The members of the meeting must state what is on their minds; at the same time, they must be ready to bow to the emerging consensus. The task-oriented values are espoused by the chairman, who makes his or her members realize that they must finish the agenda on schedule. Putting these values together can cause a lot of tension, especially when the public agenda is to develop a policy for promotion based on merit, while the hidden agenda is to try to chastise the "Young Turks" or sink the "Old Guard."

## The Deeper Structures of Executive Meetings

In one videotape, which depicts the behavior of a typical day in the life of an executive, the day begins with a meeting between the executive and his immediate employees, a meeting devoted essentially to the executive's reading of a speech he plans to give that evening at a local hotel. During this meeting, the executive, Bill Andrews, is going to read his speech to his team so they can check it for ''emphasis and content.'' On the surface of things, nothing particularly important seems to be happening.

But is this really the case? Just as the meeting is about to begin, Andrews interrupts himself to make some administrative arrangements, set schedules, and so on. In fact, many of the most important moves seem to happen almost parenthetically; things are happening in the ''white spaces'' between the printed formal behavior.

One possible analysis of this behavior is that the meeting is essentially a tribal assembly in which the attending managers are reassured that they are ''on the team.'' This line of argument follows the idea of an executive meeting proposed by Anthony Jay in his article ''How to Run a Meeting'' (1976). Jay sees one of the meetings's functions as the reestablishment of tribal commitment—a kind of giving and receiving homage that is a necessary part of executive life.

## Drama and Trauma: Reigning and Reining

While referring a matter to a committee can dilute authority, diffuse responsibility, and delay decisions, meetings do fulfill a deep human need. According to Jay, human resource executives should be familiar with the functions that make a meeting superior to more recent communication devices:

- A meeting provides a simple definition of the team, the group, or the unit. Those present belong to it; those absent do not.

- A meeting is the place where the group revises, updates, and adds to what it knows as a group. An enormous amount of material can be left unsaid that would have to be made explicit to an outsider.

- A meeting helps every individual understand both the collective aim of the group and the way in which every individual's work contributes to the group's success.

- A meeting creates a commitment in all present. Once something has been decided, even if you originally argued against it, your membership in the group creates an obligation to accept the decision.

- A meeting is very often the only occasion during which the team or group actually exists and works as a group.

- A meeting is a status arena. People are and should be concerned with their status relative to the other members in the group.
- To do all these things means drama, catharsis, therapy, and trauma—all of which are revealed on video.

The whole process can be quite subtle. For example, how does a CEO get advice? Some have a "Kitchen Cabinet," but more chief executives work with a formal committee that somehow facilitates the CEO's actions without preempting his or her authority. The CEO reigns; his or her top management committee "reins." If these committees are handled properly, good things can happen. In their article "How CEOs Use Top Management Committees" (1984), Richard F. Vancil and Charles H. Green point out that:

Formal committees also help to bind senior officers into a corporate management team. Most top executives work toward this end—in part by arranging social activities and corporate retreats in addition to holding regular meetings. The meetings themselves create, over time, a large base of shared experiences. As committee members work together, discussion becomes more efficient, a common database evolves, a shared jargon develops, and biases become clear. Managers who have been through many wars together can handle a heavy agenda because they need not waste a lot of time trying to understand each other. In times of crisis, a well-organized top management team can mobilize corporate resources quickly.

Most CEO's use high-level committees for drama and trauma that create a calendar-driven series of events; this keeps those who report to them off balance but productive. Top management committees have a "continual agenda" that keeps executives under review. Such committees become expert in diagnosing ill-defined issues.

### The Executive Committee

The term "group executive office" describes a management structure that has drawn much attention in the past few decades; however, there is much controversy over its usefulness as a management tool. Many major corporations have experimented with this team effort at management, with mixed results. In spite of the many failures, more and more companies are willing to take the plunge.

As N. R. Kleinfield points out in "When Many Chiefs Think as One" (1984), the concept involves replacing the top person with a committee of three or more senior officers who have decision-making power and authority. The team goes by a number of names such as executive council, office of the chairman, or office of the president. This concept springs from the idea that two heads are better than one, although experience shows that this does not always work in a business situation. Booz, Allen & Hamilton, a management consulting firm, report that of the fifty companies that started such teams in the early 1980s, approximately half have discontinued them.

Despite these startling statistics, Kleinfield points out that companies continue to establish executive councils for a number of reasons: to reduce the workload of the CEO, to assist in decision making, to select and groom individuals for key management positions, to improve corporate strategic planning, and to help a company through a transition (e.g., reorganization). The list of corporations that have tried group management is quite impressive: DuPont, Sears-Roebuck, Hewlett-Packard, Caterpillar, and Gulf Oil were among the first. Some giants that followed include IBM, Dow Chemical, Chase Manhattan, Ford, and General Electric.

Varied experiences with group executive offices have divided companies into believers and nonbelievers. The advocates of group management laud the technique as an effective mechanism for communication and facilitating decision making and a forum for voicing opinions; opponents perceive it as a hindrance to effective corporate management. Loss of leadership, unnecessary delays, and interference with decision making are a few of the problems cited.

According to Kleinfield, two models for group executive offices are common. In the first and more successful model, the members' responsibilities and areas of authority are clearly defined. Responsibility for various company divisions is delegated to individual members. Employees report to the person responsible for that part of the organization. In the second model, no group member is singled out as having more authority in any one area. They all have equal decision-making power. This tends to lead to confusion, because nobody knows who the ''boss'' is. Some executive committees may contain as many as fourteen members, such as IBM's corporate management committee. Groups of this size are not involved in making decisions; rather, their function is confined to more think-tank-type activities such as establishing corporate strategy and philosophy, such as Jack Welch established at General Electric.

## GE's Corporate Executive Council

*Interviewer:* You've dismantled GE's groups and sectors, the top levels of the corporate organization to which individual strategic business units once reported. That certainly makes the organization chart more simple—you now have 14 separate businesses reporting directly to you or your two vice chairmen. How does the new structure simplify how GE operates on a day-to-day basis?

*Jack Welch:* Cutting the groups and sectors eliminated communications filters. Today there is direct communication between the CEO and the leaders of the 14 businesses. We have very short cycle times for decisions and little interference by corporate staff. A major investment decision that used to take a year can now be made in a matter of days.

We also run a Corporate Executive Council, the CEC. For two days every quarter, we meet with the leaders of the 14 businesses and our top staff people. These aren't stuffy, formal strategic reviews. We share ideas and information candidly and openly, including programs that have failed. The important thing is that at the end of those two days everyone in the CEC has seen and discussed the same information. The CEC creates a sense of trust, a sense of personal familiarity and mutual obligation at the top of the company. We consider the CEC a piece of organizational technology that is very important for our future success. (Quoted in Tichy, 1989)

## CREATING AN IMAGE OF ACTION

We have seen that the drama of these meetings gives expression to subtle and elusive forces that defy logical explanation. A meeting, when properly conducted, always induces an imaginative response that participants find startling, vivid, and exciting. The essential ingredient of any meeting is drama linked to conflict. This conflict may take several forms: an enemy to be defeated, a contract to be signed, a production quota to be beaten, and so forth. Whatever the issue, the people in the meeting must face choices and make decisions—in other words, they must take action. Getting involved in a meeting means getting a slice of this action. The action may involve negotiation, hiring or firing people, or simply providing verbal support. Such action will need more than just "a good line"; it will require strong verbal communication that helps to resolve the conflict. Ineffective managers may be good at "shooting a line," but they cannot follow through with action. For effective managers, talk by itself is not enough; the talk must advance the action.

When viewed from a dramatic perspective, the chair's function is to induce an imaginative response, and the other actors in turn receive not an answer to a question but an experience. The art of meeting management allows the chair to develop a complex and captivating ambiance. Such an ambiance is not easily defined; nevertheless, it helps get the desired action. This executive style creates an image of action, of force, of probabilities controlled. The image sets the scene, fixing the action and determining the choice of the other actors.

### The Power of Nonverbal Communication

How can you tell whether an executive you have just met will be hostile or friendly? Studies reveal that the answer lies not only in spoken words but also in the vocal tones, facial expressions, and body postures that emerge during the initial conversation. The nonverbal element is a message that apparently carries more weight than the actual words.

The ways people look at each other reveal more than most people realize. The right amount of eye contact can determine who is going to be the dominant person in an exchange; for example, a committee member has a way of signaling an intent to claim the floor. People can instantly assert their position in the pecking hierarchy by the exchange of a single glance. One must be able to see the other person's eyes to know when he or she intends to start or stop; without this kind of feedback, it is difficult to synchronize the conversation. Furthermore, studies show that:

- People move into positions in which they can see better in order to dominate the conversation.
- Some female executives make more use of visual feedback than their male counterparts.
- Executives in general make more eye contact when listening.
- Eye contact promotes good relations only when it is associated with a friendly facial expression.
- Executives tend to look away when talking, especially when exceeding their "allotted time."
- Different ethnic groups use eye expressions in different ways.
- In meetings, members direct more comments to people seated opposite them than to people seated adjacent to them; when a strong leader is present, however, members direct their comments to adjacent individuals rather than to opposite ones.

Posture is also important; a person can establish dominance by throwing his or her head back and speaking in a loud voice. On the other hand, people who put their hands behind their backs while being addressed may be seen as taking a subordinate role.

### The "Holy Idiot" Defense

A surprising number of executive meetings are either left unchaired or are chaired by a relatively junior manager such as the second in command or an organizational development (OD) specialist. These junior managers' formats seem to give top management more space to play with. In one exercise, the OD person in charge tried to protect his "Top Dog" boss by ruling a vice president out of order. Quick as a flash, the two parties he was trying to separate allied themselves against the OD man. Strangely enough, however, the OD man seemed to relish his emergent role and promptly told a joke on himself; furthermore, everybody seemed to appreciate his capacity for self-vilification. The OD man, caught in a double bind, simply moved from the role of scapegoat into the role of "holy idiot," thereby achieving an important rapprochement.

Scientific analysis of the events in an executive meeting reveal clearly that a large proportion of conflict is expressed in these get-togethers. A good manager will use humor to reduce the tension.

Time after time, videos show that humor, especially irony, is particularly important. The nonlinear logic of the right brain must be brought into play. Executives, even good ones, often fail simply because they have lost their sense of the ridiculous.

## CONCLUSION

To win or even to survive in meetings at the top, managers may have to use a more sophisticated game strategy (see Figure 10.2). To develop such a strategy, they can follow debates, observe the techniques of motion picture and television actors, and examine their own and others' meeting behavior. Above all, to participate effectively in executive meetings, managers must understand their own style, recognize the "script," figure out the roles, watch the action, and keep up with the pace. In short, to avoid trauma, they should join in the drama.

**Figure 10.2**
**The Model of the Organization as a Corporate Theater of Action**

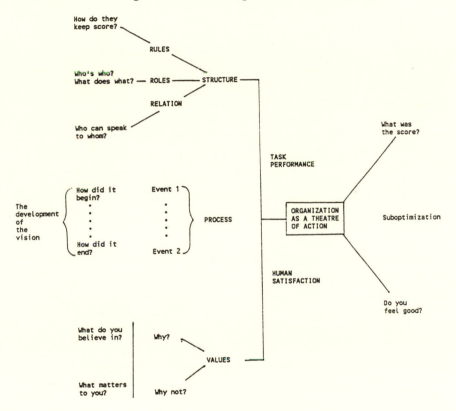

# 11

---

# The Management of
# Technological Innovation

Talking about the management of technological innovation in the future is a tricky business and takes strong nerves—a bit like walking on water. Even if you pull it off, you end up getting your feet wet.

"Futurology" has been cynically described by Ambrose Bierce in *The Devil's Dictionary* (1906) as scientific prophecy or the art and practice of selling one's credibility for future delivery. Indeed, many of the predictions about computing have a distinct fictional ring. Kind of like writing a check when you know the bank is going to stamp NSF all over it. Only in this case NSF means Not Sufficient Facts.

When you're trying to forecast the future of a computer company, it's perhaps a good idea to keep John Locke in mind and try to throw your mind into a state of tabula rasa. In other words, the more you can make your mind be like a blank slate, the more likely you are to be successful. Once you've got your blank slate, it's necessary to get your right hemisphere to write a script on it.

The right hemisphere of the brain is especially good at nonlinear logic and creative gestalt thinking. It's the right hemisphere that you use when you're painting, sculpting, dancing, or getting the idea of a computer. It's the right hemisphere that comes out with happy hunches and odd metaphors and wild creative things that sometimes work (see Figure 11.1).

In a brilliant book, *Spontaneous Apprentices: Children and Language* (1977), George A. Miller, a professor of psychology at Rockefeller University, speaks of the "left hand" subjective accidents, odd metaphors, wild guesses, and chance permutations of ideas that come from who knows where, versus "the right hand" of "order and lawfulness, technique and

**Figure 11.1**
**The Music of the Spheres: The Different Functions of the Two Hemispheres of the Brain**

| ANALYTICAL SKILLS | | | INTUITIVE SKILLS |
|---|---|---|---|
| Language | Left | Right | Intuitive spatial |
| Linear logic | hemisphere | hemisphere | relations |
| Sense of time | | | Creative gestalt |
| | | | thinking |
| | | | Simultaneous under- |
| | | | standing |
| | | | Painting |
| | | | Sculpting |
| | | | Dancing |
| | | | Body Language |
| | **THE BRAIN** | | |
| Example: | | | Example: |
| Writing a | | | Physical interven- |
| management | | | tion in a meeting |
| report | | | involving body |
| | | | language, leading |
| | | | to a policy which |
| | | | "just comes out of |
| | | | the blue" |

artifice.'' To get the left side going involves intuitive skills in nonlinear logic. This means some skill in fooling around with models—"What if" models, or contingency theory, are needed.

The physiological basis of linear and nonlinear logic has been provided by neurosurgeons from California who, in experiments with severe epileptics, have been able to demonstrate that the two hemispheres of the brain perform different cognitive functions (see Figure 11.2). Robert Ormstein, a psychologist, showed that the same basic division of labor applies to normal people. Man has a bifunctional brain.

High tech managers use the left side of their brains to analyze a problem, but there comes a time when a synergy of the capabilities of the right and left sides is necessary if they are going to develop creative, imaginative inventions. Of course, there is a danger that these categories, "left brain" and "right brain," will become unwelcome stereotypes. The message for senior management is clear: They should place a high value on intuition, creativity, and nonlinear logic in subordinates. Their view should be that there is nothing so unequal as the equal treatment of unequals.

Nonlinear logic starts with an idea, the whole. Linear logic develops the whole from an analysis of the parts. As the learning theorist E. L. Thorndike put it in the early twenties, sometimes it is better to start with

**Figure 11.2**
**A Musical Score for Invention: Stages in the Creative Process for Technological Innovation**

| Stage | Type | Behaviors | |
|-------|------|-----------|---|
| Preparation | Conscious | Saturation. Investigating the problem in all directions to become fully familiar with it, its setting, causes and effects. | Left Brain |
| | | Deliberation. Mulling over these ideas, analyzing and challenging them, viewing them from different optics. | |
| Latent Period | Unconscious | Incubation. Relaxing, switching off, and turning the problem over to the unconscious mind. | |
| | | | Right Brain |
| | | Illumination. Emerging with possible answers - dramatic, perhaps off beat, but fresh and new. | |
| Presentation | Conscious | Verification. Clarifying and fleshing out the idea, testing it against the criteria of appropriateness. | |
| | | | Left Brain |
| | | Accommodation. Trying the solution out on other people and other problems. | |

the part; sometimes the whole. It all depends on the task and whether it has been done before. Whether linear or nonlinear logic is called for is always a matter of judgment. But the Sculleys and Jobs of this high tech world have to work together.

## THE DISCIPLINE OF INNOVATION

Peter F. Drucker, in "The Discipline of Innovation" (1985), considers innovation to be an essential quality of entrepreneurship, the mechanism by which entrepreneurs create or increase wealth. By Drucker's definition, innovation is the heart of entrepreneurship: "the effort to create purposeful, focused change in an enterprise's economic or social potential."

In describing the wellspring of innovation, Drucker would add a corollary to an old adage, "necessity is the mother of invention," in that uncertainty is the mother of innovation. It arises from a purposeful search for opportunity, in situations that may exist both within and without the corporation. Unexpected occurrences, incongruities, process needs, and industry or market changes may provoke innovation within the corporation or industry. Demographic changes, changes in perception, and new knowledge may act as a catalyst outside the company in its environment.

As examples of innovation prompted by the unexpected, Drucker proffers IBM and the Ford Motor Company. IBM realized it had an unexpected success when it adapted a Univac scientific computer for payroll applications—a market rejected by Univac (at that time the industry leader). Ford, on the other hand, was driven by the unexpected failure of the Edsel to rethink its marketing strategy and produced the Mustang and Thunderbird—both outstanding successes. Innovators, he argues, examine both unexpected successes and failures for opportunities.

Closely related to and stemming from the unexpected are incongruities between assumptions and reality. A change in perspective is frequently necessary to reveal flawed assumptions—a technique that has been labeled by Edward de Bono as "lateral thinking." To illustrate the process, Drucker offers the example of the shipping industry: Despite steady technological advance in reducing fuel usage and increasing speed, by 1950 the industry lay moribund. At this juncture it was realized that the real cost of operating a vessel was incurred when the ship lay idle, not when it was working. As a result, container shipping was born (not an application of new technology, Drucker notes, but a new application of old technology) and profitability was restored.

Process needs are another source of innovation. The necessity of improving and adapting production processes to fulfill the organization's goals is a powerful impetus for change.

Industry and market changes, although not, strictly speaking, internal to the organization, also pave the way for innovation. Rapid growth in an industry gives rise to structural dislocations that can be exploited by the inventive. Such opportunities, Drucker contends, are not vigorously defended by established companies intent as they are on maintaining the status quo. The shift in the securities market to institutional investors was one such change that went all but unnoticed by major brokers during the 1960s. Donaldson, Lufkin, and Jenrette was formed for the express purpose of servicing the new market and introduced negotiated commissions —with great success.

Demographics, Drucker notes, are an oft-ignored environmental factor that is a particularly fruitful source of innovation. Managers frequently underrate them as slow-moving, but as Drucker points out, organizations that exploit them can profit handsomely. Club Med's success was founded upon the emergence of the affluent young adult and singles market during the 1970s, a phenomenon that was predictable but nonetheless ignored by many in the travel industry.

Drucker's sixth source of innovation, "changes in perception," might be more correctly labeled "changes in perspective" and is closely associated with incongruities described earlier. A simple change of viewpoint may prompt a manager to perceive possibilities that would otherwise go unnoticed. Drucker employs the well known analogy of a semi-filled glass: It may be seen as half empty or half full at the whim of the viewer. Innovation cannot germinate, implies Drucker, unless the possibility can be seen.

New knowledge is perhaps the most commonly thought of source of innovation. The archetypical entrepreneur is one who exploits scientific or technical advances for personal gain and the common good. Drucker points out that of all innovations, these are the most capricious and risky forms of innovation. The emergence of new knowledge, its application in new techniques and its introduction to markets occurs over a very long period of time: fifty years according to Drucker (this is highly debatable). More importantly, the practical application of new knowledge frequently requires the confluence of several theoretical fields. Thus, the modern computer is a result of discoveries in binary arithmetic (Babbage), symbolic logic (Russell and Whitehead), and cybernetics (Von Neuman). The erratic progress and long gestation period of knowledge-based innovation make it difficult, but not impossible, to manage.

Dispensing with the sources of innovation, Drucker turns his attention to the principles of innovation. The first is the necessity of scanning all opportunity sources—different sources will have different importance at different times. Successful innovators must also be capable of both analysis and synthesis—in Drucker's words, "use both the right and left sides of their brains." Simplicity and focus are the essence of innovation: simplicity for acceptance and focus for practicality. It follows, therefore, that innovations usually start small, but are aimed with maximum impact in mind.

Above all else, Drucker concludes, innovation requires hard, focused, purposeful work. Talent, ingenuity, and knowledge are only icing on the cake.

## THE COMPUTER ANALOGY

The first fully modern electronic computer, designed by the American mathematician John von Neumann, was introduced in 1940. The computer, which promised (or threatened, depending on your point of view) to transform our world more than any other technological advance, has reached into nearly every realm of human development; in the process it has transformed not only the shape of society but also the way people think. A new state of mind has emerged: an outlook that takes the view that man and the computer are two species of a more abstract genius called the information-processing system.

### IBM

Problem solving is the business of International Business Machines Corporation. A glance at *Fortune's* top 500 companies quickly reveals that IBM was one of the largest, most profitable, multinational organizations in the world. In the 1980s, IBM dominated the shape of the future.

One of the questions of most interest to students of management hinges around "Why is IBM so big, so successful until recently when others who started with similar technology and resources have dwindled into insignificance?" The answer is in the organizational ontology of Big Blue. Now, in the 1990s, IBM is facing real problems.

#### Apple

Apple and Silicon Valley are at the forefront of technological innovation. They are also known for their creative and unusual management styles. As mentioned by Robert Reinhold in the February 12, 1984, issue of the *New York Times,*

The methods vary widely, but they have one thing in common: a belief that the traditional hierarchical structure of older Eastern-based companies has hobbled American industry in an age when technological change is so rapid that a few weeks lost can mean the difference between success and failure.

Apple is not alone; Tandem computers has a weekly beer bust in its cafeteria. Rolm Corporation, a telecommunications manufacturer, has landscaped "campuses" instead of offices, with sports facilities and a subsidized restaurant.

### Managing Apple and the Yummies

The Yummies (Young upwardly mobile managers into existentialism and entrepreneurship) have a different attitude toward authority, computers, and ethnic minorities. They do not function in a crisply defined black-and-white geometrically defined environment. In the world of Organizational Alice, they use intuition and, in particular, the right hemisphere of the brain. Because organizations and markets behave in counterintuitive ways, it is useful to cast a glance at the executive as "ballet dancing samurai," where existentialism, entrepreneurship, intuition, and disciplined analysis are all necessary. A good example of a ballet dancing samurai is John Sculley, who is excellent in the art of corporate self-actualization.

## BIG BROTHER

IBM, in 1990, even with faltering revenues, dominated the information processing industry, which includes robots, electronic medical devices, copiers, telecommunications equipment, and electronic information services as well as computers. This enormous expansion of IBM is causing increasing concern among other manufacturers of computers. With this rise on the part of IBM, many analysts feel that the U.S. computer industry is becoming less competitive. Many believe there is a real danger that in the future there will be no real competition for IBM.

Right through the 1980s the political environment in the United States was very favorable to IBM. In 1982 the Justice Department dropped the thirteen-year antitrust suit against the company, arguing against the critics of IBM. It was generally believed that the company was superbly managed. Nevertheless, many critics are arguing that the government should reconsider its attitude toward IBM. This concern is not confined only to the United States; European governments are also disturbed by IBM's growth rate. It has been argued that IBM dominates the "computer Monopoly board," and maybe the moment has arrived to redeal the cards and play again.

As Andrew Pollack points out in "The Daunting Power of IBM" (1985), IBM's dominance is greatest in the market for large central computers and mainframes, where its share exceeds 70 percent. It is weakest in mid-sized computers, where fairly strong competition comes from Digital, Wang Laboratories, and the Data Control Corporation.

"IBM is also the leader in personal computers," according to Pollack, who also noted that many of the people he spoke to were so frightened to talk about IBM that they refused to be quoted and expressions were used like, "You quote me and I'm out of a job."

### From Punched Cards to Computers

In the 1950s electronic computers were unknown to all but a small community of mathematicians, statisticians, and scientists. This scientific intelligentsia was unanimous in its prediction that eight or ten at the most of these ingenious electronic "brains" would be quite ample to satisfy the demands and needs of not only the entire academic community but also of those few businesses that might be possessed of the skill and/or need for such a "system."

Oddly enough, Thomas Watson, Sr., and the top management of IBM were also unanimous in their underestimation of potential computer sales. However, IBM was by 1955 the predominant company in the electronic data processing (EDP) industry. This dominance pertained to electro-mechanical equipment, based on the "Hollerith" type of punched cards known as unit record systems, with only a superficial electronic knowledge attached to the punchcard sorters.

### IBM Second in Technology, First in Marketing

Contrary to popular belief, IBM was not the first corporation to produce a "computer." IBM got into the computer industry more out of force than choice. In the very late 1940s Remington-Rand came out with the Univac, a machine that rapidly revolutionized the EDP field.

### Snow White and the Seven Dwarfs

But IBM knew a lot more about marketing than did Remington-Rand. Up until that time IBM was mainly involved in manufacturing punchcard installations and tabulators, but they had market moxie to realize that potential customers would be frightened by the cost and complexity of computers. But because IBM was so knowledgeable about marketing, they trained their sales and service people to help clients to overcome any technical difficulties. By 1956 IBM had won 85 percent of the computer market in the United States. Many IBM executives resent the idea that IBM tends to be a step behind in technology.

IBM has become so successful that in the 1960s the company came to be known as "Snow White" while its competitors (Burroughs, Univac, NCR, Control Data, Honeywell, General Electric, and RCA) were referred to as the "Seven Dwarfs."

Under the direction of John Opel, who became chief executive officer in 1981, IBM had become one of the most successful companies in the world and the most profitable company in the United States. As early as 1982 IBM made profits of $4.4 billion on sales of $34.4 billion. In the 1970s many analysts regarded IBM as a corporation to be put in mothballs because the US government had launched an antitrust suit against them. But in the 1980s IBM was brought out of mothballs and became a successful company entering new markets, developing the latest technology, trimming the organizational fat, and acting in a really aggressive way.

## The Personal Computer

In August 1981, IBM introduced the personal computer, generally known simply as the PC. Already IBM has captured more than 20 percent of the $7.5 billion US market for personal computers and is now almost at level pegging with the pacesetter Apple Computers. IBM produces not only personal computers but also a wide range of products including electric typewriters that sell for $800, to data processing systems that cost in the hundreds of millions.

IBM built the PC computer from parts largely bought from outside the company. To develop the PC computer, IBM brought together a twelve-member taskforce in Boca Raton, Florida. First brought together in July 1980 and given a year to develop a competitive and easy-to-use personal computer, the taskforce broke with tradition by setting up an open architectural scheme that made PC technical specifications available to other firms. The idea behind this move was to allow other companies and individuals to write software or build equipment for the PC. One of the reasons why the personal computer was developed so easily and swiftly was that John Opel introduced a new spirit to the company and decided to create a new corporate policy-making procedure that gave greater facility for delegation. In order to achieve this goal Opel established seven independent business units. The taskforce that was brought together to develop the PC was one of these independent business units. IBM was also pursuing different business policies; for example, in 1982 IBM spent $250 million to acquire a part of Intel, a leading computer chip manufacturer located in Santa Clara, California. In 1983 IBM paid $228 million for a 15 percent stake in Rolm, a major producer of telecommunications equipment also in Santa Clara. What IBM is hoping to do with Rolm is to develop the so-called electronic office.

## IBM Had the Midas Touch

A major reason for IBM's earlier success was that the company developed the tremendous "Big Blue" corporate culture, a unique set of beliefs and principles that guided almost every action of its employees. This Big Blue culture is so strong that it also rubs off on many IBM customers.

The culture was created by Thomas Watson, Sr., who joined the computing tabulating recording corporation in 1914 and created International Business Machines in 1924. Watson had rules for almost everything; IBM employees were required to wear dark business suits, white shirts, and striped ties and were told to drink no alcohol even when they were off the job. Watson had signs posted all over the plant spelling out "THINK." The culture has changed little today even though IBM salespeople can now drink at lunch, but if they do so they are to make no further calls that day. IBM executives still dress conservatively. As is well known, IBM employees are well paid and receive generous fringe benefits. Watson was especially skilled at motivating workers and inspiring loyalty; he even commissioned a company songbook and led employees in singing company songs.

## BUNCH

From the time GE and RCA quit the computer business in the 1970s, the others were at one time collectively known by their initials as the "BUNCH." IBM became so successful in the 1960s that the Johnson Administration, in its final day in office on January 17, 1969, launched an antitrust case against IBM accusing the company of being monopolistic and engaging in anticompetitive practices. This Federal antitrust suit was like a dark cloud hanging over IBM during the whole of the 1970s, until the Justice Department abruptly dropped the suit in January 1982, saying that the case was without merit. During the seventies IBM management made good use of this time to engage in planning and consolidation.

During this period IBM faced enormous competition from companies in the Silicon Valley in California and the Route 128 area around Boston. What these companies were doing was producing smaller machines that performed a wide range of data processing functions. During this period Digital Equipment Corporation was able to raise its revenues from $265 million to about $4 billion over a ten-year period. But when IBM began the process of expanding again, it entered into the field of personal computers. In 1982 IBM sold an estimated 200,000 PCs and in 1983 they aimed to sell 800,000 more. But in 1992, IBM lost nearly $5 billion. The company's stock market value dropped from $106 billion in 1987 to $27 billion in 1993. To combat this situation, John Akers, CEO of IBM, had split the company into thirteen independent businesses to make the firm more nimble and aggressive. He also abandoned two established policies: no compulsory redundancies, no dividend cuts.

## APPLE AND THE YUMMIES

What happened almost immediately was that the IBM PC became the standard for the personal computer market. This tremendous expansion of IBM into the field of personal computers led to a confrontation with

Apple Computers. Steven Jobs, who was the chairman of Apple, always believed that IBM's entry into the personal computer market has helped Apple by driving weaker rivals like Tandy, who owns Radio Shack, into a lesser share of the market. In order to meet this competition Jobs recruited Pepsi Cola's president, John Sculley, a marketing expert, to serve as Apple's president.

An understanding of these stages of development will help managers to cope more effectively. But to cope with change, Apple management has to focus on the rapidly changing quality of the environment. Change arising from computer technology and electronic technology (e.g., evaluating the opportunities and hazards of the hybrid domestic computer–copying machine–videotape recorder expected in the mid-1990s), the proliferation of rapid transit systems, the development of new managerial technologies, the growth of international trade, and the demand for ethnic and sexual equality are turning organizations upside down. A sophisticated Apple board, not prepared to wait it out and let such changes dominate them, is entering into the spirit of the times and trying to exploit these change options.

The essence of the matter is really that Apple's top management are able to infuse their values into the system through Yummies.

Yummies are executives who thrive on innovation and start-ups and who seek out interesting and financially rewarding problems. All this means is that they are heavily involved in problem solving. Nevertheless, most of these masters of corporate invention seem to have a Midas touch, and everything they touch has made money for them. These Yummies seem to thrive on turning around seemingly impossible situations; they are often likened to war-time generals or emergency room surgeons. American management styles are changing, and perhaps it will be useful to look at this in more detail.

This new managerial style is often described in the aphorism "I'm O.K., you're O.K., but I'm still the boss." In effect what has happened is that the autocratic executive style is being relaxed and power to a degree has been decentralized. The new style in management tries to focus individual initiative and resourcefulness and tries to mobilize the energies of colleagues.

Under Jobs' "outlaw" regimen, the Macintosh team assembled a computer that was every inch the commercial success that the Lisa had failed to be. In addition the Macintosh was technically superior to its rival, the IBM PC, and was far easier for the untrained user to operate.

Was there a basic conflict between Jobs and Sculley? Was the difference ultimately cultural? In what ways?

| Jobs | Sculley |
| --- | --- |
| Visionary | Professional |
| Charismatic | Bureaucratic |

Technological    Marketing

Existential      Classical

Culturally, Jobs is an existentialist; culturally, Sculley is a manager. The question may be asked, Why could Jobs not change the culture at Apple?

As Apple became bigger, it became just another company. It had to produce a good ROI; produce new products; provide effective servicing; and operate in a very competitive market. This is the culture of big business. Jobs is an innovator out of place as the chief executive.

## GETTING BEYOND *IN SEARCH OF EXCELLENCE*

Thomas J. Peters and Robert H. Waterman, Jr., after spending a year looking at companies in the United States and studying their corporate strategies, wrote a book entitled *In Search of Excellence: Lessons from America's Best Run Companies* (1982). In this book Peters and Waterman, who had worked as management consultants, argue that these top companies—including Proctor and Gamble, McDonald's, Frit-O-Lay, IBM, Kodak, and Johnson and Johnson—focus on certain basic principles. These principles are: a preference for action over talk; genuine close customer attention; encouragement of autonomy and entrepreneurship; belief in people productivity; strong company values; simple structure and lean staff; and a certain fanaticism on a few central values. What Peters and Waterman found was the company cultures were strong but not stifling. In these excellent companies management does not allow workers to get away with slip-shod work but provides support and security for those who produce. And furthermore, the managers of these companies are average people, not Harvard MBAs, and they promote from within rather than recruit from other companies. What it amounts to in these successful companies is that they generate an excitement that a visitor can feel. For example, when IBM wanted to congratulate its sales force, it rented a stadium; as the salespeople ran onto the field their names flashed on the scoreboards in lights and their relatives stood up and cheered. These companies care about the people who work for them and manage to make those people care about the work they do.

## PUTTING CREATIVE CRAZINESS TO WORK

To get beyond *In Search of Excellence*, it is necessary to ask the rhetorical question, ''Are small firms innately superior in the art of innovation, or is it simply a technique that larger firms discard as they grow?'' In attempting to address this and other issues that surround the subject, James Brian Quinn (1985) has undertaken an examination of the innovation records of a sample of corporations both large and small. Preliminary results suggest that successful innovators have adopted common approaches to management regardless of size or culture.

The caricature of the small, lithe inventive firm has its origins in inescapable economic reality: the larger the corporation, the more visible its failure. Small corporations that fail from lack of innovation go unnoticed; large corporations face a myriad of penalties. Successful small firms tend to revolve around a highly zealous "guru," motivated by a powerful desire for achievement. Such a figure can supply the momentum necessary to overcome obstacles encountered in the early stages of the venture, while retaining flexibility and adaptability. This person is by nature not a "satisficer"; his or her eyes are fixed on personal fulfillment, however long that may take. After leaving Apple, Steven P. Jobs set up Next, which was financed by Jobs, Japan's Canon, IBM, and Ross Perot. In terms of software (Nextstep program), his firm has been a success, but not in terms of workstations. Jobs, who is known as a hardware junkie, has shown his flexibility by his ability to switch into software. These gurus, like Jobs, know how to adjust.

A majority of large corporations have unwittingly erected barriers to innovation. The inevitable gap between upper management and the factory floor as the organization grows larger, the preference for "team players" (typically the entrepreneur is just the opposite), incentive systems that encourage ephemeral strategy, and a preoccupation with rational justification all act to strangle or impede the progress of original thinking. There are some, however, that have artfully maintained their prowess for innovation. This is the group that drew Quinn's attention.

Quinn has attempted to isolate the common threads that run through the management practices of such noted innovators as Sony, Intel, Honda, and Pilkington Brothers. The most notable common factor was a corporate culture that encouraged unconventional and long-term thinking, frequently relics of the company's early years. In spite of this, successful innovators pay close attention to the marketplace and ensure that market intelligence is rapidly disseminated throughout the organization. Their organization is "flat" rather than "tall," the better to ensure that small tightly knit groups ("skunk-works") are able to function with a maximum of latitude; a common tactic is to assign several such groups a common objective and allow internal competition to be the winner. These strategies allow the organization to duplicate the culture and "feel" of a small corporation while simultaneously curtailing risk through redundancy.

### Some Advice for Big Blue

What then are the implications for other large companies? Quinn prescribes a "strategy for innovation" in the broadest terms: an emphasis on the active search for opportunity, coupling structure to strategy and a portfolio approach to planning. "Perhaps the most difficult task for top managers," he writes, "is to balance the needs of existing lines against the need of potential lines. This problem requires a portfolio strategy much more complex than the popular four box Boston Consulting Group matrix found in most strategy tests."

Rigid planning and implementation is generally eschewed by successful innovators, Quinn has found. Usually the introduction of innovation proceeds in a series of fits and starts, a process that he has christened "logical incrementalism." To innovate is by definition to venture into the unknown; its goals are therefore sketchy to begin with but clarify as the program proceeds. Multiple routes to the solution of problems can be explored and discarded with a minimum waste of effort.

Quinn is careful to note the psychological implications of incrementalism. Broadly defined goals are likely to find an equally broad base of support; the commitment that builds as a program advances and crystallizes prevents it from losing momentum. Abortive routes can be retraced without endangering employee morale.

The successful management of innovation is, therefore, the antithesis of deliberate rational planning: probabilistic and opportunistic. Control is best exercised sparingly and obliquely, to set objectives and select personnel. The idea, Quinn believes, is "chaos with guidelines."

## MANUFACTURING MANAGERS: NEW ELITE

A new elite is emerging among managers who are mainly engineers. This executive elite is using computers to transform assembly lines into extremely efficient manufacturing systems. A good example of this act of technological transformation can be seen at John Deere's new tractor assembly plant in northeast Iowa, where management set out to build one of the most advanced manufacturing systems in the world.

What Deere planned to do was to build a flexible manufacturing system that transformed the factory as we know it. They set out to develop an interlocking complex of robots and computers that would transform the factory into a really efficient system. At Deere's new Iowa plant they manufacture ten different models of tractor transmissions and five dozen configurations of tractors. When the project began, top management was not fully aware of how they could, in fact, tie computers and robots together to drive the whole thing. What they discovered was that in the economic recession of the early 1970s they were able to cope with problems more effectively than their rivals, International Harvester Company and Massey Ferguson, who both lost hundreds of millions of dollars during the same period.

This new manufacturing technology is moving us into a second industrial revolution created by computers and robots. A quick look at the new top managers of top companies reveals that there is a tremendous reemphasis on production and process engineering. And American management is only too conscious of the fact that they have been unable to cope with Japanese competition in terms of technology. What is important to keep in mind is that this new flexible factory is expensive; Deere paid nearly $2 billion for the complex it built in northeast Iowa.

It seems clear now that while the United States remains the leader in developing new factory technology, the Japanese continue to develop and apply what America invents. Flexible manufacturing, of course, represents a risk and has to be properly planned for. The object of the exercise is to build the new flexible factory that allows low volume output of custom tailored product for a profit. This new form of small batch production is appropriate to our new society with its emphasis on "small is beautiful."

In an article in the *New York Times* on December 18, 1983, entitled "The New Allure of Manufacturing" by John Holusha, it was pointed out that four companies in the United States have taken this new bold stand of developing flexible manufacturing. As we have already noted, one of these companies is John Deere of Waterloo, Iowa, which has pioneered one of the nation's most automated factories where just-in-time technology is used to cut inventory. New flexible manufacturing technology has been used by General Electric in Erie, Pennsylvania, which produces locomotive trains. What General Electric is able to do at Erie is to produce one locomotive train a day untouched by human hands, whereas it took seventy skilled mechanics sixteen days to produce the same product previously. Again this is a very expensive project for General Electric. It cost $300 million to build the plant. Another example is provided by General Motors in Kokomo, Indiana, where a high-speed manufacturing plant produces radios. GM has been able to offset high labor cost and bring back its radio operation from Singapore and in the process has created twelve hundred new jobs. A third example is the Western Electric Plant in Richmond, Virginia, where computer controlled manufacturing systems produce print circuit boards that yield productivity gains of up to 16 percent.

When you have flexibility you can produce customized products using batch production and do the whole thing quite comfortably. In these new plants product quality is an extremely important factor. Using this new product manufacturing technology it is possible to marry quality and flexibility. Many examples of this new technology can be seen in General Motors plants. For example, in the General Motors plant in Pontiac, Michigan, 85 percent of the welding is done by automatic machines, which allows General Motors enough flexibility to handle Cadillacs, Buicks, and Oldsmobiles fitted with GM's "C" body.

The question being raised is, Why are companies not switching over faster to this new flexible manufacturing technology. One major explanation is that top decision making in many companies is dominated by managers with a financial, legal, or marketing background. What it amounts to is that "technology people" have been denied access to top management for too long. And now senior management is trying to make greater use of people who are experienced in manufacturing management. All this has taken place while the technological gap closed between the United States and Japan. Now we can look forward to a situation where new manufacturing technology will begin to appear in American factories on a larger scale.

At places like the Harvard Business School a special effort has been made to develop courses and do research in manufacturing management. One of the leading lights in this field is Professor William Abernathy, who has argued that the industrial revolution has gone through five distinct stages. The first phase in the first half or three quarters of the nineteenth century was the development of factories mainly concerned with the manufacture of firearms, clocks and watches, and so on. The second phase began in the last quarter of the nineteenth century when Isaac N. Singer began to produce different types of sewing machines. The third phase was brought in by Samuel Colt who decided that the competitive edge could be won by constantly upgrading existing products. Thus Colt was able to present the world with a new type of revolver from time to time. The fourth phase of manufacturing technology, which began at the turn of the century, was the development of manufactured bicycles and automobiles where the greatest reliance was placed on "buying in" most of the parts. Henry Ford, who developed assemblyline production, was a master of this field. The fifth phase emerged with the application of automation to assemblyline production. But what Abernathy and his colleagues at Harvard argue in their book *Industrial Renaissance* (1984) is that America is in the sixth stage, which is based on flexible manufacturing. This phase, which got into its stride in the 1980s, depends on the special combination of computers and robots to break down the old barriers among marketing, design, and production—all to produce innovative products and profits.

As George Bernard Shaw once said, a reasonable man adapts himself to society; the unreasonable man tries to change society; therefore all progress depends on the unreasonable people. North Americans can often be extremely unreasonable, but this unreasonableness can be the basis of an entrepreneurial society.

# 12

# Executive Pay and Performance

## LOUISE KELLY

How much should a company's top executives be paid? In Plato's view, no one should earn more than five times the pay of the lowest-paid workers in a community. In the United States, Roberto C. Goizueta, chief executive officer of the Coca-Cola Co., was paid $86 million in 1991—including a deferred stock option worth $82 million—which works out to $41,346 per hour. This is in a country where the average hourly wage is $10.56. Such disparities have moved a lot of people to wonder what is going on here.

Among the rites of spring each year, the annual general meeting season inevitably elicits a certain amount of CEO pay bashing. While the content of the attacks changes little from year to year, the intensity seems to be increasing. Shareholders have not only become more vocal, but they are also willing to follow through with suits against management and boards they believe are not acting in their own best interests. The headlines express our collective dismay about the widening gap between senior executive pay and lower and middle management compensation. What many wonder, therefore, is whether the 1990s will be a decade of marked change in senior executive compensation.

The headlines notwithstanding, is the question of executive pay merely a misleading MacGuffin? In the world of Alfred Hitchcock, the MacGuffin is the device, meaningless in itself, that sets the plot rolling. What we are really concerned with is the question of whether our present corporate governance structure is producing industries that are internationally competitive in the long run. "The only way for capitalism to work is for the owners to take responsibility," declares Lester Thurow, dean of the Massachusetts Institute of Technology's Sloane School of Management. In short, Thurow is arguing for big institutional investors becoming more involved in running the companies whose shares they hold. Recent initiatives by big public pension funds indicate a desire to move in that direction. Investors like the California Public Employees Retirement System, or Calpers, should be sitting on the board, not having occasional meetings with CEOs, according to Thurow. The reforms that Calpers and other big funds are advocating, from executive pay to putting more outsiders in positions of power, are an attempt to send a message to companies. As Bowman, chief investment officer of Calpers puts it: "We can't bail out easily, so the only way we can improve our performance is to prod corporate America into better performance—taking a long-term view and managing in the interests of the shareholders. We have found that poor corporate performance is indicative of a lack of openness in corporate governance." What the hue and cry over excessive pay is really reflecting is a general rethinking of how strategic choices are made and implemented—a calling into question of the very process of corporate governance.

## PAY AND CHIEF EXECUTIVES

Increasing concern has been shown in the United States about the pay of chief executives, particularly since the compensation system is not widely seen as structured properly for the best performance of managers. For example, in 1990 Steven Ross, the chief executive of Time Warner, made between $39 million and $78 million, depending on how his pay is calculated, while Stephen Watts, chairman of United Airlines, made more than $18 million and John Sculley of Apple made $16.7 million. Although these figures are not typical, the average pay in 1990 of the American chief executive was $1.4 million, which includes salaries, bonuses, and special share deals.

What is of particular concern is the gap between chief executive pay and those of shop floor operators. A study by Graef Crystal, a professor at the University of California at Berkeley, found that 1973–75 chief executives (from randomly selected US companies) had cash earnings twenty-nine times that of the average US worker. By 1987–89 this had grown to fifty-three times. When these figures are compared with those of Japanese chief executives, it is found that they earn just seventeen times their average worker's pay. In the United Kingdom a multiple of thirty-three to thirty-five is common. Nevertheless, Michael Jensen of the Harvard Business School points out in real terms that the pay of chief executives is only now catching up to the level of fifty years ago.

Martin Dickson, in the *Financial Times* (1991) in an article entitled "New Soft Options for Oliver Twist" pointed out "that it is more essential for a stronger, more independent board of directors" to monitor CEO pay. As for the best compensation method, while there are as many theories as experts, there is considerable common ground. First, there is general agreement that it is desirable for executives to own a large stake in the business. Some consultants suggest that companies should set a target for share ownership, say, ten times the CEO's base salary. Second, incentive schemes involving little or no risk should be scrapped. Some radicals say scrap all incentives on the grounds that they destroy teamwork. Third, in setting performance targets, boards should use measures that would reflect the returns received by shareholders since managers are supposed to be working for the good of companies' owners.

## CEO COMPENSATION

The problem with the pay of CEOs does not lie in its amount; excessive pay is not the problem. The real issue is how they are paid. Michael C. Jensen and Kevin J. Murphy made a study of 2,505 CEOs in 1,400 companies from 1974 through 1988 with reference to their pay, bonuses, stock options, and stock ownership. In their report, "CEO Compensation: It's Not How Much You Pay, But How" (1990), they point out that top executives are not receiving record pay or bonuses, and that while salaries and bonuses have increased, they are, as mentioned previously, only now catching up with what they were fifty years ago. And surprise, surprise: salaries do not reflect changes in performance.

Jensen and Murphy recommend that some combination of three basic policies will create the right monetary incentives for CEOs to maximize the value of their companies.

1. Boards can require that CEOs become substantial owners of company stock.
2. Salaries, bonuses, and stock options can be structured so as to provide big rewards for superior performance and big penalties for poor performance.
3. The threat of dismissal for poor performance can be made real.

The argument that CEOs should own substantial amounts of company stock is not borne out by the facts. As stated in the article:

As a percentage of total corporate value, CEO share ownership has never been very high. The median CEO of one of the nation's 250 largest public companies owns shares worth just over $2.4 million—again, less than 0.07% of the company's market value. Also, 9 out of 10 CEOs own less than 1% of their company's stock, while fewer than 1 in 20 owns more than 5% of the company's outstanding shares.

Very large companies like IBM, GM, or GE will always be unable to grant their CEOs a meaningful share of equity.

And further, poor performance is difficult to punish. For example, "Baseball managers often get fired after one losing season. CEOs stay on the job despite years of underperformance" (Jensen and Murphy, 1990).

In terms of pay for performance,

The results are striking. Measured in 1988 constant dollars, CEOs in top quartile public companies earned an average salary and bonus of $882,000 in the 1930s—more than the 1982 through 1988 average of $843,000 and significantly more than the 1974 through 1981 average of $642,000. Over this same time period, there has been a tripling (after inflation) of the market value of top quartile companies—from $1.7 billion in the 1930s to $5.9 billion in 1982 through 1988. Coupled with the decline in salaries, the ratio of CEO pay to total company value has fallen significantly—from 0.11% in the 1930s to 0.03% in the 1980s.

And to this question, "Are current levels of CEO compensation high enough to attract the best and the brightest?" Probably not.

In short, as the authors argue, money isn't everything but the incentives are pointing CEOs in the wrong direction.

## THE COMPENSATION PROCESS

To get some insight into the executive pay/performance rubric, let us consider the sequence of events that leads to the compensation decision. If we were to write a play depicting the corporate governance structure that has resulted in the present system of excessive pay of top executives in North America, it would be called: "The Rubber Stamp Board and the Iron-fisted Chief Executive." How shall we describe the quaint social ritual that is the meeting of the compensation committee of the board of directors? First, the members of the corporate board would fly in the night before, dine with their old friend, the chief executive, sharing after-dinner brandy and camaraderie. Each director would receive a slender binder of briefing papers that get only a cursory read before the formality of the next morning's board meeting. Typically, the compensation committee is the least desired assignment, due perhaps to a lingering association of the supernumerary with all personnel functions (the most sought after position being in the executive committee that concerns itself with strategic issues). The result is that often the more junior members sit on the compensation committee, the Chief Executive calls the tune, and the board hums along. So we have the anomalous situation of the piper, rather than he who pays the piper, calling the tune.

## CULTURAL PREFERENCES AND DISTRIBUTIVE PRINCIPLES

However, it is important to note that this compensation ritual is played out within the larger context of a set of social relations and norms of conduct. Allocation principles are the rules that members of social units have regarding distributive behavior. They are the standards against which the distribution of rewards and resources, such as pay, promotion, and informal favors, are evaluated as fair and just. Research has indicated that there are a large number of distributive principles that vary as a function of social norms. The most widely followed distributive principles are based on equity, equality, and needs. Equity invokes the principle of proportionality between one's input and output among comparable cohorts. Equality is the rule of equal share for every member. The needs principle allows for allocation not according to performance but as a function of need.

In our Western society dominated by corporate capitalism, status, not contribution, has traditionally been the basis for the numbers on employees' paychecks. As Rosabeth Moss Kanter points out (1987), traditionally each job in a company comes with a pay level that stays about the same regardless of how well the job is performed or what the real organizational value of that performance is. The determinants of the pay scale include characteristics such as decision making responsibility, importance to the organization, and number of subordinates. The merit component is usually negligible. As a result, often the only way to increase one's pay is to change employers or get promoted. So it can be argued that the market forces are not effectively linking compensation to contribution; all the market achieves is a tendency toward making people with similar experience and education be worth about the same. According to the circular logic of the market, people are worth what they are paid in the job market, but what people cost in the market is a function of what they are worth. The market is in effect fulfilling its macroeconomic function of allocating labor, but failing to meet the microeconomic productivity challenge of matching contribution and compensation.

## THE BEGINNING OF A NEW CORPORATE GOVERNANCE PROCESS

The current economic, social, and organizational climate has resulted in a significant trend toward loosening the arbitrary relationship between job assignment and pay level. Instead, the principles of equity, cost, productivity, and the rewards of entrepreneurship are becoming the most important determinants of worth and remuneration. This is the theory behind such new approaches to compensation as profit sharing. Currently, in the United States about a half million companies have some form of profit sharing. In private enterprises other than those categorized as small businesses, government statistics indicate that as of 1983, 19 percent of all production employees, 27 percent of all technical and clerical employees, and 23 percent of all professional and administrative employees were covered by profit-sharing agreements (Kanter, 1990). Gain sharing takes the profit-sharing principle one step further by rewarding specific groups of employees differentially according to their assessed contributions to corporate performance. A well-known example of gain sharing is the Scanlon Plan, which distributes 75 percent of all gains to employees and 25 percent to the company. One criticism of the alternative of bonuses linked to fair indicators of performance is that this type of compensation is more likely to benefit top executives than employees. The general trend, however, is moving in the direction of more varied individual compensation based on people's own efforts, and the top management team will not be exempt from this principle.

The forces of change are shaking up the entire corporate governance process. In the 1992 proxy season, investors, like fed-up voters, are raring to send a message. Where corporate performance is poor, pay excessive, or management unresponsive, investors are acting for change. Changing corporate leadership or dislodging corporate directors is a tricky process. Shareholders are generally offered only one slate of candidates, and they only vote by withholding votes from would-be board members.

The idea of shareholder activism has gained appeal after the executive-pay flap spilled onto the front pages in January 1992. 1992 is seen as a breakthrough year on the corporate governance front, radicalizing a lot of shareholders. "This season marks the beginning of a new governance process," declares John Pound, an economist at Harvard University's John F. Kennedy School of Government. This can be viewed as the seeds of what will happen in the post-takeover era.

The $68 billion California Public Employees' Retirement System (Calpers) is withholding votes from directors at IBM and Sears, among others. Corporate compensation, especially a focus on pay structure, disclosure, and accountability is almost always on the agenda. Stock option and bonus plans are getting careful scrutiny, especially at companies that reduced cash compensation but made up the difference—or more—with generous stock plans. Shareholders are voting not only against the plans but also against the boards that approved the plans.

Many proxy resolutions have resulted in significant corporate change. A new resolution filed by shareholders asks Sears to elect a chairman separate from the chief executive. Last March General Motors' directors staged a boardroom coup. What happened at General Motors was a direct result of proxy motions put in place in previous years. Examples of these motions include those dealing with confidential voting and a majority of independent directors.

Chairman of General Motors, Roger C. Stempel, was ousted by this proxy governance initiative. In April 1992 at a GM board meeting, Stempel, only two years on the job, was stripped of the chairmanship of the powerful executive committee of the board and told to replace two underperforming top executives, including the president and chief executive officer Lloyd Reuss. John F. (Jack) Smith took over from Reuss, and so Smith is the effective boss of the giant automaker. Nothing like this has ever happened in the boardroom of General Motors before. But few corporations have performed as badly as General Motors in the last five years. GM lost $4.5 billion the United States in 1991, most of it in its US operations, which employs 370,000.

Although a coup in a large company seems dramatic, this is the way the system is supposed to work. Boards of directors are supposed to be watchdogs for shareholders between annual meetings. In a sense, they are put in place to keep the company's managers in line. The system breaks down when, as is often the case, boards of directors of publicly traded companies become the reserved territory of management, because many of the managers sit on the boards themselves. And in many instances, management chooses the outside directors as well, effectively cementing their control of the directors.

## THE CANADIAN EXAMPLE

Attending the annual meetings of three Canadian banks in one week revealed some insights into the Canadian corporate governance process. In all three cases—the Bank of Montreal, The Royal Bank of Canada, and the Laurentian Bank—there were positive assessments of corporate performance. However, the issue of disclosure of the salaries of their senior executives was not dealt with. It is a controversial issue because Canada is a much more conservative, less open society than the United States when it comes to public disclosure. It was only a decade ago that Parliament passed an access-to-information law, long after the Americans had adopted one. Although the issue is hotly debated in the United States, it does not seem to raise as much passion in Canada. This is despite a report from the University of Ontario that pushed for more public debate on the issue. The research by Arthur Earle (1990), a former corporate executive, concluded that there was little link between chief executive cash compensation and corporate profitability. Furthermore, Earle criticizes the way compensation (salary plus bonuses or share options) is determined. Senior executives go to great lengths to ensure that the salaries of their employees are determined by objective standards. But typically, as in the United States, when it comes to their own compensation, they control the board committee that sets it. There is recent public debate on proposed legislation to reverse the requirements of compensation disclosure. It seems that once again American corporate governance reforms are more radical and wide-ranging.

Disclosure laws for Canadian companies listed on our stock exchanges are particularly loose compared with disclosure laws in the United States. As a result, it is only the Canadian companies that are interlisted on the American stock exchanges that disclose top executive compensation with any degree of clarity and detail. For the governance system to work, it is clear that shareholders need better, more detailed information from senior management. There is a sense that the input of outside directors on board decisions will contribute to the long run competitive advantage of the western industrial democracies.

The industrial structure of Canada does not lend itself easily to the type of shareholder activism that is occurring in the United States. Corporate Canada, if anything, is a vast web of interlocking companies owned by a handful of wealthy families—the Bronfmans, Reichmanns, and Belz-bergs, for example. Typically, one family group takes stakes in the operations of another, and, as a result, puzzling out who owns what and from where profits and losses do or don't flow is akin to peeling away the layers of the proverbial onion. There seems to be a gentlemen's agreement behind the latest pay-disclosure proposal by the Ontario Securities Commission that top bosses have the right to keep their salaries hidden from the public's prying eyes.

The scheme, which would exempt Canadian companies from US disclosure laws, purports to be a sensible (a very Canadian concept) compromise between the rights of the investors in the shares of Canadian publicly traded companies to know whether the top brass is paying itself too handsomely and the general right to privacy of all Canadians. In the United States, where individual privacy as a rule is rated rather lower than in Canada, companies trading on Wall Street have been required to disclose the individual earnings of their five highest-paid executives. Interestingly enough, this legislation has had no noticeable impact on the size of those executives' annual pay. The pay of top executives of US companies is, in general, much higher than in Canada where individual salaries are not necessarily disclosed, unless the company is interlisted on the NYSE.

## STRATEGY AND PAY-PERFORMANCE LINK

The question of the methods of assessing the worth and contribution of the top management team is a telling one for the student of strategy. For therein lies a real key to understanding how strategy is formulated, implemented, and the resulting performance tallied. A common per-ception is that executives are making many millions of dollars a year even when stock prices go down, dividends are cut, and book value is reduced. The purpose of this chapter is to assess the basic pay-performance relationship at the policy level, with a view to developing a model of the strategy-performance loop.

## WHO'S IN CHARGE HERE?

To grasp the implications of the pay-performance link with strategy information, it is necessary to take a step back and frame the question in terms of corporate governance theory. The essence of the problem of corporate governance (Blair, 1991) is to devise systems of finance and control that provide flexibility and financial strength, while at the same time ensuring that corporate management is encouraged to use the company's resources and is accountable for its performance. The ultimate goal of corporate governance should be the creation of a healthy economy through the development of business enterprises that operate for the long term and compete successfully in the world economy. Perhaps the most essential point of corporate governance is that it serves as a mechanism for assuring long-term performance. From this perspective, performance is the only meaningful measurement of corporate governance.

Corporate governance issues are often viewed in terms of that game called organizational power. To understand this dynamic we must know specifically who are the players, what are the means or systems of influence they use to gain power and what are the goals and goal systems that result from their efforts (Mintzberg, 1983). A useful paradigm to get at the workings of corporate governance is that proposed by Cyert and March (1963). They developed a theory of the firm that is an attempt to reconcile the economic and behavioral theory of management. They view the firm as a coalition of individuals bargaining among themselves to determine the organization's goals. The firm is no longer tidily monolithic but is more like a multiple-goal coalition with shifting participants, shifting needs, and shifting power within the coalitions.

We can see the dynamics of these shifting coalitions in the current debate on executive compensation. The financial excesses of the corporate takeovers of the 1980s have resulted in a shift in the power structure of corporate governance away from traditional corporate management to the financial markets (Blair, 1991). Shareholders, and particularly institutional investors, have gained considerable economic and political power in relation to corporate management. A growing number of institutional investors are banding together to increase their involvement in corporate operations. During the 1991 proxy season, institutional investors and organized shareholder groups sponsored 153 corporate governance proposals mainly urging companies to drop antitakeover defenses, overhaul executive compensation packages, and guarantee that boards will consist of a majority of independent directors. The popular consensus is that boards must compensate the CEO and management with plans that link compensation to shareholders' objectives. To achieve this goal much more attention must be paid to evaluating board processes and performance. Of particular concern is that the current corporate governance structure minimizes communication amongst management, the directors, and the shareholders. One proposition is that regulatory bodies, such as the Securities and Exchange Commission in the United States, should stiffen compensation disclosure requirements and open the proxy voting processes to allow more direct input from shareholders on management compensation.

In keeping with Cyert and March's view of the coalition, it would be useful at this point to determine who the players are in this particular power game. Rechner and Dalton (1991) conducted a longitudinal analysis of the choices regarding board leadership structure for 141 US corporations over the period 1978–83. They argue that firms opting for independent leadership outperformed those firms relying on CEO duality (allowing the CEO to serve as chairperson of the board of directors). A recent article in *Fortune* (Colvin, 1992) maintains that most CEOs appoint their own directors, presenting only their nominees to the shareholders for a vote and that, in fact, 63 percent of public US companies rely on CEO duality.

There is a growing public consensus that the irrationality of American and Canadian executive compensation is having an insidious effect on our national competitiveness. Meredith (1991) concludes from a meta-analysis of the literature on compensation that CEOs are overpaid, there is little link between CEO pay and company performance, and stock incentives do not work. Jensen and Murphy (1990) conducted an analysis of performance pay and top management incentives for over two thousand CEOs in three samples spanning fifty years. The results indicated that CEO wealth changes $3.25 for every $1 change in shareholder wealth. They argue that the reason stock incentives do not work is that most CEOs hold trivial fractions of their company's stocks, the median ownership of CEOs of large firms is 0.14 percent.

Such data, in our view, is not particularly revealing of the process of executive compensation and how this dynamic can increase our understanding of the strategy formation dynamic seen from the context of corporate governance issues. A recent article in the *Administrative Science Quarterly* (1989) by H. L. Tosi puts forth an agency theory model to explain the decoupling of CEO pay and performance. They analyze the monitoring and incentive alignment of CEO compensation as well as influence patterns of various actors on CEO pay as a function of ownership distribution within the firm. They conclude that the level of monitoring and incentive-alignment was greater in owner-controlled firms than in management-controlled firms. In owner-controlled firms, there was more influence over CEO pay by major stockholders and boards of directors. However, they identify a gap in the literature, and point out that a behavioral approach to explaining the decoupling of pay and performance can offer new insights into the process used to determine CEO pay. Jay Lorsch in a recent debate in the *Harvard Business Review* in 1991 argued that the evaluation of the CEO's performance by the outside members of the board will be constructive only if there is a mechanism for communicating the results back to the CEO. The theme that is emerging is that the pay-performance conundrum cannot be understood strictly in quantitative terms, but must be viewed holistically in context as a communication and behavioral process.

## EXECUTIVE STOCK OWNERSHIP; DOES IT IMPROVE SHAREHOLDER RETURN?

The issue is whether there is a positive relationship between shareholder return and the degree of executive ownership in large public companies. Is there an incentive effect of executive stock ownership as well as option plans that impacts positively on the long-run average shareholder return?

Stock options first came to executive compensation in the United States in the 1950s, when Congress passed legislation granting them preferred tax treatment. The rationale behind stock options was that companies should tie their executive pay to the key determinant of shareholders' wealth: the market price of the stock. The question is whether the market price of the company's stock is the appropriate measure of executive performance. As J. P. Morgan pointed out at the turn of the century, stock prices will rise and fall. The volatility of the stock market, especially after the 1970s brought to an end the longest sustained bull market, inspired companies to cast about for alternative forms of executive compensation.

## REFORMING THE SYSTEM

There is a growing consensus that there are some major problems in the realm of executive compensation. North American senior executives are paid so far in excess of their workers as to raise fundamental questions concerning equity, and in some minds decency. A further source of concern is that the gap is growing, not shrinking. The gap is also growing between the pay of North American senior executives and their counterparts in other major industrialized countries. Chief executives at large US companies make 160 times an average worker's pay, while Japanese executives make only twenty times that country's average.

In the Canadian case, legislation has been tabled that would further loosen the executive compensation requirements. In the United States senior executives are insulating themselves effectively from pay risk. In many compensation packages, there exists almost no financial scenario that would minimize the CEO's pay package, while there are an infinite number of scenarios that lead to maximum pay-out.

What are the options for reforming the system? One possible solution is to endorse government regulation of senior executive pay packages. Although this option has begun to be explored in the United States, it does not seem to be in keeping with the current economic zeitgeist that favors free market forces. John Kenneth Galbraith argues in his most recent book, *The Culture of Contentment* (1992), for a return to the mixed economy, with a strong role for government in supporting a vibrant economy; but his is a lone voice of the socialist iconoclast. As Mikhail Gorbachev can now attest, there seems to be no adequate substitute for the free market, where prices are set by the forces of demand and supply.

How can measures be put into place that will strengthen the ability of the market forces to regulate executive compensation and bring remuneration in line with the goal of long-term competitiveness. In order to strengthen the operation of the market forces within the firm, it is essential that the compensation committee of the company's board of directors be structured as a true countervailing force (Cyert and March, 1963). Typically the top management team has ample resources on their side of the table when it comes to negotiating their pay package. Principal among these resources is an outside compensation consultant, as well as an in-house director of compensation. Both of these consultants can be perceived as having a conflict of interest, since they work for the company and can be summarily fired by the top management team. One option to strengthen the objectivity and authority of the compensation committee is to engage their own compensation consultant.

A guiding principle underlying the reports of these consultants should be to demonstrate the degree of sensitivity of the pay package of the CEO and other senior executives to both short- and long-term accounting and stock performance. Sensitivity analysis of these types should be undertaken by the compensation committee to ascertain to what extent a compensation plan incorporates risk. Examples of the type of "heads I win, tails you lose" executive compensation packages include restricted stock plans and tandem grants of restricted stock and stock options.

An annual written analysis of the pay of the company's top management team would be more meaningful if it included a comparison of the top management team's pay with the pay of the ordinary workers in the company, as well as with the pay of the top management teams of major companies in such key countries as Japan, Germany, France, and the United Kingdom.

Graef Crystal, in *In Search of Excess* (1991), advises that the name of the compensation consultant should be required to be divulged in the company's proxy statement each year. He takes this idea further by advocating that there be a required statement if the committee fires the consultant, indicating the reason for this action. This is similar to the protection that is afforded a company's auditors. The idea invokes the principles of Cyert and March's theory of the firm that views large complex organizations as a series of coalitions of individuals bargaining among themselves to arrive at organizational goals. The existence of shared power bases and multiple authorities and voices within an organization means that goal formation becomes a power game in which many coalitions vie for possible payoffs. The implications of Crystal's suggestions are to enact a redistribution of power in the executive compensation process to allow for a countervailing coalition representing objective outside forces to assess the payoff of the top management team.

## THE ARGUMENTS FOR AND AGAINST SHAREHOLDER DIRECT MANAGEMENT

Those who are firm believers in free market economics will argue that no limit should be placed on how much an executive can earn in salary, stock options, and perks. The responsibility for deciding such matters, they argue, belongs to the boards of directors of corporations. They reason that the majority of stockholders do not have the time, the interest, or the information needed to become involved in trying to micromanage such corporate decisions. The appropriate medium for the shareholders to make their views known to the members of the board of directors is by voting in new directors, or they can manifest their displeasure by voting with their feet, that is, they can sell their stock in the company.

The argument is that in the modern competitive worldwide economy, boards of directors need the flexibility to attract the best management that companies can afford. So, in effect, they need to be given free reign to pay at the margin, just enough and no more, to attract the required talent and to provide incentives for performance. The fact that a majority of nations all over the world is moving away from centrally planned economies to the greater freedom of the market system reinforces this point of view. The basic tenet of this argument is that appropriate levels of salaries, along with the correct level for prices, wages, and profits, are best determined by the market.

The countervailing view argues that the market is not operating efficiently with executive compensation. If executive compensation was actually set by market forces, top managers' pay would be related to their companies' performance. In fact, several studies have found little relationship between executive pay and performance. The compensation mechanism is flawed because pay levels are set by corporate boards of directors filled with company insiders and the chief executive's friends. Furthermore, if the performance-related stock options do not increase in value because the stock price has not increased, many boards are only too willing to replace those worthless options with new valuable ones. So instead of an incentive to perform, executives get a guaranteed payoff. Meanwhile, nothing protects the shareholder from a fall in the stock price.

Finally, the option of divesting as a means of registering stockholder dissatisfaction with executive pay or performance must be examined more closely. Large stockholders like the New York City pension funds, with $44.5 billion in assets, take a long-term approach to investing. Jumping in and out of stocks based on short-term results is bad for the pension funds, for the companies, and for the strength of the economy as a whole. The goal has to be for shareholders to build long-term partnerships with managers and to provide the capital that is needed to build their businesses. Although no one is arguing that shareholders do not need to be involved in the day-to-day operations of the company, shareholders do need the assurance that the compensation system rewards managers when they do well and holds them accountable when they do not deliver. The idea is that when strong boards full of independent directors set executive compensation based on performance, only then will it be possible for market forces to start influencing top managers' pay.

## EXECUTIVE PAY: SOME GENERAL CONCLUSIONS

Companies have long been concerned with one fundamental fairness issue—the relative compensation of employees in general. Now, however, they face two new issues that are complex and will prove difficult to resolve. The first, evident in the debate over shareholder and manager-controlled firms, sets up what shareholders receive against what managers receive for their efforts. The second, evident in the debate over the independence of the boards of directors, is how groups managing the organization fare in relation to each other. At the very least, these issues call for better measurement systems or new principles on which the various constituencies can agree. If executive pay practices continue to move toward contribution as the basis for earnings, as it seems it will, the change will unleash a set of forces that could transform corporate governance relationships as we know them now. If the gap between the pay levels of the top management team and the rest of the organization diminishes—this is called pay compression—the resultant power shifts will have implications for the present hierarchy and corporate governance process. What is known is that executives need to think strategically about the organizational implications of every change in compensation practices.

# Part III

---

## Policy, the New Executive, and a Critique

# 13

Leadership Style at the
Policy Level

## INTRODUCTION

Our corporate prima donnas, are they in for a lifetime? In other words can organizations in the 80s afford to have CEOs running the show for fifteen or twenty years—in different seasons? Can our organizations survive with the values and philosophies of the entrepreneur in maturity, decline, or turnaround? Can the typical executive in maturity with his or her conservative view turn his or her organization around? In an attempt to answer these questions let us examine the state of leadership research, and that of corporate strategy as a choice of top management.

It goes without saying almost that there is disagreement in the academic community as to the state of leadership research, principally because there are anomalies which the present paradigm does not address. For T. S. Kuhn, philosopher of science, anomalies inexplicable by the current paradigm lead to crisis, to a proliferation of competing articulations, explicit discontent, debate over fundamentals, and ultimately that form of scientific revolution we describe as paradigm shift. It is on the verge of this state that research in leadership finds itself today. This research focuses on a required paradigm shift and investigates the relation between executive personality and values on the one hand, as revealed in videos of actual executive behavior, and organization's strategy or life cycle stages on the other hand.

Special thanks to A. B. Ibrahim for his comments and contribution to this chapter.

## GENERALLY ACCEPTED PARADIGM WHICH DOES NOT SEEM TO WORK

Many studies have been undertaken to investigate the personality of the leader. For example, it has been reported that the leader tends to have some of the following characteristics: analytical, intelligent, keen, aggressive, enthusiastic, dominant, extroverted and persuasive.

Other studies analyzed the leader's behavior according to two dimensions, initiating structure and consideration.

Fiedler's empirical works postulate three important dimensions of the total situation which structure that leader's role: leader-member relations, task structure, and position power.

Finally, House (1971) in his path-goal theory identified four kinds of leadership behavior: directive, supportive, participative, and achievement oriented.

As scholars, most leadership researchers are thoroughly familiar with the classical scientific research model as stated by Kaplan and Kuhn. In brief, observation is followed by theory, theory is followed by applied research, modified with a view toward application of valid behavioral science knowledge. By any objective assessment, leadership theories have failed to produce generally accepted, practically useful, and widely applied scientific knowledge. Thus, we are in a position of having a generally accepted paradigm, which does not seem to work. Why?

The major criticism of leadership theories from executives is that they are essentially academic, and no significant effort has been made to apply the finding to actual management operation as a means of improving corporate performance.

## A PARADIGM SHIFT

A different approach to organizational leadership seems to be emerging now in the area of business policy that focuses on the fit and match between the executive on one hand and organizational strategy or life cycle stages on the other hand (Khandwalla, Ansoff, Adizes, Wissema et al., and Miller, 1977). This marriage of organization behavior and policy represents a paradigm shift in leadership research. However it must be noted that little empirical research has been reported.

To understand the link or fit between organization strategy and leadership let us examine now the research on strategy.

## CORPORATE STRATEGY: A CHOICE OF TOP MANAGEMENT

There are many factors which shape the formulation of strategy or influence the decision maker. Environmental factors, including economic trends, industry structure, competition, and so on, are very important in deciding what course of action the organization should pursue. The internal capability of the firm, ''corporate resources,'' is another aspect in shaping strategic decision; factors such as the financial position of the firm and the strengths and weaknesses in different functional areas have to be considered. In essence, a situational audit of the internal and external capability of the organization is an essential part of the strategic decision.

However, these factors though important are just ingredients in the decision making process. Executives in charge of corporate destinies do not look only at these factors, they in most cases are heavily influenced by what they personally want to achieve. In other words strategic decision is a choice of top management. For example, Chandler defines strategy as the determination of the basic long-term goals of an organization, while Ansoff defines it as a rule for making decisions. Hofer and Schendel define strategy as a pattern of objectives, purposes or goals defining what business we are in or should be. Mintzberg defines strategy as a pattern in streams of organizational decisions or ''actions.''

In effect, strategy is a decision, a clinical decision, a choice made by a leader, and like any decision-making process is filtered by our perception, personalities, motivation and expectations. This relationship could be described by the following proposed model (see Figure 13.1). Accordingly, one way to study strategy is to study the decision maker, the strategist, his personality, values and motivation. In other words his leadership style.

## STRATEGY-LEADER FIT

The proposed paradigm shift in leadership/strategy research is not without support. Research by Wissema, Vander Pol and Messer link

**Figure 13.1**
**A Proposed Strategy Formulation Model**

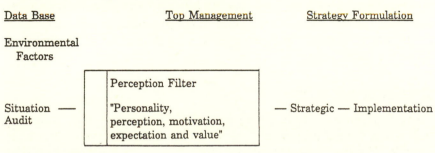

| Data Base | Top Management | Strategy Formulation |
| --- | --- | --- |

Environmental
   Factors

Situation — [ Perception Filter / ''Personality, perception, motivation, expectation and value'' ] — Strategic — Implementation
Audit

Corporate Resources

specific strategy and a certain style or personality of the leader. In fact their typology is based on the idea that certain behavioral characteristics are necessary for different strategic directions. Wissema et al. reported six strategic directions and the type of leader or manager to match each strategy.

For Wissema et al., if the strategic direction is explosive growth, then the best type of manager to fit such a strategy would be a "pioneer" type of strategist in their own terms. The "pioneer" type manager has certain personality characteristics: he is very flexible, very creative, divergent, very extroverted, hyperactive, restless, dare-devil, intuitive and irrational. These characteristics are completely different under a "contracting" type of strategy. The managerial style here is what the researchers termed "insistent diplomat" who is flexible, with fixed objective, considerate, broad, relativistic, many-sided.

Miller, Kets de Vries, and Toulouse studied thirty-three organizations in the Montreal area and reported similar findings. Entrepreneurial type executives were found to have different distinct personalities (i.e., more innovative and creative).

Khandwalla, based on a study of different Canadian firms, reported similar findings to those of Wissema et al. Effectiveness of different managerial styles under different environments was investigated. The researchers reported seven managerial styles each with behavioral dimensions to fit a certain type of environment.

Miles and Snow explored the need for congruence or fit between top management, environment and their four different strategic directions: defender, prospector, analyzer, and reactor.

Ansoff suggested that "general management capability" should be modified to match different stages in the organization life cycle. Ansoff discussed three different components to achieve management capability: "culture," "competence," and "capacity," and described different attributes and skills required for each component.

Adizes reported that different skills are needed in different stages of the organization life cycle. The authors of this research strongly believe that the organization life cycle greatly influences organization strategic direction. Certainly the infancy stage of the organization life cycle needs a different personality and managerial style from that of the death or declining stage.

## RESEARCH METHOD

The Ibrahim and Kelly (1986) study tracks strategy and leadership succession over a period of 15 years in four large firms in Montreal, Canada. The first organization is a large firm in the food retail and self services department stores; the second firm is a large conglomerate which offers a broad range of services and products in the following categories: financial services, pulp, paper and packaging; the third is a large corporation which, directly and through subsidiaries, carries on transportation and related operations, consisting of rail, telecommunication, airlines, and hotels; and the fourth organization is engaged in the motor transport business, real estate and vehicle rental and leasing.

Leadership succession and strategic directions in each organization were carefully identified. Twelve CEOs, presidents, and SBU managers were studied.

The research study is based on interviews, study of documents, as well as videotapes. Dramatic new development in video technology has allowed management researchers the opportunity to study executives more effectively.

The methodology utilized to identify the corporate strategic direction was a form of direct research developed at McGill University and can be summarized as follows: (1) listing key decisions or actions made by each organization over a period of time under study; (2) inference of the strategic direction from the previous listing; (3) final periods of change are thoroughly analyzed. In addition to the McGill approach, sixty executives and MBA students were shown the videotapes and other related documents and were asked to answer a questionnaire concerning leadership styles of different CEOs, presidents, and SBU managers in the four organizations under study.

## STUDY FINDINGS

Although there were obvious dissimilarities in strategy and executive styles adopted by these four organizations, a sufficient number of commonalities and themes appear with reasonable consistency to facilitate development of a model of strategy/leader fit. Four distinct executive styles were identified that match different strategic directions. The following is a description based on the research findings.

1. *The Entrepreneur*. This proposed style fits executives managing organizations that have been described in the strategy literature as "stars" (Boston Consulting Group); "explosive growth" and "expansion"; "prospectors" or under the general term "growth strategy," be it expansion, mergers, and/or acquisitions. The entrepreneur can be described as very innovative, creative, intuitive, flexible, extroverted, optimistic, motivated, excitable, dominant, and a risk-taker. The entrepreneur fits organizations in the developing and aggressive-growth stages.

2. *The Professional*. This proposed style fits executives managing organizations that have been described in the strategy literature as "cash cows"; "continued growth"; "defenders"; and strategic directions such as holding, or harvesting (General Electric). The professional can be

described as a team player, bureaucratic, conformist, systematic, stable, calm, cautious, mature, friendly, and conservative. The professional is slow to change and to meet increases in threat. The professional fits organizations in the maturity stage of the organizational life cycle with a stable domain.

3. *The Caretaker*. This proposed style fits executives managing organizations that have been described in the strategy literature as "dogs," "contraction strategy" and generally "retrenchment strategy," be it divesting, holding, liquidating or harvesting. The caretaker can be described as strong, dominant, tolerant, calculative, selfish, specialized, hard-nosed, budget efficient, priority-oriented, legalistic, introverted, dogmatic, and a "status quo" person. The caretaker fits organizations in the declining stage (retrenchment) where cash flow is the name of the game.

4. *The Visionary*. This proposed style fits executives managing organizations that have been described in the strategy literature as "turnaround." The visionary can be described as a strong, hard-nosed leader/manager with flair and an analytical mind. Visionaries accept challenges and take calculated risks; they set flexible assignment of resources and short communication channels; their main goal is to be a winner. These executives are persons of vision. The visionary fits organizations that have been able to move from a stagnant decline to growth again.

Table 13.1 presents a model of strategy-leader fit based on the research findings.

## IMPLICATIONS—HUMAN RESOURCE STRATEGY

As Tichy pointed out, our organizations need to apply more strategically oriented approaches to human resource management to gain competitive edge in the 1990s. The model described in this research achieves such alignment between strategy and human resources. The model could be utilized by many firms, specifically firms that are in a process of changing strategic direction, or entering a different stage in the organization life cycle. Human resource management could play an important role in implementing this model. We suggest the following propositions:

1. The assessment center methods should be utilized in managerial selection of key tasks. The method has been used successfully to identify potential executives that fit different organization climates.

2. Human resource management must constantly scan the external and internal environment looking for the right people to achieve effective alignment with corporate strategy. This requires an efficient and possibly computerized data base that provides the organization with profiles and assessments about executives.

**Table 13.1**
**Strategic Fit: A Model of Strategy-Leader Fit**

|   |   | Strategic Direction | Characteristics of the style |
|---|---|---|---|
| 1. | The Entrepreneur | Developing/ Aggressive Growth | Innovative, creative, intuitive, flexible, extroverted, optimistic, motivated, excitable, dominant, risk taker, and little consultation with employees. |
| 2. | The Professional | Maturity/ Stable Domain (Neutral) | Team player, bureaucratic, conformist systematic, stable, calm, cautious, mature, friendly, conservative, decisions are based on facts and consultation, slow to change and to meet increases in threat, a skilled executive. |
| 3. | The Caretaker | Decline/ Retrenchment | Strong, tolerant, calculative, selfish, specialized, budget efficient, hard-nosed, priority-oriented. |
| 4. | The Visionary | Turnaround | Strong, hard-nosed, analytical, seeks challenge and takes calculative risk, replace mediocrity, very demanding, flexible assignment of resources, short communication channels, non-conformity, main goal is to be a winner. |

3. The promotional pattern should be modified to match the intended strategy. Executive promotion should be based on the values and skills required under different strategic directions. Again assessment center reports could be helpful here.

4. The reward system should also be modified to match the intended change in strategy. Specifically the reward system should be able to support both short and long term strategic goals. The key to an effective reward system is to ensure that people under different strategic directions continue to perceive that significant career opportunities are available to them.

5. Training and development. The purpose of this step is to reorient and introduce human resources to the critical thrust of the strategic change and what kind of organization should follow. Skills, attitudes and values are the core of such induction and training.

## CONCLUSION

The purpose of this chapter is to present some findings from a research project that investigates the relation between executive personality and values on one hand and the corporate strategic direction on the other hand. Four distinct leadership styles that match different strategic direction have been proposed in this research: the entrepreneur; the professional; the caretaker; and the visionary.

# 14

---

# An Invitation to Existentialism
# for the Executive

A new player has joined the marketing game and perhaps some older players are also beginning to reveal their true colors. The "new" existential manager has been brought on the board of corporate realpolitik. The new player is amused by *In Search of Excellence*, so dearly loved by his or her boss, who believes if we only could. . . . Our executive immigrant has a new set of "zany, sexy, sensate, sensuous" corporate needs that he or she may have to conceal from bosses in the traditional industries but not in the companies in the Silicon valleys of North America and Europe.

This is a new executive generation with a different optic, with different executive manners, which often behaves in quite unmanagerial ways. Many of these young executives cannot penetrate their own nature to ascertain where their deepest choices are made. Indeed, the existential executive could easily agree with the great biographer James Boswell that he or she feels like "a lunatic in a lucid interval contemplating a mad spell." But the existential executive is thinking of corporate life, not eighteenth-century London. Somehow the new liberated manager has arrived to concentrate his or her own craziness enough to realize that it takes craziness to beat craziness in the executive suite.

In the mid-1950s, W. H. Whyte painted a portrait of *The Organization Man* just as he was going into a decline. Like Sloan Wilson's "man in the gray flannel suit," he was essentially a conformist, keen to win over colleagues and influence superiors, was a product of bureaucracy that came of age in World War II and was dying by the mid-1960s. Organization man started to make his exit not because society didn't like his looks or his dedication to achievement, affluence, and aggression, but because a new manager was emerging.

A new generation of managers is emerging, particularly in marketing, that wants to participate in decision making and that does not want merely to be on the receiving end of *faits accomplis*. But before proceeding further into our saga, it would perhaps be useful to put down a few words about existentialism, which, we hope, will create the zany tone; set out the sensuous, sexy setting; refer to some of the props; introduce the existentialist; and supply other facts necessary to our drama—for drama it is. But first of all it is necessary to present you with the invitation.

## AN INVITATION TO EXISTENTIALISM

This "Invitation to Existentialism" is meant to be a temptation to open the door to the unknown—to the mystery, mythology, and magic of this new lifestyle that is permeating our lives. The sorcerer's apprentice is the adman who has sold his soul to the highest bidder for knowledge, knowledge of how to plumb the final, awesome secrets of humankind, so the consumer can be manipulated out of his or her seat in front of the TV and be powerhoused to the nearest store. The adman has now learned the last lesson of this unique and arduous apprenticeship: he has met the last enemy, the ultimate consumer, the existentialist, the man who stares back at him every morning while he shaves, the man who has a new set of zany, sexy, sensuous needs, the man who wants to stop the world to surf, to ski, to play tennis, to meditate, to glide, to write poetry, to sex it up, to be himself, to get out of himself, to drop out—to be in the existential swim. Existentialism is for poets and tennis players. But what is existentialism?

The definition of existentialism can be reconstructed from the advertising copy floating around like solar debris in magazines such as *Time, People*, and the *New York Times Magazine*. Only the ads are trying to sell vodka, menthol cigarettes, and Canadian whiskey. My argument is that they are selling a substitute—a substitute for existentialism. Now you know the answer to existentialism. But what are the questions? Like the Audi ad, it seems the tighter the anxiety, the looser the language. And these days the word "existentialism" is almost as inflated as the yen. The fact is, existentialism, like the Audi, is a luxury philosophy at a reasonable price, handles easily, and rides smoothly. Basically this is true for one reason: French engineering and Danish craftsmanship. Specifically for reasons like these, the premises are orthopedically designed to fit any philosophy, optic, perspective, or posture and to prevent not only fatigue but boredom and ennui, so much legroom and headroom you can stretch yourself any way to reach your self-actualizing limit. Luxury, lassitude, leisure, love and angst, anxiety, apprehension, alienation, anomie—that's existentialism. No question about it.

## THE MAN IN THE AD

### Every Person Has an Existentialist Inside Fighting to Get Out

What is being argued or at least alluded to is that the advertising people who write copy are writing letters to an imaginary existential character. Copywriters have a fascination with the existentialist who they rightly imagine is inside every one of their readers trying to get out. A good example of this phenomenon is an ad by Mobil showing a tightrope walker on an existential excursion between the twin towers of New York's World Trade Center. The motif in this ad takes as its point of departure the identity crisis, but in pursuing its swift trajectory it quickly moves across the sky, spelling out the message, "WHO dares, wins."

## THE EXISTENTIALIST'S COGNITIVE STYLE

The existential manager will have a strong preference for a divergent, rather than a convergent, cognitive style. A manager with a convergent style is more likely to use a conceptual frame of reference that tackles problems by working toward "the answer at the back of the book."

The existential executive tends to utilize a divergent style with a strong preference for problems that have open-ended spectra of answers. He or she rarely views a decision as being the product of "a no-alternative situation" and is particularly interested in computer simulations and artificial intelligence.

The contemporary executive is very sensitive to linguistic, social, and even sartorial changes. Nobody ever said it was easy to be an existentialist. It takes more than that delicate combination of body-fitting shirts, cavalry boots, tennis and *je ne sais quoi* (money).

What these existential managers want is more joy in their work, to live and work more fully, to have authentic and aware relations with co-workers. These managers want to be "turned on" to work the way Alec Comfort turned them on to sex through *The Joy of Sex*. Thus the potent, alive, and kicking executives are often described as "sexy," precisely because they are responsive, creative, experimental, and myth makers.

The existential style is essentially a search for an alternative and a supplement to the analytic style that is good for problem solving but has nothing to say about either problem finding or solution implementation. Getting beyond the analytic style (which is highly numerate, preoccupied with decomposing problems into components and convergence) requires an effort in lateral or divergent thinking. Instead of moving vertically in a linear train of A, B, Cs, the existential executives try to move laterally in a mental context where intelligence and feel (a compound of hunch, hypothesis, hype, vibes, and experience) count—to try to find the real problem. To try to find out if "there is a crisis"; to find out "what we really want."

In cognitive terms, existential executives are trying to turn on their metaphoric, intuitive, and analogic processes, which means switching on their right cerebral hemispheres that have been left in cold storage. What our system is good at (and our business schools best of all) is switching on the left cerebral hemisphere, which is good at linear, rational, and digital thought—the kind of intellectual activity that takes place when someone says "Let's be logical about this."

What existential executives are trying to do is to supplement and find alternatives to analytic skills. They wish to develop an "intuitive-synthetic" cognitive style that has an inventive mode and an integrative mode.

Traditionally, existentialism turns about such fundamental questions of identity as, "Who am I?" "Where am I going?" "Why?"

The essence of the existential approach argues that a person ought to decide what destiny decided him or her to be, and to be that person. The corollary of this thesis of being yourself is to find an organizational role that will allow you to be you. Ideally, the organization should be designed for the individual, not the individual redesigned for the organization. Secondly, if you can't respect yourself as you are, you can't respect other people. And it is this corporate world of "choose or die" that many executives face today. They want to make their mark or stand out before they pass away.

This is what the word *exsistere* in Latin means: "to stand out, to emerge." The existential person wants to stand out, to count, to be somebody. This is what the existential writer, artist, or playwright focuses on—a person in the process of becoming or emerging.

From the challenging complexities of the net of human encounters that make up corporate life, existential executives are confronted with psychological subtleties that fascinate and irritate them with questions that evade final answers. Yet out of these encounters executives begin to form an idea of themselves, a sense of being.

This fragmented voyage of discovery is not much concerned with mapping out ego. For Freud, the ego, a reflection of the outside world, was the battleground of the mind where the id warred with the superego. The ego kept the person in touch with reality.

## THE NEW EXISTENTIAL VALUE SYSTEM

Now, with a sense that the mainline North American and Western European value systems are bankrupt, many existential executives are challenging the establishment. Out of this challenge has emerged a counterculture that is opposed to male chauvinism; the worship of science and technology; and the adoration of affluence, achievement, and aggression.

One reason for the challenge of this counterculture may be a new concern for ecology, for an environment where the death of any life diminishes all. The counterculture has developed an existential culture, a new cosmological sense, and a broad romantic vision.

It is a pervasive value system, infusing every wheel of life, defining not only work and household habits, but also sexual habits and attitudes. Above all it is religious. What the counterculture provides is mysticism, mystery, and the magic of transcendental experience that gives new meaning to life. At the heart of this religious fervor is a deep perception that humans and their world are more complex than behavioral scientists believed. Thus, existentialists wish to mobilize the energies of transcendence and develop a sacramental consciousness.

## MOVING THE RIGHT HEMISPHERE

A new view of counterdependent executives is emerging that recognizes both their intractability and their potentiality. The executives' potentiality is recognized in the new ethic of intention based on the simple proposition that each person be held responsible for his or her own actions.

Rather than regarding executives as "naked apes," existentialism deals with how executives can become more active forces in shaping their own destinies. The need for choice, the capacity to control (or at least to influence) the key decisions of one's life is the central desire of the existentialists. The "will to meaning" is stronger than the "will to pleasure."

The idea of picking up the tabs, psychic or otherwise, is a tough road to follow, but it is central to the existential approach. Will and decision represent the core of the existential concept of personality. Existential managers have to move beyond the analytical approaches to new values.

While traditional executives were busy learning about participation, creativity, and commitment, along came the system approach where the central problem of organization became the management of information. The new system's values were openness, controlling the level of surprise, and the rejection of linear causal trains. Now the road is open for the development of the new existential value system. Executives have moved from achievement ("making it"), aggression ("watch it"), affluence ("having it"), and alienation ("being out of it," "the captain's a lonely figure on the bridge") to the new existential values: self-actualization ("what I can be, I must"), self-expression ("do your own thing"), interdependence ("let's pull together"), and joy ("right on, brother").

## THE EXISTENTIALIST AND AUTHORITY

For older top managers the paradigm of rationality, the notion that logical analysis rather than personalities should determine roles, rules, and relations, seems to have worked. But somewhere along the line, probably in the mid-1960s, something happened. Things started to go awry. The roles were still there but the relations began to change. Children started cheeking parents, patients suing their doctors, students chasing presidents out of their offices and smoking their cigars. The agonizing reappraisal had begun. The breakdown of authority was beginning.

Then the whole apparatus of authority with its ideas of total responsibility—"I shall hold you totally responsible"—came tumbling down. Managers had moved out of optical space, which is essentially made up of clearly defined fields with sharp black-and-white markers where "things" such as jobs are as separate as buildings bounded by space. In this classical world, managerial space is a kind of optical geometry where functions can be focused in lines of you do "this" and I'll do "that." Instructions go down the line through a series of amplifiers that show up more small print at each level, and reports flow up the line through a series of condensers that remove small print and leave only headlines. The system moves from "here" to "there." "Here" appears to both manager and the managed to be separate in time as well as in space from "there."

## KOTTER'S EXISTENTIAL MANAGERS

John Kotter's study (see chapter 3) showed that general managers do not function in a crisply defined black-and-white, geometrically defined environment. They do not direct through formally delineated organizational channels, nor do they systematically set and follow formal plans. Instead, their actual managerial behavior is characterized by long hours, fragmented episodes, and oral communication.

Such behavior differs substantially from the traditional notions of what top managers do (or should do). It is hard to fit their behavior into categories such as "planning," "controlling," "organizing," "directing," and so on. This gap raises serious questions about the kind of formal planning and performance appraisal commonly in use today. Furthermore, it raises questions about management education, which relies heavily on management "theory" and produces more than sixty thousand new MBAs each year.

Kotter's managers behave in an essentially existential way; they treat each day as a separate event to be lived out, where decision making is prime, and moral issues of loyalty are basic.

In "How Senior Managers Think" (1984), Daniel J. Isenberg has argued that "the higher you go in a company, the more important it is that you combine intuition and rationality, act while thinking, and see problems as interrelated." Isenberg found that

Most successful senior managers do not closely follow the classical rational model of first clarifying goals, assessing the situation, formulating options, estimating likelihoods of success, making their decision, and only then taking action to implement the decision. Nor do top managers select one problem at a time to solve, as the rational model implies.

Instead of having precise goals and objectives, successful senior executives have general overriding concerns and think more often about how to do things than about what is being accomplished. In addition to depending on their ability to analyze, they also rely heavily on a mix of intuition and disciplined analysis in their decision-making and incorporate their action on a problem into their diagnosis of it.

Isenberg also reminds us of René Descartes' appropriate remark: "It is not enough to have a good mind. The main thing is to use it well."

But their behavior has also gone beyond the laws of logic, for so much of what is happening in organizations goes beyond logic. For our contemporary executives, like Sartre and Camus, the absurd bears the stamp of truth, for the unexpected, by its very lack of probability, appears to have enhanced its probability. "What else is new?" would be the executive's response to this nonlogical statement.

In this topsy-turvy world, the absurd moves into the realm of the possible. And in this world of Organizational Alice no one is guilty or responsible. When people cannot be held exclusively responsible, classical management with its managerial mandates ("I hold you totally responsible for . . . ") ceases to be relevant. We are into a new management world view called existential systems theory.

## EXISTENTIAL SYSTEMS THEORY

### Handling Complexity without Complexes

You can't get anywhere in the corporate life without accepting that the whole thing can be rather complex (crazy?). It is best to start from the simple existential proposition that the whole thing is a giant garbage can filled with loosely connected organized anarchies. The idea that you can describe a business with an organization chart, with every position neatly tied up like a present under a Christmas tree, is so much window dressing. The organization chart stands there in the chairman's office like something from Leonardo da Vinci's early notebooks, line relations in unbroken lines, functional relations in broken lines. A whole science was invented around the span of control, with mathematical formulae to tell what is the optimal number of people to have reporting to you.

Continuing only with the classical form, with its presumption of one employee–one boss, defined delegation and authority commensurate with responsibility, it is easy to recognize the "how many angels can you get on the end of a pin" syndrome. Unfortunately organizations do not behave like pin factories. But the first thing to recognize about organizations is that they are complex systems run by existential managers, who see themselves riding out each day to do battle with the system—in a sort of constant crisis.

## THE CRISIS AND CLIMAX OF THE ORGANIZATION

In these executive encounters, crisis stresses the activity of the corporate forces opposing our existential hero, the executive. Here the exciting and also destructive force is "The Organization," that giant pantechnicon where information and existentialism meet to do battle for the executive's soul. The object of organization theory is to build up a vivid portrait of a beautiful, intensely isolated land called "the organization," which for the modern manager is as fascinating and unique as the face of the moon. Organization theory tries to put together a taste of everything there is down there in that mysterious, strange, surrealistic world.

Organizations, of course, have stereotypes about other organizations. For a long time it was fondly believed that all organizations—the Mafia, the Marines, IBM, the Communist party, the Bank of England, the Kennedys—were built the same way. The organizational stereotype was a cross between the structure of an infantry division and the first organization chart for General Motors. In this phantasmagoric web of line, function, and staff, connected by a chain of command of one man–one boss, with maximum delegation, clearly defined authority and responsibility, business was in fact transmitted by the informal organization. The informal apparatus got the stuff out the gate while the management theologians counted how many subordinate angels could be gotten on the head of an organizational pin.

### Organizations Behave in Counter-Intuitive Ways

On the basis of extensive research, Derek Pugh (1976) comes to a pessimistic conclusion that suggests that organizations are a lot more complex than was at first thought.

Complex systems differ from simple ones in being "counterintuitive," i.e., not behaving as one might expect them to. They are remarkably insensitive to changes in many system parameters, i.e., ultrastable. They stubbornly resist policy changes. They contain influential pressure points, often in unexpected places, which can alter system steady states dramatically. They are able to compensate for externally applied efforts to correct them by reducing internal activity that corresponds to those efforts. They often react to a policy change in the long run in a way opposite to their reaction in the short run.

The next part of the argument is particularly relevant: "Intuition and judgment generated by a lifetime of experience with the simple systems that surround one's every action create a network of expectations and perceptions that could hardly be better designed to mislead the unwary when he moves into the realm of complex systems'' (Pugh, 1976).

How do modern effective managers deal with this complexity? And why do general managers not plan but react on a minute-to-minute basis? The answers lie in the complexity of the situation.

### Existential Structure: The Relativity of Boxes and Bubbles

David K. Hurst describes the change in his company's management style when faced with financial collapse (1984). Hugh Russel, Inc. was a large industrial distributor with sales of $535 million in 1979. In 1980 this publicly traded firm was purchased through a 100 percent leveraged buyout by a privately held, and unprofitable, steel fabricator, York Steel Construction Ltd. In a very short time the executives of Hugh Russel found that their old style of management could not cope with the new situation.

Because circumstances changed after the acquisition, our framework fell apart almost immediately. Overnight we went from working for a growth company to working for one whose only objective was survival. Our old decentralized organization was cumbersome and expensive; our new organization needed cash, not profits. Bankers and suppliers swarmed all over us, and the quiet life of a management-controlled public company was gone.

The authoritarian ''hard box'' management style required augmentation if the company was to survive. The management teams turned to the organizational theories of Henry Mintzberg and Edgar Schein for a framework of the decision process.

The most useful framework we used was the one Ichak Adize developed for decision-making roles. In his view, a successful management team needs to play four distinct parts. The first is that of producer of results. A *producer* is action oriented and knowledgeable in his or her field; he or she helps compile plans with an eye to the implementability. The *administrator* supervises the system and manages the detail. The *entrepreneur* is a creative risk taker who initiates action, comes up with new ideas, and challenges existing policies. And the *integrator* brings people together socially and their ideas intellectually, and interprets the significance of events. The integrator gives the team a sense of direction and shared experience.

Before the merger, decisions were made at the highest level and information was tightly controlled. The crisis created by the merger forced management to consult lower level managers and their unions. The emphasis changed from structure to group dynamics. Obedience became trust, independence became autonomy, and the formal structure became informal groups.

When the bank realized the precarious financial situation the company was in, its relationship with York Steel changed.

As the corporation's financial position deteriorated, our relationship with the bank became increasingly adversarial. The responsibility for our account rose steadily up the bank's hierarchy, . . . and we received tougher and tougher "banker's speeches" from successively more senior executives. It remained for us to gain the confidence of our contacts, exchange candid views of our positions, and present options that addressed the corporation's problems in the bank's context and dealt with the bank's interests.

In the new "soft bubble" system, decision implementation is postponed while the decision is accepted by the "key players." Under the hard, rational model this "creative stall" would have been considered procrastination. The new framework influenced every facet of decision making, including employee benefits, relations with suppliers, customers, and shareholders.

The following lists illustrate the difference between the hard rational box approach and the soft bubble approach.

| Hard | Soft | Hard | Soft |
|------|------|------|------|
| objectives | values | serious | humorous |
| policies | norms | rational | intuitive |
| right | useful | learn | remember |
| target | direction | lens | mirror |
| precise | vague | words | pictures |
| necessary | sufficient | objects | symbols |

The creative thought process led to some unusual but useful perceptual changes. For example, when divisions were sold, the process was considered as acquiring a purchaser, which led to better marketing strategies: "For us, the theory in the bubble is our managerial theory of relativity. At the macro level it reminds us that how management phenomena appear depends on one's perspective and biases. At the micro level we remember that all jobs have both hard and soft components."

This new theory of managerial relativity argues for holarchies rather than hierarchies.

## Holarchy

The structures of our world are ordered into hierarchies or holarchies, as they are called by Arthur Koestler. Arguing against the view that all behavior can be reduced to a simple set of reflexes, Koestler has come up with the idea of a "holon," which, as the name suggests, is both a self-contained entity and an element of the next level. According to Koestler, "The holons are . . . Janus-like entities: the face turned toward the higher levels in the holarchy is that of a subordinate part in a larger system; the face turned toward the lower levels shows a quasi-autonomous whole in its own right."

Is there a corporate life for the CEO in these holarchies? The answer is "Yes" in the sense that the most successful firms recovering from the excesses of the strategic plans of the 1970s are being led by chief executives who have been described as "monomaniacs with a mission." Their mission is to succeed; their mania is a brilliant new combination of existentialism, entrepreneurship, intuition, and disciplined analysis—in that order.

## SOME EXISTENTIAL CONCLUSIONS

Existential managers have their own special style that makes them appear to be above the law of organizational logic.

1. Existential managers operate in holarchies where their Janus-like skills link one holarchy to others.
2. Existential managers use the "soft bubble" system.
3. Existential managers, like other people, find it difficult to control the ancient brain, the center of emotions.
4. Existential managers wear bifocals to "look up" and to "look down" the organization.
5. Existential managers need a well developed right hemisphere to do nonlinear logic like "planning."

### Organizations

1. Organizations are ultimately unknowable and they often behave in counter-intuitive ways.
2. Organized anarchy is a response to this ambiguity.
3. Garbage can theory demands opportunism.
4. All the organization is a stage; all managers are actors. And these managers behave like Michael Macoby's "gamesmen."

### Their Style

As Macoby points out, "The modern gamesman is cooperative but competitive; detached and playful but compulsively driven to succeed; a team player but a would-be superstar; a team leader but often a rebel against bureaucratic hierarchy. . . . His main goal is to be known as a winner, and his deepest fear is to be labeled a loser" (1976).

# 15

A Critique of Executive
Behavior: Its Facts,
Fictions, Paradigms

As every management Ph.D. knows, executive behavior is an interpretative science, a science in search of meaning: the aim is to make meaningful, at least in this particular case, "the facts of executive life." In brief, executive behavior is at once empirical, interpretative, and critical. The critical knowledge of "what managers do and with whom" transcends both empiricism and interpretation and is intended to produce the emancipating effect of freeing us from false consciousness and eliminating forces beyond our control. The whole point in dealing with the critical aspect of managerial behavior is, if not to provide a guide to revolutionary action, at least to allow the executive to make a fresh start with a clear eye.

The moral of this story is that we still need the facts of managerial life; we still need to be able to interpret these facts in the light of the paradigm of the observer; but above all, we need to free ourselves from the confines of our present view of executive life, be able to take positive action. The object of this book has been to look behind the facts, examine the interpretations, and focus the critical aspects of executive behavior.

## METHODS OF STUDYING EXECUTIVE BEHAVIOR

To do this it is necessary to look at the methods of studying business behavior.

The distinctive scientific feature of the science of what managers do is that it focuses on behavior, a commodity that can be observed, measured, and objectively analyzed—the behavior of people in organizations. But it is important to keep in mind that it is about what lies behind executive behavior. The aim is to catch a glimpse of the logos, ethos, and pathos of executive behavior.

A major difficulty in the study of executive life is the problem of framing questions that are simple enough. Questions relevant to the study of executive behavior include: What do executives do? How do they allocate their time to different functions? How much time do they spend alone and how much communicating with others? What methods of communication do they use? It is one of the oddities of managerial literature that we know so little about the behavior of executives in any significant detail.

Direct studies of executives are few in number, largely on account of difficulties required to be overcome to get the research started.

## HOW ARE EXECUTIVE STUDIES CARRIED OUT?

In studying executive behavior, asking the right questions is the key to success. The question "Who are you?" is frequently used for selection purposes, because the sequence in which a person lists his or her roles can help reveal how such a person might be best employed.

In studying executive behavior, the eyewitness or trained observer is preferred. Observational studies are less likely to make a priori decisions about causality and provide a description of a sequence of events, and thus they are process oriented.

Researchers have tried to answer the question "What do managers do?" by asking managers questions and by observing their behavior. Most managers find it difficult to let a researcher record what they do. In addition, it takes time to explain to an observer what the executive is actually doing.

Once all data has been collected it must be grouped under activities (programing, technical, personnel), interactions (with whom: superior, peer, subordinates), and method of communication (phone, letter, face to face). Finally, a conclusion must be reached. There are many anecdotal accounts of executive behavior, but few studies of managerial behavior using scientific techniques of recording. Scientifically, data may be collected by observation, by the subject keeping records, or by activity sampling procedures, as opposed to the method of continuous observation.

### The Case Study

Traditionally, case studies have represented a valuable source of information about organizational life. But the behavioral scientist would criticize case studies as a source of scientific data about organizational life (not necessarily as a teaching instrument) on the following counts:

1. It has obviously been dramatized to heighten the reader's interest; phrases are used such as "Jake Morgan, foreman, leaned back in his swivel chair. He was thinking hard." It is the dramatic presentation that makes case studies such excellent teaching devices, but drama and data are sometimes incompatible.
2. Much of the conversation has the ring of invention, which, of course helps in terms of continuity and interest, if not in terms of credibility.
3. There is a lack of properly collected behavioral information. At least there is rarely any specification of the research method employed.
4. Motives and attitudes were ascribed to the people involved.
5. The story with a beginning and an end arouses, if not suspicion, the feeling that the whole situation is just too neat. Unfortunately, case studies can be used to prove virtually anything.

## The Scientific Approach

To develop a more effective organizational science, it is necessary to replace the case study with more scientific studies of executives. To achieve the scientific approach in the study of administrative behavior, Luther Gulick (1937) argues that the following requirements must be observed:

1. Analysis of phenomena from which we may derive standard nomenclature, measurable elements, and rational concepts;
2. The development of extensive scientific documentation based on these analyses; and
3. The encouragement of an imaginative approach to social phenomena and the circulation of hypotheses so that they may be scrutinized by others in the light of experience, now and in future years.

This need for documentation focuses attention on empirical studies of executive behavior, but before empirical studies can be carried out it is necessary to ascertain what we are looking for, how it can be described and measured.

## The Self-Recording Technique

Before we discuss actual studies in detail it would perhaps be best to say something about self-recording procedures, or the diary technique, to give it its more usual title. The self-recording method has been used extensively as a means of providing information about how executives spend their time, with whom they interact and how they distribute their work within the department. Tom Burns, Sune Carlson, and Rosemary

Stewart have all made extensive use of diaries as a means of gaining insight into how executives utilize their time. In this research approach, the object is to produce a detailed record of how each executive spends his or her time each day over a specified period (usually four or five weeks). In order to facilitate the collection of standard and uniform data, it is usually necessary to design a record form; the executives are allowed to describe their activities by marking one of the several prearranged codes referring to particular categories of behavior. Inevitably the kind of information contained in a precoded diary is limited. To some extent comprehensiveness and precision have been sacrificed, but the diary technique as a research instrument has the supreme virtue of allowing large numbers to be studied simultaneously. Some managers find the task of self-recording extremely difficult and somewhat time-consuming. In some research the data supplied fell off somewhat in accuracy after a few days. The accuracy of diaries must always be suspect. In my experience in a self-recording exercise carried out with a group of shop stewards, it was found that the shop stewards overestimated the actual time they spent on union business, as compared with the data that emerged from a study carried out by observers.

Rosemary Stewart, a British social scientist who has made extensive use of diaries, has listed the advantages and the disadvantages of using diaries for recording executive behavior:

1. *Advantages*:
   a. Greatly increases the possible coverage of: number and types of managers; geographical and industrial distribution, and length of time, unless only a small number are observed for a long period.
   b. Classification is made by the man who knows what he is doing. It is hard for an observer to follow all that is being done without interrupting the manager, even if he is familiar with the job he is observing. The difficulties of classification become much greater when observing an unfamiliar, and especially a highly technical, job.
   c. All time can be recorded, whereas an observer may be excluded from confidential discussions.
2. *Disadvantages*:
   a. There are great limitations on what can be studied if one is aiming at comparability. The limitations are not quite as great if one is studying a homogeneous group of managers.
   b. It is probably impossible to get a random sample, especially in different companies, as one is relying on volunteers or members of courses. (This is probably also true, though perhaps to a lesser extent, of observation.)

c. However great the care and restricted the objectives, there will still be some unreliability in recording. This will mean the exclusion of some diaries and will probably invalidate conclusions based on small percentage differences.

## Activity Sampling

Activity sampling was developed in the late 1920s. This observational technique was used in the textile industry to obtain data on a large number of machines and workers spread over a considerable area. The actual research technique requires that the behavior to be observed should be analyzed into a number of categories, and that then a number of momentary observations at randomly determined times be made; that the executive should not be affected by the observer's presence; and that the categories of event, behavior, and communications act to be observed should be carefully defined. For these reasons it is usually regarded as essential to conduct a pilot study.

The advantages of activity sampling include: a number of executives can be studied at the same time; observations can be made over a period of days or weeks, which reduces the chance of day-to-day or week-to-week variations affecting the result; executives are not under close surveillance for long periods of time; measurements may be made with a preassigned degree of accuracy; and the results are easier to analyze. The disadvantages include: the executive being studied may change behavior when he or she sights the observer; behavior sampling does not produce as much detailed information as continuous study. There are, in addition, the dangers of using an incorrect sample size or of failing to ensure the randomness of observations; and further, the research may also be invalidated through lack of careful definition of the behavior to be studied.

## Access

Before using an activity sampling procedure as a means of studying executive behavior, it is, of course, necessary to gain the approval not only of the executives being studied but also their superior and usually the personnel manager. Normally in these circumstances, it is easy to gain the approval of the latter parties, but, perhaps not too surprisingly, the executives to be studied exhibit a certain degree of reservation about their roles. As might be anticipated, their behavior at this stage is high in defensiveness, and they usually require assurance that "the investigation will not make serious inroads on their managerial tasks." It has always somewhat surprised me that many managers, when they are presented with the details of the actual procedure, seem to regain some of their confidence, apparently from the fact that they assume because the observations are intermittent, they will not be continuously under observation. While this, in fact, is the case, the observations are fairly frequent—sometimes as frequent as once every four minutes on the average. Activity sampling is an excellent technique, and when selectively used it can be a very powerful technique for resolving some of our dilemmas about organizational behavior.

## A STUDY OF A DEPARTMENTAL MANAGEMENT GROUP

A well thought out and carefully executed study of the departmental manager and his immediate subordinates was made by Professor Tom Burns, a sociologist at Edinburgh University who used the self-recording technique to study the behavior of four managers in a British engineering factory. In this brilliant study, widely regarded as a classic, the subjects were the departmental manager and the two production engineers and a designer who were all directly responsible to him. The actual department consisted of 128 people, more than half of whom were women.

Burns' objective was to apply Carlson's technique to study their activities, and in particular to get a record of the pattern of interaction. He was especially interested in their methods of communication; these were classified as face-to-face; by letter, memorandum, or telephone; and by drawings or other nonverbal means. Burns recorded his data in the form of episodes. Each person contacted required a separate record. If the people involved in an interaction changed, then a separate record form had to be used. Some idea of the data generated by this study may be gained from the fact that episodes lasting from one to two minutes were frequently recorded. A major research skill in conducting executive behavior studies lies in the development of an appropriate classification system.

## THE USE OF VIDEO

### The Deeper Structures of Executive Behavior

Scientific studies of executive behavior by observation have been available for some thirty years. The first and most important study was made by Sune Carlson who conducted a study of ten managing directors. When he began his work he thought of chief executives as conductors of an orchestra who wave their wands and other executives play the tune. After completing his work, Carlson came to the view that the top executive was more like a marionette puppet, with all the subordinates pulling the strings. Carlson carried out his studies in the late 1940s, mainly by direct observation. But now in the 1990s an increasing number of these investigations are being carried out by videotape recording. The most striking single finding of some of these studies is that the executives being videoed seem to be pulling the strings of the experimenters.

### Style versus Action

What video studies of actual conferences reveal is style: how to make and receive dramatic impact. How an executive creates this style is at least as important as the content of his or her behavior. All this style versus content is very obvious as we watch a CEO do battle with the Seven Samurai VPs who also want to be the CEO's successor. The CEO shows his or her brilliance in converting hard balls into soft balls and all by style—a technique many executives would like to emulate.

But what does the video show that goes beyond the spoken word? Television debates started with the contest in 1960 between John F. Kennedy and Richard M. Nixon, and it was widely believed that Kennedy with his patrician manners triumphed over Nixon. But polls showed that people who heard the debate on radio voted Nixon the winner. What the TV communicated was Kennedy's courage, or what he called "grace under pressure."

The same point can be made about videos of executive get-togethers. It is the extra nuance, the body language, the slight sideways movement of the head that accompanies the spoken word that makes the decisive difference.

For example, it is fair to surmise that Jimmy Carter lost the 1980 debate against Ronald Reagan when Carter stridently attacked Reagan for being a warmonger and Reagan retorted with that now-immortal jibe, "There you go again." On video it was fatal for Carter.

The same point can be seen in videos of executives at work, talking. The script tells you one thing, often something quite trivial, but when you see the action, it is something else again. Subordinates addressed by their bosses literally retreat across the room.

One of the most striking characteristics of traditional observational studies of executive behavior is the fact that the researchers are not surprised by what they see. Executive life appears to be busy, slow, middle-brow, genteel, much ado about nothing. Videos of executive life are full of tension, energy, puzzlement. These videos come close to a realization of the idea of "camera-stylo" or "camera-pen." But here is the point, it is the executive being videoed who is writing with the camera-stylo.

### Video Conclusion

This new technique of using video to study meetings has enabled us to bring familiar information into fresh combination and to draw out unexpected and interesting findings. The video allows us to enlarge our understanding of meetings and allows us to review the evidence in tranquility and to work out the deeper structures of the executive narrative.

Video studies enable us to take a longer, wider view of the dramas of meetings. What is revealed is an adventure story sustained by continuing interplay of driving energy, bold executive personalities, and recurring accidents. The video allows the viewer to study the background and character of these executive meetings and to focus attention on the structure and meaning of their work. The videos are like a painting by Brueghel done with a delight in people, showing executives with a consuming interest in the whole business of managing, and filled with movement.

The video allows an extended voyage of discovery into deeper structures that lie behind executive behavior—it goes beyond the arithmetical collection of data provided us by people like Carlson and looks at the calculus of behavior; it looks at the differentials and integrals of behavioral change. Now we have executive behavior with many cunning passages, but the main line is clear enough. It is necessary to distinguish between observation and facts as Daniel J. Boorstin in *The Discoverers* (1983) has pointed out. Observation, according to an Italian source, is essentially "feminine" whereas facts are "masculine." With this new technique of research it is possible to go from quantity to quality, from hunch to logical deduction.

The moral of this study of executive behavior by video is that we still need the facts, we still need to be able to interpret these facts in the light paradigm of the observer, but above all, we need to free ourselves from the confines of our present view of executive life to be able to take effective action. The object of this model is to fuse the facts, the interpretations, and the critical aspects of executive behavior.

What the video study of executive meetings enables a manager to do is to move away from the whole idea of doing meetings in a wholly mechanical fashion. Hence, the emphasis in this type of research is on drama. What the manager must learn to do is to step out of his or her role and respond to the drama of the meeting.

Executive behavior as studied by video is a field of inquiry that is only just beginning. All sorts of interesting problems await exploration and creative solutions. A whole new field is mushrooming in a way that is going to have dramatic effects, both for the traditional, academic management scientist and for the executive.

### A Caveat

At one time film and videos were the allies of truth. They seemed to show us corporate reality reflected in a flawless mirror. No longer. Since the Abscam Scandal of the early 1980s, we have finally learned to be aware of the hidden agenda of the video camera. Managers have to treat video data as images like any others, loaded with the implicit biases of their makers and their culture. The camera makes stars and stooges, kings and knaves—it is all a question of "what's going down." However tentative and aesthetically unsatisfying much of today's executive video art may seem, there is no denying we stand on the edge of a brave new world of executive image making. Video *verité*'s claim on reality has to be summarily negated. What does it all mean? Who knows? Authenticity is in the eye of the beholder.

## BUSINESS BEHAVIOR BEHAVIORALLY VIEWED

Most senior managers, while skeptical of what university business schools "discover," are only too aware of the inadequacies of the managerial mythology contained in such books as *In Search of Excellence* (Peters and Waterman, 1982). But the answers of executive behavior studies are unlikely to be simple, comprehensive, and appropriate in all contexts and technologies. In fact, looking for definitive closure may well be premature and misleading. To my mind the most important single notion to emerge from the study of executive behavior is the realization that what counts is "double take," that is, the ability to tease out and underline the relevant facts and findings, develop appropriate categories, suggest possible relations (usually both complex and complicated), and simplify the problem (usually with a model with a number of "black boxes"). Stop and mull it over. And make a number of predictions, collect data, and then start again.

As John Kotter points out, in *General Managers*

Sound theories must recognize that the context in which at least some managers work is very complex and can vary significantly in many dimensions in different situations. One of the key reasons that the vast amount of leadership research conducted in this century adds up to so little is probably because it has been guided by theories that, even when context is taken into account, treat context in incredibly simplistic ways. (1982)

## THE NEED FOR SCIENTIFIC THEORY

It is not enough to record behavior, no matter how accurate and detailed these data may be, or even to supplement these data with clinical interviews or surveys of their beliefs by scientifically constructed attitude scales. This by itself does not constitute science; executive behavior science demands the development of a coherent edifice of concepts and hypotheses about the managerial process that makes sense to practicing managers. Too few managers, nevertheless, seem to realize that nothing is better than a valid theory, or to appreciate the supreme importance that theory plays in the development of a science.

## MODELS OF THE INDIVIDUAL AND EXECUTIVE BEHAVIOR

All executive behavior studies seem to imply some sort of model of the individual. Both organization theorists and managers who subscribe to these theories carry around in their heads, albeit in some cases intuitively, a model that structures in their minds how a person energizes, sustains, and directs his or her behavior.

Reviewing this unobvious characteristic of executive behavior can help to define the subject and provide useful clues on how experts in this field think. Organizational behavior people tend to be somewhat suspicious, indeed paranoid, of commonsensical explanations of events. They tend to regard such explanations as facile, if not simple-minded. They believe there is always something going on below the surface that is not obvious to the "untrained" eye.

To understand events, organizational behavior people believe, it is necessary to discover the hidden model as opposed to the public one. Figure 15.1 shows a list of models employed by the different researchers in this book.

## ACCURACY OF EXECUTIVE BEHAVIOR STUDIES

Executive behavior studies are often reported as if they were, in fact, scientific, whereas, perhaps, it is more realistic to think of them as being an art form. For example, what the researcher chooses to admit is hardly less important than what he or she excludes. Perhaps it would be better if students of executive behavior could provide us, like biographers, with a synthesis of all the facts about the friendships, conversations, dress, habits, tastes, food preferences, and money of their subjects so that this information could be taken into consideration when we study the pattern of behavior and interaction of a particular executive.

Kotter has some very useful guidance on research methods that challenges the whole scientific basis of executive behavior studies. In reviewing his research, Kotter links his work methods to those of William Foote Whyte, whose famous *Street Corner Society* (1943) research revealed how urban gangs functioned. The point is that to gain acceptance the observer changes into participant-observer, and scientific "facts" give way to the "low down" on reality. Science and the truth are not always compatible in executive behavior research. A kind of Heisenberg Principle of uncertainty seems to apply where the closer you try to specify the behavioral dimension of executive behavior, the more likely the observer

**Figure 15.1**
**Organization Theory and Model of Manager Are Linked**

| Organization Theory | Researcher | Model of Manager |
|---|---|---|
| | | Conductor |
| Classical Theory ——— Carlson | | Marionnette |
| Human Relations ——— Whyte | | - Organization Man |
| Systems ——— Mintzberg | | Input-Output Systems - Set of Roles |
| | Burns | - Horizontal Executive |
| | Kotter | - Vulnerable Power |
| Existential-Systems Theory ——— Macoby | | - Gamesman |
| | Kelly | - Existential Executive |

| Level | Researcher | Model of Manager |
|---|---|---|
| Chief Executive | Carlson | Conductor - Before Marionnette - After |
| Executive Behavior - Strategy Fit | Ibrahim | Missionary vs. Visionary |
| Presidents | Whyte | Organization Man |
| Presidents | Mintzberg | Input-Output System - A Set of Roles |
| General Managers | Kotter | Vulnerable Power |
| Middle Managers | Burns | Horizontal Executive |
| Section Managers | Kelly | Political Tea Party |
| All Managers | Macoby | Gamesman |

will end up part of the executive gang. By being so closely involved, Kotter is able to "discover" important findings such as the need to minimize the feeling that some of his general managers had an "I can do anything" syndrome—shades of self-destructiveness euphoria.

Then there is the vital problem of the validity of the evidence. Much of the researcher's time is, or should be, spent comparing one piece of evidence with another, and one occurrence of an event with another. Also, it is quite probable that the diaries of executives are not necessarily truthful.

Basically, what it amounts to is that management researchers ought to be more critical and follow the criteria for receiving evidence used in the courts. For example, eyewitness accounts, as has often been shown in courtroom testimony, are often unreliable. Memories of past events should only be accepted with confirmation. Researchers in this field ought to operate on the basis that they have not always been told the incontrovertible truth. As we know from literary biographies, there is no such thing as final truth. Researchers in this field ought to make it much clearer how they, in fact, weigh the evidence, select and reject facts, choose a particular stand, and adopt a specific paradigm.

Thus the critical knowledge of executive behavior transcends both empiricism and interpretation, and it produces an emancipating effect (see Figure 15.2).

We still need facts; we still need to be able to interpret these facts; to be able to take innovative action. This book has been devoted to fathoming the facts, the interpretations, and the critical aspects of organizational behavior.

Thus the contingency model for the study of executive behavior is based on an imaginative integration of facts, interpretation, and critique. The object of the model is to get managers away from the idea of viewing and doing things in a wholly mechanical fashion. Hence the emphasis in on critique.

What this amounts to is that the manager must learn to step out of one's established role and respond to the drama of the research. But no drama is going to do any good unless the manager has the appropriate information, understands the model, and is ready to critique. To go forward, the manager has to adopt an essentially existential view of the world.

**Figure 15.2**
**Executive Behavior Is Empirical, Interpretive, and Critical**

```
                    Empirical--facts of "what managers do"

Executive           Interpretive--relates facts to the paradigms of observers
Behavior
                    Critical--frees us from false consciousness and allows us
                    to take "revoluntionary" action
```

# References

Abernathy, W. *Industrial Renaissance*. New York: Basic Books, 1984.

Adizes, I. "Organizational Passages: Diagnosing and Treating Life Cycle Problems of Organizations," *Organizational Dynamics*, vol. 8, no. 1, 1979, pp. 3–21.

Allison, G. T. *Essence of Decision: Explaining the Cuban Missile Crisis*. Boston: Little, Brown, 1971.

Allport, G. W. *Personality: A Psychological Interpretation*. New York: Holt, Rinehart & Winston, 1937.

——— . *Pattern and Growth in Personality*. New York: Holt, Rinehart and Winston, 1961.

Ansoff, I. H. *Corporate Strategy: An Analytical Approach to Business Policy for Growth and Expansion*. New York: McGraw-Hill, 1965.

——— . "Corporate Capability for Managing Change," SRI International, 1978.

Bales, R. F. "In Conference," *Harvard Business Review*, vol. 32, no. 2, April 1954, pp. 44–50.

Barnard, C. I. *The Function of the Executive*. Cambridge, Mass.: Harvard University Press, 1938.

Bauer, D. "Why Big Business Is Firing the Boss," *New York Times*, March 8, 1981.

Bettman, J., and B. Weitz. "Attributions in the Boardroom: Causal Reasoning in Corporate Annual Reports," *Administrative Science Quarterly*. Vol. 28, 1983, pp. 165–183.

Bierce, A. *The Devil's Dictionary*. Owings Mills, Md.: Stemmer House, 1978.

Blair, M. M. "Who's in Charge Here? How Changes in Corporate Finance Are Shaping Corporate Governance," *Brookings Review*, vol. 4, no. 4, Fall, 1991, pp. 8–13.

Blumenson, M. *The Patton Paper*. New York: Houghton Mifflin, 1974.

Boorstin, D. J. *The Discoverers*. New York: Brandon House, 1983.

Boyle, R. J. "Wrestling with Jellyfish," *Harvard Business Review*, January–February 1984.

Brickley, J., S. Bhagat, and R. Lease. "The Impact of Long-range Managerial Compensation Plans on Shareholders' Wealth," *Journal of Accounting and Economics*, vol. 7, 1985, pp. 115–129.

Burns, J. M. *Leadership*. New York: Harper & Row, 1978.

Burns, T. "The Directions of Activity and Communications in a Departmental Executive Group," *Human Relations*, vol. 7, 1954.

——— . "The Reference of Conduct in Small Groups: Cliques and Cabals in Occupational Milieux," *Human Relations*, vol. 8, 1955, pp. 467–486.

Byrne, J. A., D. Foust, and L. Therrien. "Executive Pay," *Business Week*, March, 1992, pp. 52–58.

Carey, J., and E. T. Smith. "The Pepsi Generation Heads for the Corner Office," *Business Week*, September 25, 1989, p. 170.

Carlisle, A. E. "Mac Gregor," *Organizational Dynamics*, Summer, 1976, pp. 50–58.

Carlson, R. E. "Selection Interview Decisions," *Personnel Psychology*, vol. 20, no. 3, 1967.

Carlson, S. *Executive Behavior*. Stockholm: Strombergs, 1951.

Carnegie, D. *How to Win Friends and Influence People*. New York: Pocket Books, 1958.

Carson, T., and J. A. Byrne. "Fast Track Kids," *Business Week*, November 10, 1986.

Chandler, A. D. *Strategy and Structure: Chapters in the History of the American Industrial Enterprise*. Cambridge, Mass.: MIT Press, 1962.

Chung, K. H., et al. "Do Insiders Make Better CEOs than Outsiders?" *The Academy of Management Executive*, vol. 1, no. 4, 1987, pp. 323–329.

Colvin, G. "How to Pay the CEO Right," *Fortune*, April 16, 1992.

Conger, J. A. "Leadership: The Art of Empowering Others," *The Academy of Management Executive*, vol. 3, no. 1, 1989, pp. 17–24.

Crystal, G. *In Search of Excess*. New York: Norton, 1991.

Cyert, R. M., and J. G. March. *A Behavioral Theory of the Firm*. Englewood Cliffs, N.J.: Prentice-Hall, 1963.

Dale, E., and L. F. Urwick. *Staff in Management*. New York: McGraw-Hill, 1960.

Dalton, M. *Men Who Manage*. New York: John Wiley & Sons, 1959.

DeAngelo, H., and A. DeAngelo. "Proxy Contests and the Governance of Publicly Held Corporations," *Journal of Financial Economics*, vol. 23, 1989, pp. 29–59.

Drucker, P. F. "The Discipline of Innovation," *Harvard Business Review*, May–June, 1985.

Dubin, R. *The World of Work*. Englewood Cliffs, N.J.: Prentice-Hall, 1958.

——— . "Business Behavior Behaviorally Viewed," in *Social Science Approaches to Business Behavior*, G. B. Strother, ed. Homewood, Ill.: Richard D. Irwin, 1962.

Earle, A. *Compensation for CEOs*. London, Canada: National Centre for Management Research and Development, University of Western Ontario, 1990.

Ehrenreich, B. "A Feminist View of the New Man," *New York Times Magazine*, May 20, 1984.

Fiedler, F. E. *A Theory of Leadership Effectiveness*. New York: McGraw-Hill, 1967.

Gabarro, J. J. "When a New Manager Takes Charge," *Harvard Business Review*, May–June, 1985.

——— . "The Development of Working Relationships," in *A Handbook of Organizational Behavior*, J. Lorsch, ed. Englewood Cliffs, N.J.: Prentice-Hall, 1987.

Garvin, D. A. "Quality on the Line," *Harvard Business Review*, September–October, 1983, pp. 65–75.

Gratch, A. "Testing for Traits that Make a Manager," *New York Times*, February 3, 1985.

Gulick, L. "Notes on the Theory of Organization," in L. Gulick and L. F. Urwick, eds., *Papers on the Science of Administration*. New York: Institute of Public Administration, 1937.

Halpin, A. W., and B. J. Winer. "A Factorial Study of the Leader Behavior Descriptions," in *Leader Behavior: Its Description and Measurement*, R. M. Stodgill and A. E. Coons, eds., *Bureau of Business Research*, monograph 88. Columbus: Ohio State University Press, 1957.

Hart, G. L., and P. H. Thompson. "Assessment Centres: For Selection or Development?" *Organizational Dynamics*, Spring, 1979.

Heller, J. *Catch 22*. New York: Simon & Schuster, 1961.

——— . *Something Happened*. New York: Alfred A. Knopf, 1974.

Hofer, C. W., and D. Schendel. *Strategy Formulation: Analytical Concepts*. St. Paul: West Publishing, 1978.

House, R. T. "A Path-Goal Theory of Leadership Effectiveness," *Administrative Science Quarterly*, 1971, pp. 331–338.

Hurst, D. K. "Of Boxes, Bubbles, and Effective Management," *Harvard Business Review*, May–June, 1984.

Iacocca, L. *Iacocca: An Autobiography*. New York: Bantam Books, 1984.

Ibrahim, A. B., and J. Kelly. "Leadership Style at the Policy Level," *Journal of General Management*, vol. 2, no. 3, Spring 1986, pp. 37–46.

Isenberg, D. J. "How Senior Managers Think," *Harvard Business Review*, November–December, 1984.

Jacques, E. *The Changing Culture of a Factory*. London: Tavistock Publications Ltd., 1951.

Jay, A. "How to Run a Meeting," *Harvard Business Review*, March–April, 1976.

Jennings, E. "Mobicentric Man," *Psychology Today*, July, 1970.

Jensen, M. C., and K. J. Murphy. "CEO Compensation: It's Not How Much You Pay, But How," *Harvard Business Review*, May–June, 1990, pp. 138–153.

Jones, H. S., R. E. Fry, and S. Srivastva. "The Person of the CEO: Understanding the Executive," *The Academy of Management Executive*, vol. 3, no. 3, 1989, pp. 205–215.

Judis, J. B. "The Guru Who Forgot What He Said," *London Sunday Times Business World*, 1990.

Kahn, R. L., and D. Katz. "Leadership Practices in Relation to Productivity and Morale," in *Group Dynamics*, D. Cartwright and A. Zander, eds. New York: Harper & Row, 1960.

Kanter, R. M. "The Attack on Pay," *Harvard Business Review*, March–April, 1987, pp. 60–67.

Kaplan, A. *The Conduct of Inquiry: Methodology for Behavioral Science*. New York: Harper & Row, 1961.

Kelly, J. "The Study of Executive Behavior by Activity Sampling," *Human Relations*, vol. 17, no. 3, 1964.

——— . *Is Scientific Management Possible?* London: Faber & Faber, Ltd., 1968.

—— . "Make Conflict Work for You," *Harvard Business Review*, July–August, 1970.

—— . "The Turnaround Manager," *Strategic Directions*, November, 1976.

—— . *How Managers Manage*. Englewood Cliffs, N.J.: Prentice-Hall, 1980.

—— . *Organizational Behavior*. Homewood, Ill.: Irwin, 1980.

—— . "Productivity and Participation," in *Matrix Management Systems Handbook*, D. I. Van Nostrand, ed. New York: Reinhold Company, 1984.

—— . "The Use of Assessment Centre Simulations to Evaluate Decision-making Skills," in *Advances in Management Education*, C. Cox and J. Beck, eds. New York: Wiley, 1984.

—— . "The Corporate Theater of Action," *Business Horizons*, January–February, 1986, pp. 67–74.

—— . "Surviving and Thriving in Top Management Meetings," *The Personnel Magazine, AMACOM*, June, 1987.

—— . "An Invitation to Existentialism for the Marketing Manager," *Irish Marketing Review*, December, 1989.

—— . "Yummies in the New Entrepreneurial Style," in *Small Business and Entrepreneurship*, A. B. Ibrahim. Dubuque, Iowa: Kendall, Hunt, 1990.

—— . "A Critique of Executive Behavior," *Business Horizons*, March–April, 1991.

Kelly, J., with B. Ibrahim. "Beyond Strategic Planning," *Strategic Direction*, no. 10, August, 1986.

—— . "Leadership at the Policy Level: A Strategic Fit," *Journal of General Management*, Spring 1986.

Kelly, J. with K. Khozan. "Participative Mangement: Can It Work?" *Business Horizons*, August, 1980.

Kerr, S., et al. "The First Line Supervisor: Phasing Out or Here to Stay?" *Academy of Management Review*, vol. 2, no. 1, 1986.

Khandwalla, P. N. "Some Top Management Styles: Their Context and Performance," *Organization and Administrative Sciences*, vol. 7, no. 4, 1977, pp. 21–51.

Kirkpatrick, S. A., and E. A. Locke. "Leadership: Do Traits Matter?" *Academy of Management Executive*, vol. 5, no. 2, 1991, pp. 48–60.

Klein, J. "Why Supervisors Resist Employee Involvement," *Harvard Business Review*, Sept.–Oct. 1984, pp. 87–95.

Kleinfield, N. R. "When Many Chiefs Think as One," *New York Times*, Oct. 28, 1984.

Koestler, A. *Janus: A Summing Up*. New York: Random House, 1978.

Kotter, J. P. "Power, Dependence and Effective Management," *Harvard Business Review*, July–August, 1977.

—— . *The General Managers*. New York: Free Press, 1982.

—— . "What Effective Managers Really Do," *Harvard Business Review*, November–December, 1982.

Kuhn, T. S. *The Structure of Scientific Revolutions*. Chicago: University of Chicago Press, 1970.

Loomis, C. J. "Can John Akers Save IBM?" *Fortune Magazine*, July 1991.

Lueck, T. J. "Why Jack Welch Is Changing G.E.," *New York Times*, May 5, 1985.

Luthans, F. "Successful Versus Effective Real Managers," *Academy of Management Executive*, vol, 2, no. 2, 1988, pp. 127–132.

McClelland, D., and D. H. Burnham. "Power Is the Great Motivator," *Harvard Business Review*, March–April, 1976.

McGregor, D. M. *The Human Side of the Enterprise*. New York: McGraw-Hill, 1960.

Macoby, M. *The Gamesman*. New York: Simon and Schuster, 1976.

Main, J. "The Recovery Skips Middle Managers," *Fortune*, February 6, 1984.

Meredith, D. R. "CEO Compensation," *Chief Executive*, issue 70, September 1991.

Miles, R., C. Snow, A. Meyer, and H. Coleman, Jr. "Organizational Strategy, Structure and Process," *Academy of Management Review*, vol. 7, no. 3, 1978, pp. 546–562.

Miles, R. E. "Human Relations of Human Resources," *Harvard Business Review*, vol. 43, no. 4, July–August, 1963, pp. 148–57.

Miller, D., M. Kets de Vries, and J. M. Toulouse. "Top Executive Focus of Control and Its Relationship to Strategy-Making, Structure and Environment," *Academy of Management Journal*, vol. 25, no. 2, 1982, pp. 237–253.

Miller, G. A. *Spontaneous Apprentices: Children and Language*. San Francisco: Seabury Press, 1977.

Mintzberg, H. "The Manager at Work: Determining His Activities, Roles and Programs by Structured Observation," Ph.D. dissertation, Sloan School of Management, Massachusetts Institute of Technology, Cambridge, Mass., 1968.

——— . *The Nature of Managerial Work*, New York: Harper & Row, 1973.

——— . "Planning on the Left Side and Managing on the Right," *Harvard Business Review*, July–August, 1976.

——— . *Power In and Around Organizations*. Englewood Cliffs, N.J.: Prentice-Hall, 1983.

Mintzberg, H., and J. Waters. *Tracking Strategy in an Entrepreneurial Firm*. Montreal: McGill University, 1980.

Muczyk, J. P., and B. C. Reimann. "The Case for Directive Leadership," *The Academy of Management Executive*, vol. 1, no. 4, 1987, pp. 301–311.

Payne, R., and D. S. Pugh. "Organizational Structure and Climate," in *Handbook of Industrial and Organizational Psychology*, M. D. Dunnette, ed. New York: Rand, McNally, 1976.

Pepper, C. W. "Interview with Laurence Olivier," *New York Times Magazine*, March 25, 1979.

Peter, L. J., and R. Hull. *The Peter Principle*. New York: Morrow, 1969.

Peters, T. J., and R. H. Waterman, Jr., *In Search of Excellence: Lessons from America's Best Run Companies*. New York: Harper and Row, 1982.

Pfeffer, J. "Size and Composition of Corporate Board of Directors," *Administrative Science Quarterly*, vol. 30, 1972, pp. 218–228.

——— . "Do Leaders Really Matter?" *Academy of Management Review*, January, 1977, pp. 104–112.

Pollack, A. "The Daunting Power of IBM," *New York Times*, January 20, 1985.

——— . "One Day, Junior Got Too Big for His Boots," *New York Times*, business section, August 4, 1991.

Posner, B. Z., and W. H. Schmidt. "Values and the American Manager," *California Management Review*, vol. 26, no. 3, Spring, 1984.

Prokesch, S. "America's Imperial Chief Executive," *New York Times*, October 12, 1986, p. 12.

Pugh, D. S., and R. Payne. "Organizational Structure and Climate," in *Handbook of Industrial and Organizational Psychology*, M. D. Dunnette, ed. Chicago: Rand McNally, 1976.

Quinn, J. B. "Managing Innovation-Controlled Chaos," *Harvard Business Review*, May–June, 1985.

Quinn Mills, D. "Bridging the Corporate Generation Gap," *New York Times*, April 7, 1985.

Raskin, A. H. "The Workers in the Executive Suite," *The New York Times*, January 4, 1976.

Rechner, P. L., and D. R. Dalton. "CEO Quality and Organizational Performance," *Strategic Management Journal*, vol. 12, February 1991.

Rose, F. *West of Eden*, New York: Viking Penguin, 1989.

Sank, L. "Effective and Ineffective Managerial Traits Obtained as Naturalistic Descriptions from Executive Members of a Super Corporation," *Personnel Psychology*, vol. 27, 1974, pp. 423–434.

Sayles, L. *Managerial Behavior*. New York: McGraw-Hill, 1964.

Schelling, T. C. *Strategy of Conflict*. Cambridge, Mass.: Harvard University Press, 1966.

Schendel, E., and C. W. Hofer. *Strategic Management: A New View of Business Policy and Planning*. Boston: Little, Brown, 1979.

Simon, H. A. *Administrative Behaviour: A Study of Decision-Making Processes in Organizations*. New York: Free Press, 1947.

Stewart, R. "The Use of Diaries to Study Managers' Jobs," *The Journal of Management Studies*, vol. 2, no. 2, May 1965, pp. 228–235.

——. "Middle Managers: Their Job and Behaviors," in *Handbook of Organizational Behavior*, J. W. Lorsch, ed. Englewood Cliffs, N.J.: Prentice-Hall, 1987.

Stewart, T. A. "GE Keeps Those Ideas Coming," *Fortune*, August 12, 1991.

Stodgill, R. M. *Handbook of Leadership: A Survey of Theory and Research*. New York: Free Press, 1974.

Stodgill, R. M., and A. E. Coons. *Leader Behavior: Its Description and Measurement*, Research Monograph no. 66. Columbus: Ohio State University, Bureau of Business Research, 1957.

Stybel, L. J. "Linking Strategy Planning and Management Manpower Planning," *California Management Review*, vol. 25, no. 1, 1982, pp. 48–56.

Taylor, Frederick W. *Principles of Scientific Management*. New York: Harper, 1947.

Tichy, N. *Managing Strategic Change: Technical, Political and Cultural Dynamics*. New York: Wiley, 1983.

Tichy, N., and R. Charan. "Speed, Simplicity, Self-Confidence: An Interview with Jack Welch," *Harvard Business Review*, September–October, 1989.

Tichy, N., C. Fombrun, and M. A. Devanna. "Strategic Human Resource Management," *Sloan Management Review*, Winter, 1982, pp. 47–60.

Tichy, N. N., and D. O. Ulrich. "The Leadership Challenge: A Call for the Transformational Leader," *Sloan Management Review*, Fall, 1984, pp. 59–68.

Tosi, H. L., and L. R. Gomez-Mejia. "The Decoupling of CEO Pay and Performance," *Administrative Science Quarterly*, vol. 34, no. 2, June 1989.

Ulrich, D. *Organizational Capability: Competing from the Inside Out*. New York: Wiley, 1991.

Vancil, R. F. "A Look at CEO Succession," *Harvard Business Review*, March–April 1987.

Vancil, R. F., and C. H. Green. "How CEOs Use Top Management Committees," *Harvard Business Review*, January–February, 1984.

Vroom, V. H., and P. W. Yetton. *Leadership and Decision-Making*. Pittsburgh: University of Pittsburgh, 1973.

Watson, T. J., Jr., and P. Petre. *Father, Son and Company*. New York: Bantam, 1990.

Webster, E. *Decision Making in the Employment Interview*. Montreal: Industrial Relations Centre, McGill University, 1964.

Whyte, W. F. *Street Corner Society: The Social Structure of an Italian Slum*. Chicago: University of Chicago Press, 1943.

Whyte, W. H., Jr. "How Hard Do Executives Work," *Fortune*, January, 1954.

—— . *The Organization Man*. New York: Simon and Schuster, 1956.

Wissema, J. G., H. W. Vander Pol, and H. M. Messer. "Strategic Management Archetypes," *Strategic Management Journal*, vol. 1, 1980, pp. 37–47.

Zaleznik, A. "The Leadership Gap," *Academy of Management Executives*, vol. 4, February, 1990, pp. 7–27.

# Name Index

# Subject Index

## About the Author

JOE KELLY is a Professor of Management at Concordia University, Montreal. He is the author of a number of books on management and organizational behavior and has had articles published in journals such as *Harvard Business Review, Journal of General Management,* and *Journal of Industrial Economics.* He has considerable experience as an organizational behavior consultant in the fields of restructuring organizations, structured training, and executive development.